~~CHAS~~

CREATING

~~THE~~

YOUR

~~AMERICAN~~

LIMITLESS

~~DREAM~~

LIFE

...ON YOUR TERMS!

DR. ESTHER ZELEDÓN

~~CHASING~~ CREATING ~~THE~~ YOUR ~~AMERICAN~~ LIMITLESS ~~DREAM~~ LIFE

... ON YOUR TERMS!

First published in 2023 by Dean Publishing
PO Box 119
Mt. Macedon, Victoria, 3441
Australia
deanpublishing.com

Cataloguing-in-Publication Data
National Library of Australia
Title: Creating Your Limitless Life ... On Your Terms!
Edition: 1st edn
ISBN: 978-1-925452-67-9
Category: Self-help / Personal Growth / Success

The stories and opinions in this book reflect the author's recollection of events and personal way of working. Some specific names, locations, and identifying characteristics have been changed to protect the privacy of those depicted.

Dialogue and some encounters or experiences have been recreated from the author's memory. This book deals with personal growth and purpose and isn't a substitute for professional advice in relation to one's mental health or psychological issues. The information provided in this book is designed to provide helpful information on the subjects discussed using the author's personal experiences. This book is not meant to be used, nor should it be used, to diagnose or treat any physical, emotional, or psychological medical condition. This book is about making personal choices and being responsible for your actions and results, and is not a source for treating any medical problem or condition. Always consult your own professional health expert for advice regarding your mental or emotional health.

The publisher and author are not responsible for any specific health or psychological needs and are not liable for any damages or negative consequences from any treatment, action, application, or preparation to any person reading or following the information in this book. References are provided for informational purposes only and do not constitute endorsement of any websites or other sources. Neither the publisher nor the individual author(s) shall be liable for any physical, psychological, emotional, financial, or commercial damages, including, but not limited to, special, incidental, consequential, or other damages. Our views and rights are the same: you are responsible for your own choices, actions, and results.

To my sixteen-year-old
self who almost gave up.
I'm so glad you didn't ...

CONTENTS

"PEOPLE HESITATE TO DISCOVER THEIR PURPOSE BECAUSE THEY'RE AFRAID."

Dr. EZ

INTRODUCTION: YOU ARE LIMITLESS

While lying on the floor of my apartment, my long hair trailing on the carpet, I stared at the ceiling, watching the blades of the fan spin around. Out of the corner of my eye, I could see the mess accumulating in my apartment, and I knew why it was mounting: my lack of motivation. The dull humming of the air conditioner and the footsteps of the neighbors echoed in my head. I thought to myself, *Where did I go wrong?*

By any measure, I should have been blissfully happy. I had all the check marks: PhD from a top university, attractive, fit, married to a handsome Latino man, with family and friends that supported me. But I was so unhappy, and worse—misaligned. I had followed the template of the American dream and achieved everything that I was supposed to, and all at the proper time. But my life wasn't mine.

I had given my energy, my time, and my life to everyone else and had helped them follow their dreams. *Why did I defer my own dreams to chase some ideal of the American dream? And what happens now?*

As social activist and novelist Langston Hughes once wrote, "What happens to a dream deferred? Does it dry up like a raisin in the sun? ... Or does it explode?"[1] My dreams had become dried up raisins, and I knew the only way for them to come to life again was to let them explode …

Before I arrived at that pivotal moment in my life, I had been coaching, facilitating, and mentoring thousands of people. Whether it was elementary school kids when I was in high school, friends, students, and individuals from vulnerable communities in college, high school and college students in graduate school, or close family and people in need, it was the lens through which I saw the world. It's something innate within me. It might sound strange and mysterious, but I can see and feel misalignment. It's my superpower! And yet, in that moment so many years ago, it was hard to see my own misalignment. I had to undertake the work of understanding my own larger purpose and aligning my actions to it.

Today, I live and breathe purpose. Actually, my entire purpose in life is to help people discover and have the opportunity to live their purpose.

My superpower is kind of like those strange 3D optical images. You know, the ones that you squint and look at trying so hard to see the image lurking in the blur. Then when you finally stop trying—presto! You see the image. My lens is set on alignment, and I can see through the blur and optical illusions. I can help people discover their true reason for being, their ultimate purpose, the authentic version of themselves and strategically realign themselves to begin living their limitless lives.

I have integrated this approach throughout every level of my career: retail and service worker, teacher, professor, international diplomat, environmental scientist, expert on global climate change and localization, and now entrepreneur. I've worked with individuals, groups, leading corporations, and even nations at multiple levels. I've led international teams and advised global leaders on purpose and cohesion.

So, you can imagine how painful it is for me to see people's dreams and purpose wither and die from lack of nourishment and attention. Or to hear the words, "It's too late for me." It's even more painful because I actually experienced it myself. But I know in my heart that no one needs to live an unfulfilled life and the possibility of a limitless life is within your grasp.

Throughout my career, I have seen the transformation that comes when dreams explode into a fiery passion that cannot be extinguished, setting the soul on fire. After helping thousands of people, I can tell you that the only difference between dreams that die and dreams that remain alive is the fuel and direction they are given: time, attention, passion, belief, action, and taking them seriously. Without this fuel, they die. With it, they flourish. It really is that simple.

But sometimes our dreams and purpose get clouded because, along the way, we are given other people's dreams and purpose, passed down from generations of regrets and ambitions that were left not pursued or through society as check marks to achieve, aka *Chasing the American Dream*—and we don't even realize it. Worse yet, we start to live our dreams, and then we are bullied; our voice is silenced, and we give up. We then can't sort in our minds what we were told to be and who we really are, and, to compensate, we start focusing on our day-to-day and what we can control. We get comfortable with our lives and fear uncertainty. As Paulo Coelho states, "You are what you believe yourself to be" and, "There is only one thing that makes a dream impossible to achieve: the fear of failure."[2]

Our bodies start to show us the signs first.
Our minds catch up later.
We then finally wake up one day
and realize we are **MISALIGNED.**
We are functioning in one direction on the outside
with a different direction on the inside.
We are **MISMATCHED.**

Do you know this feeling? Sometimes, it's hard to differentiate. We realize something doesn't feel quite right, and we start to feel stuck, overwhelmed, exhausted, unfulfilled, like we just want more. Or worse, we knew it all along, and we feel guilty or scared or ungrateful for wanting more than we already have. So, we feel that we have no other choice but to live with misalignment.

When we are misaligned, we fail to thrive. We become like tropical flowers trying to flourish in the desert, parched and dry from lack of nourishment. We find ourselves in situations—jobs, relationships, locations—where we know we don't belong, where our minds, souls, and bodies aren't receiving the sustenance they need to thrive.

And I want you to thrive, to feel that your external actions are in harmony with your internal compass, driving you to become the greatest possible expression of who you are. When I talk about alignment, I mean the process of creating the conditions that allow and inspire *you* to thrive. I want you to be limitless, to reach your highest dreams and aspirations and find that peace that only you can bring to yourself.

On that note, did you know there's a phenomenon that occurs, known as the spring tide, when the Sun, Moon, and Earth are completely aligned with one another? This complete alignment creates the greatest gravitational pull on the Earth and brings the largest tides. The same type of force can happen for you when you are ALIGNED inside and out. I know this. I've seen it happen to so many people.

I am here to help make YOUR (not anyone else's) dreams and purpose real, to take them from invisible to visible. Do you know that feeling when everything just feels perfect, when the stars align? You can have that feeling every day and, even more, be the boss of your own life so you can build your personal empire, make a difference in the world, reduce stress, and live a fulfilled life. In other words, you can be limitless.

Why would I make such a bold statement? Because this book is for people who want more out of life. Those who have an inner calling to live their full potential and leave an impact in the world. The awake dreamers who may not have all the answers but have a deep desire to fulfill dreams, give more, and live life on their terms. The ones who have that little voice inside their head telling them they are meant for more. There's a reason why MVP (most valuable player) also stands for mission, vision, and purpose. It's time for MVP to refer to things outside of sports and include the true and deepest mission, vision, and purpose for our lives.

So, what is it that you want? I mean *really* want?

What will make you have true alignment? Where is your inner compass directing you? Is it toward more free time or financial freedom? Or perhaps it's toward launching a new business or finding your forever soulmate. Maybe you want to leave a legacy for your kids and grandchildren. Or perhaps you want to get your spark back in life and stop putting your dreams on the back burner.

Regardless of what your dreams are, I can tell you right now that there is a tried-and-tested formula that I have used and honed over decades of working with people. This formula will not only help you fulfill your dreams and step into purpose and alignment but sustain them—forever!

I know that may sound like a pretty big claim in the first pages of this book, but it's the truth. And I'm proof that it's possible.

There is a way you can have your dream life, have purpose, and feel aligned if you're willing to give it the time, attention, and consistent action it deserves.

There is a life compass you can use to navigate your life and give attention to all the things that are important to you.

Yes, I will bust the myth that says you can't have it all. Because with the right know-how—you can! How do I know? Because I was there... I was on the floor, so lost, confused, and dark.

I've had times when I didn't think I'd be able to juggle my work, family, and dreams. Many times, I was bullied and silenced when I started to live out my true purpose. I overcame many massive challenges and soul-searching times when I was misaligned. I now believe that what happens to you helps you define what's important, helps you discover what you're made of, and helps you crystallize what and who you really want in your life. I have it all, and so can you!

We must change impossible to "I am possible."

This is my mantra in life. I live it every day, even when it's hard. I have seen the power of making the impossible doable with the people, communities, and organizations I work with.

It starts with clarity of purpose, a vision and mission, and a solid plan that works for you. From high school, to college, to graduate school, to the workplace, people have always questioned my dreams. It's fair to say that I've had more naysayers than champions, but I have consistently proven all of them wrong. Hard work is a given—don't fool yourself into thinking that you can achieve your dreams, purpose, and alignment without putting in the work. But it takes so much more than that. With infinite possibilities, what direction do you choose? How do you know that you're making progress? How do you keep advancing toward your dreams when life gets tough? How do you differentiate other people's wants and dreams from your own? How do you stand tall when you pursue a purpose outside of the common path? How do you balance all the competing demands on your energy and time?

For me, at every stage of my life, the answer—**the formula**—my secret sauce has always been the same:

1. Analyze my purpose
2. Plot out the steps that take me in that direction
3. Align my actions to that purpose

Like many formulas, it seems so simple, but making it happen takes dedication, action, and systems. In the coming pages, I'll help you define the actions that advance your purpose and build the systems to see your progress every day and celebrate the accomplishments that will continue to fuel your dedication.

With passion and commitment, I made it happen. More importantly, I have complete alignment, which brings me happiness, balance, joy, and peace in my every day. No more overthinking and no more spinning thoughts. Alignment gives me the ability to thrive, not just survive.

Now, I'm certainly not saying there won't be challenges. I'm saying that with a solid plan, it *is* possible. One thing people often say is, "Esther, all I need is to get organized… Can't you just help me organize my to-do list and calendar?" I know that so many of you buy a new planner every year, with high hopes of "getting organized" so you can make progress on your dreams. And every year, from around March onwards, that planner stays empty. Your to-do list is just a set of tasks without priorities. Your to-do list isn't part of a plan or strategy, doesn't advance your purpose, and doesn't help you reach alignment. That's why you quit. Because, at the end of the day, you're right back where you started. We can do better.

My experience has proven that this potent formula I am about to show you for mapping your purpose doesn't only belong to individuals. I've used this mapping process successfully in communities, corporations, and even for entire countries. **Yes, it's not your ordinary purpose map!** It's designed to help you (or your organization or group) discover your passion and purpose, align your ultimate legacy, and enable you to thrive and scale your lifelong impact. It helps you get more out of life without giving up your dreams, sacrificing time with loved ones, or falling into a habit of overwork or self-neglect. Once you have full alignment, the sky's the limit.

See past today and get ready to unleash the life you love.

I'm going to show you how to design your own purpose map, which I call the Purpose Sun, so you can take charge of your life and do these three things on purpose:

- Multiply your productivity
- Reduce stress
- Thrive while building the life of your dreams

Make no mistake—I'm specifically talking about YOUR dream and purpose. I'm not talking about the cookie-cutter "American dream" or any other prepackaged goal that society, culture, or family says should be your dream. I'm interested in what lights you up, what sets fire to your soul, what makes you feel purposeful, significant, and valued. And I don't mean an Instagram-ready version of a "dream life," where you have to portray an image of perfection. It's not an image of a manufactured moment in time. Rather, it's a way of life, where you live with the certainty that your time and talents matter, and you naturally attract the people and energy that align with your purpose.

As the saying goes, "Create a life you don't need a vacation from."

What is that limitless life and vision for *you*?

PART ONE:

A SECOND CHANCE

Before we delve into mapping your purpose and starting your new journey, I'd like to share with you how this book came about. It wasn't an idea that spontaneously downloaded into my mind. It has been a lifelong journey that gave me the practical tools and applied knowledge to know that this works. Full disclosure—I'm going to share my personal and professional story with you so you can see the ways in which I applied this in my life, the struggles I had, and the ways I climbed out and pushed through. Like you, I've had my ups and downs, and it's the pendulum of life to which no one is immune. But despite life's natural uncertainty, I believe there's a way that we can plan and chart the course of our lives to be fully aligned and resilient to the challenges that life places before us. As the adage goes, "We cannot direct the wind, but we can adjust the sails." I'll teach you how to ride and overcome the waves, while *you* adjust the sails. Deal?

THE LEGACY OF DREAMS

I was born in Nicaragua during a time of civil war and revolution. My father was a prominent figure, and we lived in the nation's capital, Managua. Helping others and striving for positive change in the world, literally fighting for justice, is in my family's blood and in its history. My great grandfather, Dr. Benjamín Zeledón, believed deeply in the importance of Nicaraguan freedom and sovereignty. A brilliant writer and politician, he said (translated by the author):

> Without Freedom there is no life; without equality there is no light; without national autonomy, chaos reigns ... We fight because Freedom gives us life, Equality gives us Light

> and because effective national Autonomy, regained, makes disappear the chaos through which we sail.[1]

More than just words, he lived his beliefs. He became a leader in the revolution, defending his country against what he saw as treason by its own government. Dr. Zeledón was killed by U.S. Marines during the Battle of Coyotepe Hill in 1912, and his body was dragged through the streets around the country to strike fear into the hearts of those who supported the revolution. Instead, Dr. Zeledón became the enduring symbol of pride, patriotism, and bravery that still lives on in the hearts and minds of the Nicaraguan people. His image is emblazoned on the national currency, and his unwavering passion courses through the veins of his descendants. My great grandfather's strength and courage lives within me.

When I was born, I was a very sickly child, and my mom often had to take me to Costa Rica for medical care. I had several health problems, but a critical point arrived when I turned visibly yellow, as though I had been poisoned. A doctor diagnosed me with a small urethra, which made urination difficult and caused a buildup of toxic chemicals in my body. If I didn't get surgery to correct the issue, I would die. The surgeons in Costa Rica and Nicaragua couldn't perform the complex operation, so I would need to go to the children's hospital in Miami and spend six months there. My parents, however, didn't have the money, and the situation in Nicaragua had become extremely dicey. With no clear options available, everyone thought I was going to die. Sometimes, in moments like these, fate intervenes.

My father, although not a religious man, is a big believer in fate, and I get a lot of my beliefs from him. We believe in destiny. We are also practical enough to know that sometimes for fate to intervene, it just needs a little nudge. You have to tell the universe what you want! I was so sick, and Dad was desperate. He wanted to buy a lottery ticket, but Mom said it was not a priority and too expensive. But Dad didn't give up there. He split the cost with my mom's sister, took the biggest gamble of his life, and bet everything on a game of chance, the outcome of which would determine whether I would live or die. It's interesting looking back on this now because he is equally a high achiever, overthinker, and risk-averse, but he just knew I was special and worth it. He asked me to choose the numbers because, according to him, I was the "lucky one." Lottery ticket in hand, Dad sat back and hoped that the winds of fate would blow in a favorable direction—and they did. He won the money needed to save my life.

Once we received the payout, Mom took me to Miami, where we stayed for six months. During that time, we spent all of the money on medical treatment, but I got the lifesaving surgery I needed, and I survived. My mom also sacrificed those months for me and left my sister in Nicaragua. Fate intervened in a favorable way, but the ideal conditions wouldn't have existed if it weren't for my father's persistence and willingness to take a risk. Call it fate, divine intervention, or just dumb luck—either way, Dad's big gamble and Mom's sacrifice are the reasons why I survived to tell this story and why I put an enormous amount of guilt and expectation on myself.

"I knew it was the future, even if no one else could see it."

LEAVING HOME FOR SAFER SHORES

After we returned home, the situation in Nicaragua deteriorated, and life got more dangerous. The country was still recovering from decades of unrest, dictatorial regimes, and civil war, and Dad received a serious bomb threat. He didn't agree with some of the government's policies and actions, which made him a target. He has the same defiant spirit that my great grandfather showed during the uprising of the early 1900s. (So do I, but more on that later). But when you criticize the government in Nicaragua or anyone in power, you better be ready to protect your life. The country was no longer safe for us, and we had to leave.

Luckily, Dad already had alternate plans. He would get a scholarship to either complete his PhD or go to law school overseas. He applied to several graduate schools and received offers from Oxford, Kent, McGill, Harvard, and UC Berkeley. After considering all of the options, he settled on UC Berkeley, and we moved to the United States and made California our new home. I was around four years old.

Mind you, my parents had already left Nicaragua twice before and returned. They spent four years in Europe, where Dad studied at Oxford and Mom worked as an au pair. During those years, they left my older brother with my grandma. Later, they went to Ohio for Dad's master's to study and publish the story of Afro-Nicaraguans on the Atlantic coast, only to learn a month later that the government didn't have enough money to fund them. This didn't stop my dad. He worked five jobs, and my mom gave up her scholarship so they could help bring this history to light. My dad was not driven by money, and together they returned to Nicaragua to help the country and its people, only to have to leave once again. After losing three homes and all their money, Mom vowed to never return. Dad did end up moving back for a time, but more on that later.

Because of my earlier health issues, my parents always treated me as if I were fragile and weak. But they weren't like this with my older sister, Sonia. At the time, they saw Sonia as the strong one. In my parents' minds, she would go on to do great things and perhaps even become president one day, but I, Esther, just needed to live and not get sick. I mean, it was a close call. But that was my initial assigned purpose in life: to live.

Adopting a mindset like that comes with negative side effects, and my parents never pushed me as hard as they did Sonia. They never encouraged me to dream big, create lofty goals, or have oversized ambitions. I just had to live, go to college, and get married. Because of this, I developed a "fixed mindset" early on, and transitioning to a "growth mindset" took time and a lot of work. (We'll discuss mindset in depth at the beginning of Part Two). Before you judge my parents, it's really hard to have a sick kid and when I became a mom, I understood the reasons why. I learned how scary it is to almost lose your kid and how traumatic it could be as a parent to face that again. The fear is all-consuming and exhausting. You never want to go through that again or see them suffer. I was meant for more than just living, college, and marriage, but it would take some time for them, and for me, to realize it.

When we first arrived in California, I took a test to determine my English proficiency, as I mainly spoke Spanish. It soon became clear that I wouldn't pass kindergarten with my current language skills and speech problems. I could barely speak English at all. When Mom realized I wouldn't pass, she promised the teachers that she would get me language learning cassettes and I would learn to speak English well. I was a very disciplined child, so, using the cassette tapes Mom gave me, I practiced and practiced and practiced until I was finally fluent enough to pass the test. My mom taught me how to plan and persist against all odds. It's something I still carry today. Thus, even at that age, if there was a goal, I set my eyes on it. However, once I passed, the teachers demanded that I use English only, which meant that I had to abandon Spanish completely. It was the advice-trend in the U.S. at the time. At home, my parents would speak to me in Spanish, and I would respond in English. Gradually, the language I had grown up speaking faded from memory, and I became English-only. I am now a very vocal advocate against this approach. When my daughter, whom you will learn about later, had her own speech delays, I went against that same advice and chose for her to learn both Spanish and English anyways, and I'm so glad I did. Today, I still have an accent in both languages, but I am so grateful to be bilingual and bicultural.

From kindergarten to fourth grade, we lived on the outskirts of Berkeley in a place called Walnut Creek. Those years were amazing for me. Dad was a graduate student; Mom was getting her MBA and worked at Macy's, and we lived in a small, safe, quiet suburb. Our backyard was big, and we had a lot of green space and outdoor freedom. To me, it was paradise. I would spend my afternoons daydreaming with my imaginary friends, playing outside in green space and clean air with my bestest friend, and being active. Because Dad frequently took me to the university, I got exposed to that world at a young age. Sometimes, I helped him photocopy documents and find books he needed for research, and other times I rode my bike around campus, exploring the sprawling school grounds, feeling the air on my face, and being outside. The campus had a view of the Golden Gate Bridge and ocean, which was just amazing.

At the time, my parents didn't have much money, but there were plenty of free things to do in the Bay Area. Even on a lowly grad student income, we managed to do a lot of memorable activities, such as visiting Mount Diablo to see the snow, driving near the Golden Gate Bridge, and attending free fairs. We spent a lot of time outdoors, appreciating nature, and I grew up seeing the world through an environmental lens. We never ate out or took vacations, but none of that mattered because I had my best friend, who lived across the street and was of Indonesian descent. I also had my older brother, Maximo, who would take silly videos of me. Most importantly, I had space. The time I spent exploring the natural environment as a young girl would shape the person I'd later become and the path I'd eventually take—I just didn't know it at the time. Back then, being out in nature—experiencing the greenery, life, and the natural energy—was simply a great way to spend the day and gave me the space to be grounded and aligned. I look back on those days fondly.

WHEN THE PATH GROWS DARK

Growing up in California, I didn't understand our economic situation. Sure, I noticed that we never bought anything expensive, that Maximo would mention the Ku Klux Klan was in nearby neighborhoods, and that my mom would comment on how mean people were to her when she gift wrapped presents for people at Macy's. Also, Dad had a long commute to campus, but we lived in a good house in a nice suburb, and I had everything I ever needed: lots to do, a great school, and my best friend, who was like a sister to me. My life felt like one of abundance. I had everything I needed to thrive, and I never felt poor. I did notice that we were constantly bargain hunting and using a lot of coupons, trying to do everything on the cheap, and almost never went to restaurants. I also saw how my mom both worked and was studying for her MBA at night, how my sister would be the one to make me dinner, and how Maximo would get my clothes for me on discount at the store where he worked. My job was to be the coupon cutter of the family, and I was in charge of receipts.

My parents also found a way of creating illusions of vacations when we visited family. For example, my uncle lived in Los Angeles, so we took road trips to visit him and, along the way, would visit something outdoors. I remember those trips fondly because I would ride facing backwards in the station wagon, staring at the other cars and daydreaming of the world, life, and the future. We stayed in cheap motels—Days Inn and others—and we drove long hours to minimize costs, but it was still a vacation of sorts. My parents would inspect the hotels first, and my sister and I would either share the bed or would sleep on the floor with sheets.

As a kid, I never understood why we rarely stopped at the sights. Once I was older, I understood that it was about the cost. Often, we would drive close to a sight, such as the Grand Canyon, take a picture, and Dad would tell us the history. Or we would stop in front of the Alamo but wouldn't go in. Unfortunately, not all of my memories from these trips are pleasant. I won't forget being kicked out of a restaurant and being called spics, and all of the other times when we were pulled over, with my parents being super polite to the policemen and all us kids being scared in the car. My parents always taught us that, as immigrants, we needed to stay calm, be respectful, and never ever argue back. "Keep your head down and maintain a low profile." Our life felt a lot like my favorite movies, *An American Tail* and *Elemental*, where we were a family of immigrants trying to make it in a new country full of danger and uncertainty.

In the end, though, I am super grateful for those experiences. With the little they had, my parents did everything they could to show us the world and the sights. They showed me that you can travel, immerse yourself in culture, and meet people without needing much. I remember that during those trips, I would imagine myself as Walt Disney. I loved everything about Disney. He was visionary, had huge dreams, wanted to make the world a better place, and had created this place, which was modern and safe, where dreams could come true. He was a trailblazer, ahead of his time, and saw potential in things where people saw none. I wanted to be Walt

Disney. As often as they could, my parents did save up to take me to Disney, and those trips were the most magical.

Those days, living in the Bay Area, we had one television at home, one of those big, chunky, old ones with a manual dial. I remember watching the war in Iraq and the bombs on-screen and lying there when, suddenly, the earth began shaking horrifically. Mom had begged Dad not to go on the Bay bridge that day, which he was supposed to do, but she was feeling sick. She just felt that something was off that day, and, for some reason, he decided to listen to her. As she predicted, the earth shook like I had never experienced before. The bridge fell that day at around the same time he would have driven across. Again, fate, or something, had intervened. Picture frames went flying; mirrors broke, and we experienced aftershocks all night.

During that San Francisco earthquake of 1989, Mom lost a pregnancy. She was six months pregnant at the time, but the sheer terror she felt caused her to miscarry. It was the first time I felt death so close. I had been really excited to have a younger sibling, and, outside of being with my best friend, I felt really lonely. It wasn't the last time our family would face a natural disaster.

After the earthquake, Mom finished her MBA as valedictorian, top of her class. All those evening classes, where we would pick her up listening to Whitney Houston and 80s classics and I would be passed out in the car, had finally paid off.

Within this time frame, Mom got pregnant again, this time with my little brother, Benjamin. I was older now but didn't know what this meant for us. Unfortunately, Dad's PhD scholarship ended, and what little money we had before was gone. We always lived paycheck to paycheck, and he had the never-ending burden of supporting his mom and two mentally challenged brothers in addition to all of us. Dad felt he had no other choice but to return to Nicaragua for work, but Mom refused to move back there again. She had finished her MBA at the top of her class and had dreams of being able to use it. Over the years, they had left their home country and returned three times and every single time lost everything they had built: house, possessions, bank accounts, and so on. Mom didn't want to do it a fourth time, and the fear of possibly losing it again was too much. She was exhausted and tired of sacrificing herself. I saw her midlife turn into a time of questioning and vocalizing.

The family needed a change, a new start. We had family in Miami, and they seemed to be doing OK, so moving there made sense at the time. Plus, there they were friendlier to immigrants. You could, even with an accent, utilize your MBA and education. But looking back, we are not too sure if it was the best decision. My parents often say that if Dad had chosen McGill University in Canada instead of going to UC Berkeley, perhaps things would have been better for them there, away from the devastating natural disasters, in a country with a higher level of social services and retirement benefits.

Moving us mid school year was a disaster. In the middle of fourth grade, pregnant Mom, Sonia, and I moved to Miami, while Dad returned to Nicaragua to work. My sister and I flew from

California to Miami on our own (and, yes, they sent us with no child accompaniment, since that was very expensive). It was our first taste of our new life, where we would have to learn the system and navigate ourselves. It was also the first time I had flown on an airplane since moving to California five years before. I was nine years of age. I will never forget running through the airport with my sister to catch our connecting flight, neither of us knowing whether we were doing the right thing or what to expect. I was so scared of the airplane. I had no memory of being on one before. We were just kids, and I was losing my best friend. I think that moment was what helped me understand how scary it was for my parents to send us alone, and for us as well.

We lived with my aunt for a while, which was a shock to the system because we went from having a lot of green space to being crammed into a tiny town house with multiple family members. It was also a huge sacrifice for my aunt, who had her own set of obligations, so my parents were grateful for the help. We also lost the amazing health insurance that we had under Dad's graduate school program, and Mom had to go on the government system, which, as you can imagine, was awful. My mom had a high-risk pregnancy and preeclampsia. During the birth, they refused to give her any anesthesia, and she felt that she was passing out and dying. They treated my mother like garbage. She had to yell and advocate for herself while giving birth because she was losing consciousness, all while sharing a room with several other women. Even when Mom was induced, the medical staff didn't give her an epidural or any anesthesia. She told Dad that she felt she was dying, so he went and yelled at the right people and got them to help her. This would also mark the first of many incidents where we would have to advocate and fight for medical care. I remember Dad's face that day when he came to my aunt's house. He was so traumatized and exhausted and didn't eat. I don't understand how people judge others on government medical programs—trust me, it's not a situation people want or choose to be in. There's nothing nice about it other than getting basic care.

Those days were a shock for all of us. Soon, after my new baby brother, Benjamin, spent some time in the incubator, we moved out of my aunt's place and rented a small town house of our own, but I was still mourning what we had left behind. I no longer had my green space, my best friend, or my father. Mom worked late nights at Walmart, so I rarely saw her either, and much of the responsibility for my little brother fell on my grandmother, who was already elderly, me, and my sister. My grandma moved in to both help us and for us to help her. I felt horrifically trapped in this concrete town house, where the neighbors were extremely unfriendly, and we had no private space. Worst of all, I lost access to nature and green space, which was essential to my well-being. Mom's dream of using her MBA also had to take a pause while she worked those nights at Walmart. I stopped imagining, visioning, or dreaming. I became silent. My escape was to watch telenovelas on Univision and Telemundo with my grandma at nights and talk about the characters. I learned later that watching Spanish telenovelas is a shared experience among so many people around the world, from Kosovo and Estonia to Latin America. For almost three entire years, I barely saw my parents at all, and my sister and I weren't close. Those were my dark days. I just felt numb most of the time. In

Berkeley, I was used to feeling safe whenever I walked anywhere, but Miami was a different beast. I could no longer walk home from school without being harassed. I will always remember my aunt forgetting to pick me up from school one day (before you judge her, she had a million things on her plate). After two hours of waiting, I started to walk home, weighed down by all my projects. On the way home, a man pulled up in a pickup truck. He had a California sticker, so, at first, I was like, *how cool.* But soon, he got out of his car and flashed me. He was completely naked and started to chase me. I hid in the bushes for two-plus hours and eventually made it home to hide in my room.

I told my mom after she came home from a long day. I felt guilty and horrible since she already had so much to deal with. As it was, I would sometimes find her crying alone. The school couldn't really do anything. I didn't take his license plate, and I could only describe him as a hairy old man. I remember being so angry at myself for not remembering his license plate and for feeling completely useless. I've since learned that this is a common trait of people pleasers, perfectionists, and high achievers. Rather than taking the moment to be gentle with myself because I had gone through something traumatic, my first response was to blame myself for being an added weight. The world suddenly became a scary place. On top of that, our economic situation was bad, even though both of my parents worked as much as they could. Dad was saving all the money he earned to get us a house in the suburbs, so we had to stretch every dollar as thinly as possible.

The negativity surrounding my new life in Miami affected the way I thought about the world and how I reacted to my environment. The city changed me. I lost all my dreams and just lived day-to-day. My personality also changed, and I lost my light. Sound familiar? And my sister. It was hard to watch her every day. She was this vibrant powerhouse in California. She had so much energy. She was popular, free, and bold. From the moment we moved, she became silent, quiet, and was in charge of our little brother. She also helped Mom and would pick me up from school. Suddenly, she was an adult before ever wanting to be. She had lost her spark, and we just sat there most nights in our shared room, motionless. We talk about it now a lot. Those were our dark years. And at the same time, those years changed her life. She became really close to my mom, and together we all built resilience.

In 1992, when Hurricane Andrew hit Florida, my family and I had to face the disaster without my father. Benjamin was very young at the time, and the experience—with the wind and the flooding and the chaos—was terrifying. We bunkered with my extended family and although a tragedy, I felt closer to being part of a community. This was the first time I saw my second idol, American meteorologist, Bryan Norcross, on television. He was helping us all through the crisis. I admired how he was coaching viewers by providing critical information and inspiration but also being firm. I wrote a letter to him explaining how he made a difference in our lives. I still had a lot to learn before I understood why I admired him so much.

Even though we had been through a lot, my parents taught us that there were always people experiencing worse conditions than us. They really instilled in us the belief that, when someone is struggling, you can always do something to help. When Hurricane Andrew devastated Miami, Sonia, Mom, and I spent our weekends volunteering: handing out food, offering aid, and doing whatever we could to help. But even then, I remember passing out food, thinking, *Is this what they really want and need? Are we really helping?* I always felt like it wasn't enough.

That introduction to service made me realize that I loved helping others. Those were the only times in the darkness where I felt light again. It would be brief for that moment, but it was there. As the years went by, I began taking a different exit off the public bus so I could go to the elementary school to tutor kids. In high school, I tutored students who were falling behind in class. All throughout my school years, I helped others whenever I could, and I built relationships that I still have today. Come to think about it, I have been coaching others since I was in middle school.

Sonia received a full scholarship and left for school in Massachusetts, and I began to feel more alone in Miami. Although we weren't close, she was company. This took an almost 180-degree turn later in life. I'll get to that part. I was getting into trouble a lot, hanging out with the wrong crowd, skipping school, smoking, exposing myself to things beyond my age, and generally acting out. Yes, I even had the skinny eyebrows and black lip liner look. We had moved to a house in the suburbs, but I was still hanging around with the same crowd, still finding ways to rebel against a situation I didn't want to be in. I did have a balcony at home, which was the closest thing to having green space. I would sing on my balcony and stare at the stars. I would also spend a lot of time with my close extended family primas and tias, which made things a lot more bearable. As my therapist explained to me years later, I was yearning for belonging. Plus, add in teenage hormones.

I was on a dark path that led nowhere good. I needed light, a lifeline, a new direction, but Miami wasn't the place to show me a better way forward. I'm sure many of you are confused because the Miami you see on television is beaches, bright lights, and vibrancy. But with no money or resources, I can count on my hand how many times I saw the beach. It just rained all the time, and it wasn't until college that I really saw Miami. Soon, however, I would get exactly what I needed. When I flew to Massachusetts to visit Sonia at college, I finally saw a brighter path.

"You don't owe anyone anything, and, beyond regrets, you don't get anything from sacrificing."

A TASTE OF SOMETHING BETTER

At Wellesley College, I met people who traveled the world. I met people who attended talks and conferences, always wanting to learn more, and I met people who had ambitions beyond moving out of their parents' house and getting married. Instead of gossiping and wanting to get in trouble, they discussed ideas. I saw classes where they asked the students for their analyses, where class sizes were 5–10 people, and where women spoke up and had amazing insights. These were the people I wanted to be around. These were the people I wanted to *be*.

Our economic situation and geographic location didn't inspire big dreams, but seeing this new world, knowing what might be possible, made me realize that I wanted something more from life. I wanted to take that brighter path and see where it led. I knew I needed a new circle.

Sonia lived in a dorm that had its own chef, and the food was not only amazing, but it was also all-you-can-eat. Until then, an annual birthday trip to Red Lobster was the closest I got to eating anything special. *I still to this day love Red Lobster and cheesy breads*. But now, I was eating *real* chef's food, which, as a teenager, was amazing. After spending time at Wellesley, I realized there was a world of endless possibilities and that I was limitless. I now had a new direction in life. My life in Miami didn't match the new one I imagined for myself so when I returned home, I made some serious changes. I needed to realign.

First, I changed the crowd I hung around with. This was *key* and something you'll see I've had to do several times in my life. While I felt like a new person, Miami and my friendship group were still the same. Being lumped in with my peers and trying to fit in for so long made me forget that I wasn't them and that I could have my own dreams—*big* dreams. So, I stopped hanging around with anyone who might hold me back from my new path and became closer to a select few whom I could trust to be my champions. I knew I couldn't stay in Miami long-term. I was going to university, and no one would stand in the way of me being around people who had visions, dreams, alignment, and purpose.

Our family went through a big transition, as my parents decided that it was time Dad returned from Nicaragua to be more present for us kids. They had also purchased a house in the U.S. that was theirs, a property they felt they could finally call their own. They had obtained the American dream. I had spent years missing their full support and their opinions, and the shift in our home situation came at a welcome time but was also a huge adjustment. At first, I resented Dad being home and wanted it to be just us, but I also knew we needed him around.

At the time, it was hard for me to see the magnitude of my dad's sacrifice. He was a prominent figure in Nicaragua but in Miami, he was just someone else. He started assisting immigration lawyers. He was a lawyer in Nicaragua, so he knew law. But without being a member of the bar in the U.S., he could only assist lawyers or serve as an interpreter in court, which he did for years. The stories, though, from the court weighed on him a lot, and it was often hard for him to have to watch how the judges treated immigrants.

During her time in Massachusetts, Sonia seemed to have transformed into a completely different person, and I had the privilege of witnessing her life from a new perspective. Like the story of *Encanto*, her journey was filled with sacrifices and burdens that I was just beginning to appreciate. My visit to Massachusetts had a similar effect on me. The atmosphere seemed charged with positive change, and I couldn't help but absorb it all.

Sonia took on multiple work-study jobs and went above and beyond to support me. She bought me my very first GAP bag and bodysuit, which I loved, and she revealed the secret of keeping receipts and taking advantage of price adjustments within a fourteen-day window. I was also amazed to discover that Wellesley offered a wardrobe for students on financial aid, and Sonia managed to grab some stunning designer suits that eventually got handed down to me. She also taught me invaluable mindset skills like problem-solving, the art of hustling, and just plain "figuring it out." It all felt like a dream come true, and I couldn't wait to get to college.

But I was worried. There was no way my parents could afford to send me to college, especially to a school as expensive as Wellesley. All of Sonia's friends were scholarship students, so I knew that was a viable option. I figured that with a lot of hard work, my dream was achievable. But to earn a scholarship, you have to be at the top of your class, so that became my goal. Even then, I thought like a high achiever.

Once Sonia's friends knew what I planned to do, they began mentoring me during the visit and offering advice. When they were home, Sonia and my cousin, who had also gotten a scholarship, would say things like:

"You have to be focused."

"If you want to get the scholarship, you have to get straight A's."

"You can't be wasting time with boys."

I missed being on a college campus with the people and the ideas and the electric atmosphere. The whole experience really sparked me, and I knew I had to find my way back. Not back to

Wellesley specifically, but back to an environment that excited me and animated my soul. "I'm going to make a plan," I said to myself. I didn't know exactly what that plan would entail because I wasn't supposed to have grand ambitions. I was the sickly kid with speech problems, remember? Sonia was always the smart one, the one who would succeed and fulfill her dreams, the one who could become president one day. After that trip, Sonia and I started spending more time together when she was home. We began to develop a special, unbreakable bond that we still have to this day. She trusted me, and I knew from that moment she had my best interests in mind. She was the first person to believe in me and believe that I was meant for more.

I also forgot an important part of the story. Remember when I was told to become English-only? Well, when we first moved to Miami, the other kids made fun of me because I couldn't speak Spanish. Focusing on English made sense in Berkeley, but Miami was a different demographic, and most of my peers defaulted to Spanish. So, I made another goal: I would relearn the language I had lost. At age thirteen, my grand plan was taking shape. I would learn to speak Spanish again, focus on getting good grades, and earn my ticket to a new life. But, as we know, things don't always go according to plan, and I knew nothing about planning for contingencies then.

A NEW CROWD, A NEW OUTLOOK

The timing for change was perfect because I was moving to a different school. At my new school, I enrolled in a gifted magnet program and was immediately surrounded by a very different group of people. Even though I still lived in the same neighborhood, I now had access to a whole new crew. My new circle. My peers were focused on doing well in school, getting ahead, and chasing their dreams. Finally, I had a great circle of friends, and it was exactly what I needed. I also started to dream again. I started paying attention to the magazines my dad would purchase: *Time* and *National Geographic*. One time, I saw a cover with someone who appeared to be from the United Nations. She looked so confident and was fighting for a cause. I wanted to be on that cover—I wanted to be her.

Still, high school was a difficult time for me. In order to catch the public bus, I had to get up at 5.30 a.m. for an early pickup, so I was constantly tired. I also still had many health issues related to my hormones and periods. Sometimes, I would just randomly bleed at school through all my clothes, and I would wake up horrifically nauseated in the mornings. But I knew I couldn't miss school. I had to be top of my class. I would push through horrific cramping and pain and sickness. I would bleed and have to change my clothes, and I would go to school sick. I used to try as long as possible to hide the pain from my parents to avoid being a burden, but, at one point, it became so unbearable that we went to the doctor.

As it turned out, I had a cyst the size of a baby. It scared Mom, and I ended up going on different birth control pills. I won't forget the time I told my youth Catechism teacher that I was on them for my health, and she told me it was a sin and that I shouldn't take them. It was one of the first times that I really felt the pressure of external societal influences pushing me to change who I was and how I acted. After that, I kept my condition private from my teachers.

Due to my family's financial situation, I received discounted lunch at school, but the food had to be eaten inside the cafeteria. This arbitrary rule did little more than highlight the class divide. My friends didn't eat in the cafeteria, so, in order to spend time with them, I often wouldn't eat at all. Sometimes, when Mom gave me the small amount of money I was meant to use for discounted lunches, I saved it over the course of a week and bought a pizza or something else at full price to eat wherever I wanted. The price of one item off the regular menu equaled the cost of a week's worth of discounted lunches. On weekends, I would also babysit for extra cash. What did I spend it on? School lunches, of course. Looking back, the crazy thing was that if I were honest and open and communicated my needs to my family, we probably could have found a solution and made peanut butter sandwiches or something else. But, instead, I stayed quiet to avoid burdening them and because I felt they wouldn't understand. I also didn't tell my friends because I didn't want to lose them or be bullied. I wanted to be part of the circle and have conversations about the future. I felt that the only way to keep everyone happy, be less of a burden, and be safe was to people please. I was ashamed and didn't want to lose my circle, and I felt the weight of needing to keep up appearances.

Growing up, I was taught that you don't talk about money or your financial situation with anyone, but I didn't fully understand our situation. I was a kid of highly educated parents, yet we lived paycheck to paycheck. (Later, I learned that so many immigrant families are in this situation). So, not only did I spend much of high school tired, but I was also hungry. Between walking everywhere and not eating, it's no wonder I was so skinny. I actually hadn't spoken openly about this until now and never told my family.

Even though I was hanging out with a new crowd, certain aspects of the Miami mentality stuck with me. Doing well in school was fine, but, in such a machismo culture, getting married by a certain age and having a family were the ultimate goals. Within me, the desire to have the life I wanted competed with the urge to fulfill cultural expectations, and I found myself torn between two paths. I started to give up on fighting every battle, and I decided to give in to the construct of being married.

Thus, in high school, I had a boyfriend whom I was sure I would marry. Great, I could check that box off, and then we could construct my dreams together. I was obsessed with the life we were going to create, and we planned our entire future together. This became my fantasy—check mark. I mean, he was Nicaraguan, and his family knew mine. This had to be a sign, right? Fate, right? This is the tricky thing about life. Without really knowing your true alignment and purpose, you can misread signs and interpret them how you think they should be rather than as they truly are. You start to think life is telling you one thing when it's something completely different.

I decided that once we graduated high school, we would go

to college, get married, and continue our journey through life as husband and wife. I was obsessed with the idea of what we should be rather than what we were. Plus, I loved, LOVED his family. His mom, I saw as a second mother. I even had a chance recently to see her and tell her, and it was nice to know that the feelings were mutual. So, I wanted so badly for my relationship to work because I didn't want to lose her too. Even though I had big dreams, they all revolved around the social and cultural constructs of marriage.

Worse yet, since I wanted to leave so badly and have what I saw in Wellesley, rather than listening to what he wanted to do, I pushed him into following my goal and dream to the point of even losing the romance and love around us. Not long ago, I found a letter I had written to him, supposedly a love letter. I was horrified when I read it. The letter was basically a to-do list, instruction manual, for how we would start crafting our lives. I told him in the letter what he needed to score on his SAT, that he shouldn't join the military as he wanted, and that we needed to go to college together. Definitely not a love letter.

I had not yet fully broken free of suburban Miami's influence. I wanted so badly to make both things—romance and success—fit each other at all costs but without taking the time to analyze if this was even the right fit. How could I when I was still living and growing in that problematic environment? Only a world-shattering event could sever the final ties that bound me to those cultural expectations around life and marriage.

During high school, I wanted to be a highly affectionate person, especially with my boyfriend, but it was something I really struggled with. Fear of judgment and a deeply ingrained habit of people-pleasing held me back from realizing this version of myself. I was also worried about what my parents would think—I lived in constant fear of getting in trouble and being a burden—so I suppressed the desire to show affection, to hug people, to truly be myself. I was the ultimate people pleaser. Remember, my parents spent all their money on the lottery to save me. I was given a second chance. I owed them; I owed the world, and I did everything to please everyone. I would also take any criticism from friends, siblings, anyone, and would just stay quiet.

Back then, I hadn't learned constructive ways to communicate. When I would speak up in defense of my friends or against the injustices I saw done to them, I did it in a way that was overly aggressive and sometimes hurtful, and I would lose them in return. I had no practice. So, with time, whenever the chance to express my true self or expose injustices around me arose, I would freeze and let external influences control my actions.

I also found that people were very unforgiving of any mistake I made. But I realized later it was because I gave the image that I was perfect, so any error I made seemed like a big deal. I also didn't communicate enough. It's hard now to imagine that I was the little girl who hated public speaking, never spoke in class, saw injustices and stayed quiet, and just put my head down and worked hard. As my parents put it, I was the "perfect child." What people didn't see was the enormous amount of anxiety I had, how much I put everyone else's needs before my own, and how I later became deathly afraid of showing any weakness.

Understandably, my hesitance to show affection put a strain on my relationship. I suppressed the real me and behaved in a way that

I thought was right—how a lady who was marriage material needed to act. I still won't forget that, once in school, there was a rumor started about me that I gave a blow job on the bus. I wanted to die, and I blamed myself for that rumor. I thought I must have caused it somehow. There was all this language in Miami about being one of *those girls* versus being the girl that a boy would take seriously and marry. Boys at school, my father, extended family, and friends constantly spoke about this. By the way, sex was never talked about. I think I saw my parents peck kiss once. Maybe?

Dad was also still a public figure in the Nicaraguan community, so I had to maintain a good reputation and be a respectable lady. That was the interesting part of my childhood. We had no money but had social status (remember the story about my great grandfather?), so there was a lot of pressure to maintain our image. My cousin was on the dance team, and I was so envious of her freedom to do that. She looked free and happy and was having fun. It was something I always wanted to do but the one time I expressed wanting to join the dance team, I was told no because of the bus, and there would be boys, and there was no money, and there was no time, and that wasn't something good girls did, and so on. In the end, it wasn't worth asking or insisting. I would eventually join dance groups in college, but I should have voiced my desire to join the team then, little by little, and built a case for it. You can't really thrive if you're living your life always waiting for the next stage to arrive.

Shunning your true self can only ever lead to misery and regret. My high school boyfriend, the man I was meant to marry, ended our relationship to pursue other high school girls, and I, of course, blamed myself. What's worse is that he also never communicated, and he lied, but I blamed myself for pushing him to go to college, blamed myself for my lack of affection. I was so worried about everyone else's approval and what they thought of me that my boyfriend didn't get the chance to know the true me inside. The worst part, though, was losing his family. They had become *my* family, and I felt so comfortable talking to them. I admired how open they were in conversation and how apariencias (how you appear from the outside) didn't matter as much. They knew me—the real me—and valued all of me. I still love them dearly to this day. When my relationship ended, some of my darkest days followed.

"I don't know how, but we'll make it work."

HITTING ROCK BOTTOM, SURVIVING THE FALL

The aftermath of my breakup was a disaster. We were really close. I was sixteen at the time, and I had known him since I was eleven. We had been friends at first, and, although we'd had a dysfunctional relationship (he had his issues too and was not innocent by any means, but that's his story to tell) based on poor communication and mistrust over the years, I had created a romance novel scenario in my mind in which fate had brought us together, and everything would work out in the end, no matter how different we were. Add to that the loss of my "second mom"—the whole situation was devastating.

For the first time ever, I suffered serious anxiety and hit a hard rock bottom. I started to feel confused about who was my friend and who wasn't. I didn't know whom I could trust anymore, given that some of my friends started dating my ex or had been flirting with him in the past. I realized that my positive circle was not as positive as I thought. Nor was he. I felt like I was in a Shakespearean novel, where the closest people to me were the ones who were the most harsh and traitorous. Some of them, deep down inside, had always envied me or had seen my life as "perfect" or had pretended to tolerate me. On top of which, I had a creepy teacher hitting on me.

I also realized one important mistake: I had given my life to one person and neglected myself. I realized that once I started dating him, I began to neglect my circle and friends. I had no real support group or contingency plan. I didn't have a strong network of friends or support anymore, and I felt extremely lonely. My dreams and purpose no longer felt attainable. I had gone really dark.

I still had to try to maintain a facade during the day and at family events and keep doing well in school. Maintaining this character and avatar that I had to show to the outside world was exhausting. Some days, I couldn't hide it, and I would break down in the middle of the day, making it so much worse. I couldn't keep the "show must go on" mentality anymore. This mixed with an inability to sleep at night, and the heaviness in my heart, became unbearable.

One night, I decided I couldn't take the pain anymore and I had no more gift to give to the world. I was done with my life, so I swallowed a large number of pills in a bid to end the pain. I couldn't hide my pain anymore. I didn't want to be a burden anymore. Because I had overdosed, I started to get really sick. When my parents asked what had happened, I told them I had taken some expired medication because I wanted to sleep. I started to feel much worse, the full effect of the pills hitting me hard, and Mom rushed me to the hospital.

I ended up in the ER, but I was lucky. I didn't do any permanent damage to myself, and, luckily, I didn't end my life. They gave me a lot of shots, and everything was one big cloud—a blur. Although I had fooled my parents with a fake explanation, the doctor saw right through it. Honestly, I think my sister and parents knew too. Before I left the next day, the doctor asked to speak with me alone. My parents waited outside while we talked.

"I know what you tried," he said. "Do I have to intervene, or was it a onetime thing?" I was regretful and told him that I wouldn't try it ever again. The worst had happened: I had become the burden. But instead of chastising me or making me feel guilty, he gave me a big pep talk, saying that suicide, which he explained could have been the result, wasn't worth it, and what I was feeling would eventually fade. He actually managed to change my perspective. "Every day will be better. You have your whole life ahead of you," he said. And he was right. Because that doctor had chosen to meet with me alone, we were able to have an honest conversation—I could speak freely without my family there—and his words made a huge difference. He asked me what I wanted to do with my life and encouraged me to do it. I had a goal to reach, and feeling sorry for myself wasn't a part of the plan. I hope he knows how that talk made a big difference, but I do wish the doctor had prescribed me therapy—it would have done me good then.

During my depression, I lost a lot of weight and, by the end, weighed only ninety pounds. I was skeletal. On top of that, my grades suffered, which was starting to jeopardize my dreams of earning a scholarship. At the time, Sonia was back in Miami, attending law school. She was worried about me, so she decided to get involved and started running with me. I got really into working out and started making goals around fitness. Sonia always knew how to regulate me, whether through exercise, a change in environment, or some other way. She gave me milestones to reach and was my accountability partner. I should have reached out to her for help more often. She was my coach. Even then, I didn't tell her everything going on at school, but just having her company and support helped tremendously. *Remember, she's my champion.*

She helped me devise a strategy for handling the rest of the year. I couldn't avoid my ex-boyfriend because we went to the same school and attended a lot of the same classes. I saw him almost every day, and I was subjected to watching him date girls in my circle. But he was a year older than me and would be gone when I entered my senior year.

My high school was one of the largest in the U.S., so there were plenty of other people to get to know. I started to be closer to some of the girls who rode the bus with me. It was nice because they didn't know all my drama, and it felt like a fresh start. I started hanging out with them and began eating reduced lunch again in the cafeteria. Funny thing is, I still keep in touch with both of them, and we still talk about those days at the bus stop. I got really close to one of the girls, who was also going through a breakup. Although it was a hard time, I felt supported.

I still had bullies around me though, and the aftermath of my breakup was fuel for rumors. When I unknowingly confided in the wrong person one day, she used what I had told her to spread rumors and spark rivalries. This time, though, I confronted the bully and promised myself I wouldn't let bullies get in my way anymore. It was my first lesson on limits and boundaries.

I also found a program for underserved kids that provided free SAT classes at the library. I started going and, surprisingly, reconnected with some friends from middle school. On top of that, I started going more frequently to a youth group with my cousins, where we grew closer and made new friends. Changing my circle saved me again.

At school, I also focused more on this amazing class I was taking: AP (advanced placement) environmental science. I reread the textbook multiple times, learning how people and nature were connected. It was all about systems and their connections with people. I was glued to the text, reading about how climate change would affect vulnerable communities and the poorest people. I remember feeling this hole in my gut when I thought about how unfair that was. I knew that this was the future. I knew that climate change would be one of society's greatest problems, and it was something no one was really talking about at the time. Further, I was passionate about injustices. I wanted to help and felt so drawn to this mission—I had to be part of this cause. So, I focused on improving my grades, and, with Sonia's unwavering support, I was back in the running for that scholarship.

HURRICANE MITCH HITS NICARAGUA

In 1998, Hurricane Mitch hit Nicaragua and became one of the deadliest hurricanes in recent history. Dad didn't waste a second springing into action. It was also a time when he needed to see his mom and brother.

"You're coming with me to Nicaragua," he said. "We're leaving tonight." It would be the first international trip that I remember. Now, I knew he didn't really have the money to take me, but he knew I needed this trip. The past months had really taken their toll on me, and I think he was tired of seeing me frown all day. Even though school was better, he could see that I had lost my spark, and it was time to step into service.

As we disembarked the plane, Dad stopped and took a deep breath of the fresh Nicaraguan air. "Ah, I'm home," he said. He had never wanted to leave, and, to this day, I know his heart never left Nicaragua. Although he made the choice, he felt as though he was forced to flee his home country. "I wanted to give you more opportunities," he said. "So don't waste them."

I hadn't been back to Nicaragua since I left as a young girl, and the level of disaster, poverty, and ruin in the aftermath of Hurricane Mitch affected me deeply. The destruction was unfathomable. The streets were flooded; kids were in the streets, shoeless and begging for money, and people were crying out of despair. I saw in real life what I had only read in my environmental science textbook. I saw how complicated these issues were, involving governments, people, nature, and donors and how climate change did affect the poorest the most. This was what the world would face in the future. I could imagine it, see it, feel it all around the world.

I knew that part of the reason why Dad took me back to Nicaragua was to give me some perspective after the breakup and the incident that followed—and it worked. I couldn't believe I had been so devastated by something as trivial as a breakup when these people, my people, didn't have shelter or clean water. That trip shifted my perspective, and I finally understood how lucky I was to be in the United States and the sacrifices Dad had made, leaving the home he loved to give us the best opportunities available. I also realized that no matter how much we were struggling, we were still so rich in comparison. This was the first time I felt that I had a **purpose**. I knew I needed to bring climate change to life, to the world, and bring awareness to the issue.

It's worth a small side note here to mention the impact that travel has had on my life. It started with visiting Sonia at college and then this trip to Nicaragua, but it has continued all my life. Travel for me is my way to see the connectedness among people and the common struggles and aspirations we all share, regardless of geography, language, or religion. Travel is what has made me understand that all people have a purpose and the world is a better place when people are free and empowered to pursue what fuels their souls.

While in Nicaragua, I also gained insight into my father's life there. He was taking care of his mom, who suffered from Alzheimer's. On top of that, he had a mentally challenged brother, whom he also had to support. I saw the purpose of the money Dad was sending back to Nicaragua nearly every month, which explained why we had to make so many sacrifices at home. I remember being angry at him at one point for giving some money away, and he looked at me and said, "Esther Beatriz (when the middle name comes out, you know you're in trouble, which is why I still hate being called Beatriz) have some compassion," and repeated that he would rather give them his shirt than have it himself. Seeing this taught me a lesson that I still carry with me. Even though money was tight and we made a lot of sacrifices, we still had the capacity to help those in need. I also realized that he, too, was a high achiever, heavy in perfectionism and people-pleasing, and how much burden he carried. I will never forget this lesson.

In Nicaragua, I developed a better understanding of my great grandfather's legacy and the impact it had on my dad. He carried the burden, handed down from his own father, of shepherding the family name. It was a life purpose imposed on Dad, and it was the first time I understood that the unfulfilled dreams of parents get passed on to their children. Political conditions had prevented my father's father from carrying forward the Zeledón legacy, so Dad grew up understanding that, when conditions allowed, it would be his duty, his obligation, to make sure history remembered Dr. Benjamín Zeledón and what he had done in defense of his country. So, Dad has been instrumental in having Dr. Benjamín Zeledón recognized for the sacrifices he made in his fight for liberty. When we visited his grave, saw the streets named after him, and observed his name and image on the local currency, I couldn't help but be in awe of my great grandfather. His impact had been huge, and his legacy was alive and well.

On this trip, I also learned basic things about my family that I never knew. Until then, I had never known that my parents had lived in Ohio, where Dad did a master's, or that they had lived in Europe for four years. As mentioned earlier, Dad focused his master's studies on the English-speaking Atlantic coast of Nicaragua, which was largely populated by people of African and indigenous descent. The history of the Atlantic coast was unknown to most Nicaraguans, and Dad's work was instrumental in having that history added to curricula and facilitating the integration of the Afro-Indigenous population with the Mestizos in the country. Most Nicaraguans living in the capital didn't even know there was a whole other population that spoke English and other Indigenous languages, and they were largely ignored. He was passionate about justice and freedom for all.

Through this trip, I also understood how a history of war, conflict, and insecurity continues to impact not only those who lived it but also their descendants, over decades and across countries. Like many nations around the world, Nicaragua's history is one of turbulence, plagued by colonialism, inequality, corruption, dictatorship, civil war, and revolution. Its people are strong and resilient, but there is also a tension, anxiety, and distance that comes from mistrust. History has shown them that sometimes friends are spies, what's promised is often not delivered, and situations can turn life-threatening in a matter of moments. Just a few years ago, we found a letter that my dad's father had written to him as he was heading off to boarding school that encapsulated the sentiment perfectly. It said, "Beware! Do not trust even in your own shadow."

This legacy impacts me and millions of others around the world, even today, even though we are in many ways far removed from those situations. We are taught safety and security above all else. We learn to keep our heads down, to not make waves, and to not draw attention to ourselves. We are taught that the concept of community is a fallacy because you cannot trust your neighbors, colleagues, or friends. We inherit this collective anxiety, fear, and a fierce individualism that prevents us from forming productive and positive social relationships. Today, when I hear of Latino gossip culture or machismo or when I see the Latino community struggling to make social and economic progress in the U.S., I can trace much of it to the intergenerational trauma and history of strife brought from our home countries. I understand, then, why so many buy into "the American dream," but, as time goes on, we see how that has consequences too.

Seeing the devastation caused by Hurricane Mitch strengthened the environmental lens through which I viewed the world. I saw how susceptible certain areas, particularly developing countries, were to natural disasters and the effects of climate change. The poorest people in the world would be the most impacted by this global phenomenon. It was also the first time I saw mountains and got to breathe clean air again since leaving California. I felt a peace and serenity I hadn't felt in years. That brief but formative trip back to Nicaragua would go on to influence many of my future decisions and the path I would soon take.

SENIOR YEAR AND SCHOLARSHIP DREAMS

My senior year was amazing. I felt super motivated, and I made a new circle of friends who were positive, amazing, and inspiring. With my grades back on track, I could consider where I wanted to go after graduation. I would spend hours at the library, researching colleges. I also tried a few times to see our college counselor, but that person was responsible for close to 2000 kids of my graduating class, and she just gave me information on the local college. So, I decided to use the skills I had learned from Sonia, to figure it out myself.

I found ways to visit several colleges through diversity programs, flying alone because my parents couldn't afford to go with me. I ensured that these programs would pay for all my expenses. For context, in the past, I had been accepted into summer programs at Cornell, but I couldn't attend because the tuition fees were hefty, and only part of the cost was covered. Since my parents were tight financially and the majority of our money went to Nicaragua, it was never an option for me. This is why, to this day, I don't believe in partial scholarships. They rarely provide enough help to the students who really need it. They didn't help me, and I was too young to get a loan, so I kept my sights set on a full scholarship.

With renewed determination to see my plan through to success, I continued to take all of the AP classes available and signed up for every free course I could find. I also decided it was time for me to start dating and, in dating, I needed to change how I saw it. I needed to ask more questions about potential partners' futures and ensure that we had alignment. I needed to stop the fantasy. That's when I met someone who was kind, patient, and shared the same dream of leaving Miami to go to college.

After all my effort, I graduated in the top 1 percent, number five in a graduating class of approximately 2000 students. To be honest, I was shocked. *Wait*, I thought. *How can that be possible?* Although I knew I'd put in a lot of effort, I never saw myself as one of the really smart kids, and the news took a while to sink in. Remember, I was the sickly kid who just needed to live. But, upon graduation, there was no denying that I had earned my full scholarship and a place at an elite college. I also realized I had been doubting myself all along and that the students near me in the rankings knew my worth and saw me as competition. If I hadn't gone through that bad breakup and been distracted for six months, perhaps I would have performed even better. That's a window for you into the mind of a high achiever. It was my moment of glory, and I remember thinking, angry with myself, *I could have done better*. I would bet that many of you have had similar experiences.

Although I had an amazing senior year and made new friends, I didn't yet have the courage to fight for injustices. Normally, top-ten students were featured on a plaque in the main office. This was the tradition. However, that year, the student council took it over and put up their pictures instead, and there was no recognition or pictures of the top ten. I was fueled with anger. This was a huge injustice, not only to me but also to the nine others. I think only one benefited because she was both in the student council and top ten. But I stayed quiet. I didn't have the confidence yet to fight for myself and others. But, to this day, I feel that I should have stood up and at least questioned the decision, but the situation did serve as another lesson for me later. I also had my notes stolen by students who had borrowed them, and my guidance counselor misplaced the prestigious book award I had won, so I was left out of the award ceremony. In that case, I did at least demand my trophy, but I missed out on the celebration.

I remember that week so vividly. I was so mad at myself, and I felt that the universe was conspiring against me. I almost broke down because, on top of all these small microaggressions, I had gotten super soaked on my way to work, and some male coworkers were making fun of the bra I was wearing. It was a flower print, and you could see it through my white Publix shirt. They called me a little girl because of the flower print and because all I did was study. Little did they know how happy I had been that Mom was able to get it for me on clearance. Honestly, I had no issue with the bra, but their laughing and mocking made me feel like shit. What did my bra have to do with me? I was one of their best cashiers, but they focused only on my clothes. At that moment, soaked and upset, I was on the verge of tears, passing twenty cans through the scanner when the customer in line asked me, "Are you OK? It seems like you're having a bad day."

"I wanted more. I knew I could have more."

I looked him in the eye and told him, "Yeah… today has been pretty awful." Without another word, he handed me a $20 AMC movie theater gift certificate. Back in the day, this was a crazy large amount of money, and I was in shock.

He said, "I hope this cheers you up. You need it more than I do."

I felt tears running down my face, no longer from sadness but from joy and relief. I couldn't believe a stranger would do that. Little did he know that he made my next two weeks. Little did he know how much he changed my perspective and restored my faith in good people. He gave me the energy to start thinking about the college application process and to keep pushing my plan to get the hell out. That moment is still one I think about a lot, and it's what led me to become a huge believer in the power of kindness and paying it forward.

After I enjoyed my movie theater gift card, I started to apply to college. It wasn't easy though. I felt so clueless and made so many mistakes. To start, I bought the *U.S. News & World Report* magazine, which contained the annual college rankings, from the supermarket and requested the application forms from the top schools listed, many I had never heard of. I remember, one day, when filling out the endless stacks of forms, I made an error and put Wite-Out all over my application and sent it out. Back then, getting a new copy of an application was so hard. These were pre-download and print times. If you needed a form, you had to request it through the mail. I remember feeling frustrated and thinking that my chances were slim. So, even though I managed to apply to a bunch of colleges on my own, it was really difficult to go about the whole process solo, without much guidance. One teacher did review my applications, but I wish I'd had more people give me feedback. I should have asked others. But even doing it solo, I managed to get great offers.

My parents didn't try to push me toward any particular school. The choice was entirely mine to make. The only thing my parents did say was not to select a big school. From his experience at UC Berkeley, Dad knew that, at a big school, I would largely be taught by graduate students and would not receive the same type of attention I would at a small school. I later learned that he was right. I would need attention and support.

One of the schools sent a postcard with the opportunity to go on a paid visit. It was part of their diversity efforts. I then inquired with the others, and, to my surprise, the schools flew me to visit them. It was such an incredible experience. I got to travel on my own, sleep in a dorm, and visit multiple schools. I couldn't believe it—all for *free*! I saved some money and bought a brand-new shirt to wear on the plane, feeling that my dreams were within reach. It was an incredible benefit of their affirmative action programs.

After visiting several great schools, I made my decision.

Swarthmore College in Pennsylvania was the number one liberal arts school in the country and had a huge focus on philanthropy, so that's where I wanted to go. Wellesley, where Sonia had studied, may have also been a great fit and likely would have helped me develop further confidence (their graduates include high-power figures like Senator Hillary Clinton and Secretary of State Madeleine Albright), but I would have spent my time there trying to escape my sister's shadow. Visiting Wellesley a second time, I felt intimidated. Everyone talked nonstop about how great my sister was. I understood that they would constantly be comparing me to Sonia and my achievements would always be measured against hers. Impostor syndrome on steroids. I needed a place where I could carve my own path and not be expected to mirror the accomplishments of my sister. Swarthmore College was that place. Plus, its mission focused on philanthropy, which was deep in my heart.

The first thing I wanted to do upon graduating and turning eighteen was travel. I wanted to see the world and, during my fall break, take a huge trip to Europe. But I knew that I would have to save up for months! I was working at Publix, the local supermarket near my house, and I started to save a small portion out of my paycheck for my big trip. The rest of the check went into building my computer for college (more on that tragedy later).

Although I was moving out in a few months, I knew my parents wouldn't be supportive of my dream of international travel, so I found a way to get an international student ID and book a discounted flight. I shared my plans with my friend, who worked with me. Many years later, that same friend reached out to reminisce about that summer. She told me, "At that age, I thought that was the boldest, most independent thing a kid our age could do." I did later get caught (and got in HUGE trouble), but it was something I needed to do for myself. It was my first push toward freedom.

GOING AWAY TO COLLEGE

With a full scholarship backing me up, I arrived on campus with a head full of wild ideas and a heart full of ambition. College, however, wasn't at first what I expected. My first semester was extremely difficult. Until then, I hadn't spent long periods away from home on my own, and I had grown used to having my parents there. Suddenly, I was alone, and everything was going wrong. Again, I had no contingency planning.

With the help of my amazing cousin, who was always my champion, Dad built me a computer, which was something I'd never had before. My cousin has since passed away, but I will always carry him in my heart. I had saved all my hard-earned dollars working at Publix and babysitting to buy all the parts needed for the computer, but, in transport from Miami to Philadelphia, my precious custom-made computer broke. I never got to use it. All my money had gone into it. Every single dollar I earned and all the hours my cousin put in. All the miles I had to walk to and from work getting soaked, with my feet throbbing. All of the sacrifices—wasted.

I had already spent most of my money on books and flights

and other expenses, and the broken computer set the stage for how the rest of the semester would play out. When I learned what had happened, I cried for two days straight. All my hard work and money had gone into that machine! My roommate didn't understand, and she would just hear me listening to José José (Mexican romantic "slit your wrists" music, as my sister calls it), but I felt again that this was a sign of worse things to come. I didn't communicate my struggles to my boyfriend or family because I had to make it and didn't want to disappoint them.

From the beginning, I was failing college. With the seemingly endless string of problems I faced, I couldn't just focus on school. I felt so intimidated by everyone around me, drowning in impostor syndrome. All the kids who had spent summers at math and chemistry camp and were already so much more worldly. I was just a kid who took a lot of AP classes. Even worse, I felt out of place on campus. While Miami was mostly Latinos, suddenly, at Swarthmore, I was a minority. It was a huge culture shock. I didn't understand typical American expressions and humor, and sarcasm went right over my head. Don't even get me started on idioms. I took everything literally. On top of that, Miami's tropical attire was considered provocative in Pennsylvania, and I faced ridicule from my peers for the way I dressed. Even the parents visiting would stare at me. I was harassed by college boys, who wrote sexual things on my door. I started to keep my head down and gravitated toward the minority and international groups on campus, where I felt safe. During that first semester, I was drowning, and I desperately needed a lifeline. Although I was top in Miami, I was now here with the top of the United States and had so much to catch up on.

It was overwhelming. But quitting school wasn't the answer. Failure wasn't an option.

I felt guilty because I knew there were other students who had even more financial responsibilities. Who was I to ask for help? But I had reached a point where I didn't have any other option. When you need help, you have to ask for it. So, I sought out a guidance administrator, who ended up assigning me a tutor. Initially, I thought she was going to tutor me on the subjects I was failing, but that turned out to not be the case. I told her everything that was going on in my life and how overwhelmed I felt. I also told her how much catching up I needed to do, how I felt impostor syndrome, how I didn't fit in—how would I ever succeed? Surprisingly, she recognized that my issue was more than school itself and mostly related to the hardships that came with being a low-income student on a scholarship, being on work study with multiple jobs, and living away from home for the first time. In reality, I needed *a therapist and a coach*.

"Right," she said. "This is what we're going to do." She coached me on creating a plan that would get me through the first semester and beyond, teaching me time management and focus. We made a schedule around work and study, as I had multiple work-study jobs at the time to supplement my scholarship. We then created a road map for completing assignments throughout the year, with the aim of improving my grades. She taught me how to divide a paper into sections and complete one section per day. We fine-tuned my schedule so everything fit into a specified time slot—there would be no surprises. Basically, she showed me how to strategically use a calendar. She also helped me schedule time so I could learn skills and catch up (what is referred to now as "leveling up"). We also spoke seriously about how achieving success would mean hard sacrifices—very few parties or social activities for at least the first year. It was also crucial to remind myself and have the clarity that these sacrifices were short-term, all aimed toward achieving my ultimate goal. In the end, it was the common but silent cost for people of color in these elite schools. *Funny side story: I ran into her years later in a random village in India and thanked her profusely, but how I wish I could thank her now for all her help. I've since lost track of her, but if you happen to read this—THANK YOU!*

My time working with my tutor came around the same time I discovered the work of James Redfield, author of *The Celestine Prophecy*. As time has gone on, I have come to realize how much these quotes have influenced my life: "I don't think that anything happens by coincidence ... No one is here by accident ... Everyone who crosses our path has a message for us. Otherwise they would have taken another path, or left earlier or later. The fact that these people are here means that they are here for some reason."[2] Meeting that tutor, who understood me and what I was going through at that time, was no accident, and I know we crossed paths for a reason. Although she was only in my life for a short period, she made a lifelong impact, and I make it a conscious practice to always be open to the people, lessons, and opportunities that come through my life.

I had my schedule written down on a sheet of 8.5″ x 11″ paper, and I carried it with me everywhere. Most importantly, I followed it. We met weekly to see how I was doing, and, little by little, college life got easier, and my grades improved. Previously, my weeks were a jumbled mess of work and study and this and that, but having a clear schedule created an essential level of order that can be missing when students make the jump from high school to college. She also taught me how to make the most of my time. For example, one of my jobs involved driving the evening shuttle for students to the mall and movies. Rather than just listening to music, she had me do some tasks for school while I waited at each stop. You have to customize your schedule to suit your situation. Because the plan required a year of sacrifice, I adapted it by adding rewards. For example, one of the many work-study jobs I had was calling alumni for fundraising, and we would receive gift certificates for the local shopping mall for reaching certain targets. Those evenings, I would set high targets so I could get those certificates and if I did everything in my calendar, I would take myself to the mall to spend them on clearance clothing. My boyfriend at the time didn't understand it all but for me, it was super important recognition and celebration. The other great side benefit was that the focus required to both obtain the rewards and shop for deals gave me a kind of mindfulness.

With all this in mind, I knew I wasn't going to have a traditional college experience. I wouldn't be drinking, partying, and socializing all the time because I knew that if I wanted to succeed, I needed to put in the extra effort to catch up to my peers. Because I came from the public school system but was now at a super-elite college, my writing skills were lacking. I hadn't been exposed to the same literature or range of ideas as others, so, knowing that I had to play catch-up, I couldn't have a normal college experience and still expect to succeed. This was all fine by me. Since I understood the four-year plan, I knew that little by little I could add in social time and volunteering as well. I just had to be patient and follow the plan.

The one thing I was not ready for yet was finding my own purpose and alignment. What *was* my purpose? I couldn't answer that question. I was a premed major because my parents wanted me to become a doctor, and I couldn't let them down. My dream was to buy them a big house, provide for them, and give them back everything they had invested in me. I wanted Mom to never have to worry about money and to be able to give herself endless salon days. I wanted to fix Dad's house in Nicaragua so he could sit and look at the mountains. I needed to give them breaks during the summers and give my younger brother the lens of possibilities that was given to me. I was not ready to think about myself or my alignment yet because I didn't think I deserved it. In my mind, my only purpose in the world was to serve others, and I was just lucky to have the opportunity I had.

CRAFT THE EXPERIENCE YOU DESIRE

With a plan in place to finish college, I started paying attention to the flyers posted all over campus. I wanted to do more travel but needed someone to fund it, so I started looking for summer jobs and activities that would pay me while giving me those opportunities.

I remembered my childhood and how my parents found ways to combine obligations with travel—we took the scenic route whenever we could. I wanted to do the same, earning money during the summer and seeing the world. I also talked to the students whom I drove to the mall and dorm in the shuttle at night about their plans. Some of them spoke about really cool opportunities to work with alumni, but those were unpaid internships and were not a feasible option for me.

After much searching, I found several paid jobs on flyers around the biology building, but the one that caught my attention was an opportunity with NASA. I applied and got in. So, during my first summer of college, I worked at NASA on a paid summer research internship, which was an incredible experience. I lived in a condo on the beach, made friends with an amazing group of students, and grew close to other students of color, whom I still keep in touch with to this day.

At NASA, I met my first working scientist outside of academia. He worked on environmental issues, and, with him, we developed a project that used remote sensing imagery to examine seagrass near rocket launch sites. NASA would use that data to see where endangered manatees were and which launchpad to use when. That scientist was one of my best mentors. He opened my eyes to the idea that environment could be a field of study and that someone could get a job doing that work. I thought, *Well, I can do premed, become a doctor for a few years, and then do something environmental.* There I was again, trying to reconcile other people's wants with mine and working at 500 percent.

Even so, the idea motivated me to keep pushing forward with

my degree. Clearly, the strategies my tutor had taught me were super effective and by sophomore year, my organization skills were excellent. Luckily, the first semester at Swarthmore was pass-fail, so my shaky start didn't kill my GPA.

By the time I finished my first year, I was already wanting to go to graduate school, but my family was still pressuring me to become a doctor, so I continued in the premed program. However, I quickly learned that medicine wasn't for me. *I have real hospital phobias, and the thought of working at one grossed me out* (still does). One time, I tried to voice this, but my family interpreted it incorrectly, blowing it up into something that wasn't even what I said, so I gave up. Really, I wanted to make a difference like the environmental science textbook I read in high school. I had to be an environmental… something. Unfortunately, an "environmental something" wasn't a real job title, and there were no degrees at the time that led to this imaginary role. But I knew I needed to be part of the climate change movement and bring these issues to light—this was the future. Although there was no clear-cut degree or program for what I wanted to do, I knew there was a future in the field.

So, I needed to figure out what "environmental something" would be, and I would do it by traveling overseas. I found a program called Research Experience for Undergraduates, funded by the National Science Foundation, that involved working on field ecology. There were other super interesting and amazing opportunities, but everything else was unpaid, which was something I could not do. Unpaid internships are a disadvantage for so many. So, for now, maybe this was the answer. The program would also give me the chance to improve my Spanish. At this point, I had done a minor in Spanish and was reading the Shakespeare equivalent. I still had a terrible accent, but I wanted to develop a deeper understanding of the language.

So, after my sophomore year, I went to Costa Rica for the summer and did research in the rainforest. That experience was intense. I had no idea back then what REI, North Face, or any other outdoor brands were, so I bought my first pair of binoculars, and Mom took me to Walmart to buy boots and basic field supplies. We all lived in these cabins inside the research lab, which was housed inside a large tropical rainforest. I had never done any formal hiking, so wearing gear, doing actual research on the ground, and figuring out where to go was overwhelming. I felt that the others had it all figured out, and I was still lost.

I became close friends with two students of color, whom I am still super close with, and I also became very close friends with two locals. I found myself more interested in learning about their lives, struggles, and the community than the science-based field work. I realized then that my priorities and passions gravitated to wanting to know about people, their communities, dreams, and aspirations.

During this trip, I got the opportunity to travel next door to Nicaragua again. I served as the travel guide and was able to show my new friends my home country. But along the way, I got lost, passed out, hitchhiked back to safety, and had to buy random clothes in a market. It was a crazy adventure that taught me a lot about travel preparedness.

Once I had completed my field work, I stayed on to travel in Costa Rica with Carlos, a close friend. At the end of our trip, a huge storm hit that wiped out a part of the road. We tried to find a way through, but the situation had grown precarious. Heavy rain pounded the car and the world outside. My flight home from Costa Rica was scheduled to leave the next day, and I didn't know if we would make it through or get washed away with one of the roads. We were at the mercy of the fierce storm that raged around us.

Eventually, we met some police officers who had the means to get through. The storm showed no signs of subsiding, so we had to make the decision to either press on to our destination or ask the cops for help. Carlos made the choice for me. "Go with the cops," he said, handing me a book. "This will guide you in the next part of your life." The book was *The Alchemist* by Paulo Coelho. I took my friend's advice. We parted ways, and I asked the police for help. That's when my already crazy adventure got a whole lot crazier.

The police took me to a safe place, but I had no idea what I was supposed to do next. After wandering in the rain for some time, I found another group of cops who were stopping people and offering assistance. I told them my story, and they helped me hitch a ride to the capital with some Canadian tourists. I knew my aunt's address, so I figured I would stay with her and fly out the next day. This was pre-cell-phone days, so I couldn't call ahead, and I didn't know if my friend had made it to safety. A storm of uncertainty crashed around me and with only my passport and a couple of dollars in my pocket, I didn't have a lot of options if the situation went even further sideways.

"Do what's right for you, and your true champions will come around."

During the drive, I examined the book Carlos had given me. I spent the entire trip absorbed in its pages. I was having another one of those *Celestine Prophecy* moments that would direct my next steps. By the time we reached the capital, I had read the entire book. This was the first time I thought about my purpose and my path. I started questioning what my purpose was. Was it something I loved? Was it my goal? I had recently learned how to do the thing I loved, which was dancing, with all of me. But that still didn't fulfill me. I loved helping others but although volunteering gave me fire, it wasn't what I was looking for. I would find purpose beyond what I loved, but everything felt so cloudy, especially given all my responsibilities and with so many people depending on me.

I left Costa Rica knowing that field ecology wasn't exactly what I wanted and although I appreciated my previous summer at NASA, again, it wasn't what I wanted. All I knew for sure was that I needed to finish college and find my higher purpose. But I also still felt all the external pressures, and I felt that I had to finish my check marks first. I also knew that I would continue to study abroad and see more of the world, not just Central America. I could see that there were still so many contradictions in my life. I still had a great deal to learn, and the world had a lot to teach me.

What was clear when I came back was that I would finish premed but would not pursue medicine. I found myself more and more interested in other subjects and less and less into the subjects medicine centered around. I started experimenting with other classes around food aid, biodiversity, and earth science and found myself more driven. So, I started to design my own major, an option that Swarthmore allowed and one of the reasons why I had been drawn to the school. Even before starting college, I felt that I needed that option for when I was ready. After some research, I combined classes from several different departments to form an earth and environmental science major. Fortunately, I had a solid science foundation from being a premed student, and adding other sciences and social sciences would make it a well-rounded major. *If what you want doesn't exist, create it yourself.*

But this didn't come with zero pushback. The students of color at my school mocked me for studying something that was just going to protect the trees. They would say, "Environmental science is for white people. It's so elitist." Of course, I would completely disagree. I would then continue to explain that climate change and environmental issues were real and had the potential to hit people of color the hardest. I also received pushback from my family. They were worried that my chosen career would not pay the bills and that it was too "soft." I gathered my strength, and I decided for once that I didn't care what others thought, even if it meant that my family wouldn't speak to me for a while. I knew in my heart that environmental science would give me the skills and experience to solve world problems, and I knew it was the future. *It will pay. I just know it.* I knew it was the future, even if no one else could see it. There *would* be jobs, and there *would* be a need. It was inevitable—and boy, was I right!

I felt so brave and empowered that I decided to take it a step further and think about everything I had signed up for and whether I was doing what I truly wanted or simply trying to please others. I had decided to study abroad, but I had agreed to go to Spain because Dad thought it was important for me to understand and know that side of history and colonization. Feeling empowered, I went to the school office and told them I didn't want to go to Spain. I said I wanted to travel the world, but I couldn't do boats, eliminating the very popular Semester at Sea program. *That's another story—I get seasick on closed boats.* The office administrator told me to check out a cabinet full of folders, where I found a program, the International Honors Program, that meant going to different countries *by plane.* I asked if this was something my scholarship would cover, and they said, "Yes, except for lunch." I got really worried. I was back to the lunch issue and, again, back to my strong belief that these scholarships that don't cover everything leave students in a difficult situation. Since I wouldn't be able to do work-study, I had to ask the school to give me a personal school loan to pay for my lunches and expenses while in the program. I wasn't going to let a lack of money stop me. Paying it back would be a situation for future Esther to deal with.

The International Honors Program would send me to India, South Africa, and Brazil. Perfect. I enrolled in the program and began the next part of my journey. I was about to go on a dream study abroad program, and I felt invigorated professionally. Deep down, I wanted to go solo, but I was afraid, so I told my boyfriend my plans and hesitantly encouraged him to join me. I don't know why I did this because our relationship was on the rocks. For years, we'd had a beautiful relationship—we did everything together. He was kind, like me, and we both admired, loved, and respected each other deeply. Plus, I had helped him adjust and learn to be on his own, and he helped me become a better writer and person. We grew so much together, and we loved each other's families so much. We were each other's champions, and, for a long time, our relationship was beautiful. He showed me the love and respect I deserved.

However, we were starting to realize that although we had many similarities, our values were different. We were both loyal to our causes and beliefs, with some of ours contradicting each other. Further, we had broken each other's trust with romantic situations based on my people-pleasing and not being able to say no to others and his desire for a different physical type, *which I could never be.* I had a hard time creating clear boundaries and limits with other men for fear of them not wanting to be my friend or hang out anymore. This was something I had to learn to master over the years. Yet, we remained with each other. We were both people pleasers and afraid of wasting the time we had invested in one another. Neither of us wanted to hurt the other's feelings. We cared for each other's well-being and didn't want to cause any suffering. In the end, we both hurt each other and didn't allow the other to be happy. *Folks, this is the wrong reason to stay with someone, and it's not kind.*

My people-pleasing was put to the test toward the end of that semester before we went abroad. Our relationship was extremely strained. I had caught him lying to me several times about his whereabouts, and we were distant and broken. Both of us wanted to leave the relationship—him to be free to date his type and me to find someone more entrepreneurially aligned with me. However, we were faced with the reality that we were going to be studying abroad together. Overseas. For months and months.

Invigorated professionally, I spent the preceding semester volunteering, making sandwiches at the local homeless shelter. That's when I met the man I fell in love with. He was studying economics, spoke various languages, and was from Latin America. He spoke the most eloquent Spanish and was so clear on his purpose. He had dreams of moving to China and pursuing entrepreneurship. He was so driven, passionate, and believed that you can create your own wealth and build an empire while helping others. We would spend our Fridays making sandwiches and would wake up at 5 a.m. on Saturdays to deliver them. I found myself so drawn to him and his freedom. Our values matched on every level, and all our conversations created light inside of me. With my boyfriend, I constantly felt judged as a "capitalist" whenever I shopped or did things for myself. I also felt super unattractive because he was attracted to women with darker skin and bigger curves. On top of that, I felt guilty for wanting to help people but also create my own financial success. Was that not giving back? In my circles, making money was spoken about in a dirty way. I realized later how untrue the narrative was. You *can* build an empire while helping others—inside I knew this to be true.

At that time, I knew nothing about entrepreneurship, but I felt so drawn to its endless possibilities. This other man fell in love with me too and thought I was perfect in every way possible, but I couldn't tell anyone. It would mean hurting someone I cared so deeply for. It would mean disappointing my boyfriend's family—and mine. Besides, we were about to study abroad together. After considering my options, I voted for a slow death and started to slowly disconnect from my boyfriend. To be fair, he had also voted for the same, but we never talked about it. This way, it would happen gradually and organically, and it wouldn't be that noticeable. I mean, he was equally miserable. At least, that's what I convinced myself.

But this is the thing, everyone—opportunities only come once. I still, to this day, regret the approach I took. I spent years, before healing, looking back, so angry at how much of a coward I was and how I didn't go after what I wanted. I don't know what would have happened with this other man long-term, but I didn't even give it a fair chance. The saddest part is that, much later, once I did give it a real chance, the damage was already done, and we never really recovered. It ended terribly, and it took me years to recover. Worse yet, later, when my boyfriend met his true love, he abandoned our friendship and dropped our memories as if we had never been together. Again… lesson to all readers—*you don't owe anyone anything, and, beyond regrets, you don't get anything from sacrificing*. Be happy and true to you.

Eventually, I left for my study abroad program, but it wasn't at all what I expected. The level of poverty and chaos, contrasted by the enormous wealth, I saw in India was the greatest I had ever witnessed. The smells, the disparity, and the huge population were overwhelming. Until then, I had never seen or met a child slave. Experiencing this starkly different culture further opened my eyes to the adversities people face in different parts of the world. Until you see it, believing it—let alone beginning to understand it—is difficult. My time in India led me to realize that I have a high level of empathy for disadvantaged people and their situations.

During this time, I became close to a young woman, who worked in the home of my host mom. We didn't share a language, but we spoke with hand gestures. I would spend evenings coloring with her, and we would share drawings. When I left, she gave me the biggest hug ever and cried. Most people only saw her as a servant. It was one of the hardest goodbyes I had gone through. I realized there that I can and do make an impact. I connect with people. I experienced a clear moment of wishing I had money and resources to give to her so she could live her best life and purpose.

I had some crazy adventures too, one including a bus accident in Kerala that led to meeting a wealthy woman and her family and her inviting us to stay at her home. I also had my first experience of severe illness while traveling, getting dysentery and becoming extremely ill on my flight to South Africa. When we landed, I had to go straight to get medical care.

In South Africa, I had the opportunity to live with a better-off White family and also with a Black family in one of the townships. The White experience felt very awkward. The White neighborhoods and views were beautiful—it was probably the most beautiful place I had ever been—but also very sterile, and after 5 p.m., there was no noise in the streets.

Life in the township was the polar opposite. The evenings were full of community, struggle, life and laughter, and zero views. I discovered a lot about my own identity. I was labeled "colored" in South Africa, and I often felt insecure about my safety. Even post-apartheid, races remained separated in certain situations, and I grew to understand the racial dynamics of the country a lot better. I felt similar to how I felt in the United States, where I belonged in this "brown" category that lacked cohesiveness.

I also got to explore the beauties of South Africa and learned a lot about leaders, such as Nelson Mandela, who fought for injustices and freedom. I had never seen such impressive landscapes, beautiful vineyards, and animals in the wild. Honestly, hands down, Cape Town is one of the most beautiful cities in the world.

The study abroad program had a thematic focus on cities in the twenty-first century, and the final country was Brazil. There, I got to explore Rio de Janeiro and Curitiba. Rio was amazing—the colors, culture, beaches, and food. All the weight I lost in India, I gained back, and I could wear my tropical outfits. It felt more like "home." I belonged.

At night, I often heard gunshots from the nearby *favelas* in Rio, and I could see the sparks bursting out of their guns. Several people in my program were mugged in the evenings, which brought a sense of insecurity. But I could blend in with the locals, and I enjoyed the vibrant culture and natural beauty. At the same time, I was painfully aware of the inequities.

Curitiba was also spectacular. I never knew cities like that existed. It was environmental, well-planned, green, and absolutely beautiful. They had a bus system that connected the entire city with separate bus lanes and only cost one fare to ride. They had green spaces everywhere. It was a city focused on recycling and sustainable practices. It was the first time I saw that being environmental was not limited to being "White," and it gave me hope for the world. My host family was a homosexual couple, and it made me so sad how they had to hide their relationship from everyone, including the students they hosted.

During this time, the United States was going through its "war on terror," and there were protests worldwide. My experience abroad gave me a taste of the world and international politics and how connected everything is. I learned that people everywhere had similar concerns and problems. It didn't matter what walk of life you were from—wealthy or poor or ethnic background or color—everyone had dreams and aspirations. Everyone wanted purpose. They all had goals and were navigating life as best they could. I also learned that cities were battling their own problems and challenges, and I felt very connected to my area of study. I had grown immensely as a human being.

When I returned from studying abroad, I felt energized and connected. It wasn't until this moment, when I was clearer on my mission, vision, and purpose that I was ready to put myself first (me as MVP). I tried to make things work with the guy I was in love with, but now it was complicated. He had been seeing someone the entire time I was gone, and there was resentment. Although we would see each other a few times over the years, I had lost the opportunity. Plus, I felt that he had changed and that his desire to be kind had faded. Still, I always thought of him. That's the hard part with regrets. Even later, when my sister bought me a ticket to go see him in China (where he always dreamed of living and working), an airline glitch forced me to cancel the trip, and I never saw him again.

Side note: I did eventually travel to China in 2019 as part of my healing journey to apologize for both people-pleasing and not being brave enough to go after what I wanted. But he refused to see me, so I left him a letter. I did, however, get a chance to see what he had built for himself there, which was amazing. I finally got my closure and, most importantly, forgave myself. I realized that the reason why I regretted the situation so much and why he was the one that got away was that he was the mirror of everything I wanted to achieve myself. But I didn't need the shadow of that regret, him, or anyone to make my own dreams a reality.

Professionally, things started to go in my favor. I was accepted to a research program focused on climate change and got to meet students like me with an interest in the topic. To my surprise, there were other students of color! I also applied for the Mellon Mays undergraduate fellowship program, which would help me succeed in a PhD program and expose me to other underrepresented groups in graduate programs. On top of that, I had the great fortune to be selected by an alumnus of Swarthmore to have my last year of college funded specifically because I wanted to study something related to environmental science. With this new income stream, I was able to cut work-study hours, pay back my loan, and create bigger circles. Who knew that an alum would want to fund someone with environmental interests? Again, this is why it's important to be true to who you are—there is alignment out there, and you never know who will be your champion. Once I found alignment, everything came together.

My experiences in various groups and abroad influenced where I targeted my volunteer work and gave me the confidence to expand that work. I started focusing more on underrepresented groups and communities. Initially, in college, I was tutoring in a rich area, but the neighborhood right next door was very vulnerable and underserved. So, I started going there to tutor children and give talks. Gradually, I tailored my services more toward underrepresented groups and environmental issues. With more time on my hands, I took on leadership roles in both the Latino and environmental clubs and compartmentalized my life. Slowly, I was finding alignment.

Mainstream opinion is always behind reality, and I saw what many others couldn't. I knew that environmental science would become a critical part of humanity's future, so I stuck to my plan and completed the major I created. College was a crazy and turbulent time, but also one where I grew so much. I experienced microaggressions, and I also lost friends along the way, and, again, some of the closest to me were the ones to betray me. They resented my success and visibility, and there was nothing I could do to change that. Luckily, after the lesson I had learned in high school, I had multiple circles and although the betrayals hurt immensely, I had another tight circle that had my back and still does to this day. We are still super close. Despite it all, I was on track for graduation.

FULFILLING MY FATHER'S DREAM

After graduation, I knew I would be stepping into the unknown. Finding a graduate school was always going to be difficult because no one knew my field of study. I applied to PhD and master's programs all over the country, and I started to receive offers. None of them, at the time, were a perfect match, but they had components that interested me. Luckily, I had my own funding. Several universities flew me out to visit, and I had to decide where I wanted to complete my graduate degree. Finally, I chose the University of California, Berkeley, ironically, the same place Dad had studied when I was a kid.

Berkeley was originally my last choice. I was worried about returning to a place from my childhood, but I had a good reason to do so. Over the years, Dad frequently talked about going back to Berkeley to finish his PhD, but he was a master procrastinator and never quite got there. Between his family in Nicaragua, us kids, and our financial situation, he had a lot to deal with, and returning to graduate school must have seemed unfeasible. But I wouldn't let him put it off forever. "We'll graduate together," I said. "I don't know how, but we'll make it work." This is the thing, folks: when you pass on unfulfilled purpose to your children, they carry it. Berkeley hadn't been my first choice, but I could also see *The Celestine Prophecy* and the concept of synchronicity in action, and I knew that returning to Berkeley also meant fulfilling my father's dream. After everything he had sacrificed, it was the least I could do.

> "I now knew that I deserved more and that not everything was my fault—a huge realization for a high-achieving people pleaser."

ACHIEVING EMPTY SUCCESS

Compared to college, graduate school was a completely different experience. When I got to Berkeley, I immediately plugged in to the Latino network, became president of the association, and created new groups for other Latino graduate students. You might find this a bit odd, but I also signed up for life insurance. I know, I know, who does that straight out of college, right? But let me tell you—I never wanted to be a burden on anyone, least of all my parents. The idea of them having to deal with some whopping bill if something happened to me while I was off at college was just unthinkable. But hey, every cloud has a silver lining, right? Turns out, getting life insurance that young meant I locked in a fantastic rate that's still giving me a sweet deal today. Funny how things work out, huh?

Additionally, I was hired through an EPA (Environmental Protection Agency) grant to teach kids in the inner city, focusing on environmental justice and using Google Earth to show them where all of the major polluters were in relation to their schools. I taught them how environmental issues affected them, why these things matter, and how to advocate for better rules and regulations.

Because I had put serious effort into catching up to the other students during college, graduate school was a time for me to catch my breath. Finally, with the foundation I had built through study and hard work, I felt like I was on a level playing field with everyone else, but I still felt out of place with what I was hoping to study. Although I was in one of the world's top-rated interdisciplinary departments, my research and interests were different. It was also hard to be one of the few students of color. I had so much more burden and many more life responsibilities than the other students, and most of them couldn't relate. I was responsible for my younger brother, contributed financially to my family, and was helping Dad get reaccepted into his graduate program. I was also constantly helping everyone around me with applying to college and being there for everyone who needed me. I admit that even though I felt that the other students couldn't relate, I also didn't give them a chance to understand. I didn't share or open up for fear that, if I did, they would think I wasn't serious or committed.

At the same time, my work-life balance improved greatly. I received fellowship money and not only did it pay for my tuition, but it also provided me with a salary. I now had a solid income stream, and I could afford to buy things, socialize, and eat out whenever I wanted. I also bought a car for the first time, and I was able to comfortably support my younger brother, who lived with me and extended family and friends during the summers. Graduate school was amazing.

I got my own funding to do research back in Nicaragua and spent significant time in northern Nicaragua trying to understand how the civil war had affected the region. I also got to know the mestizo and indigenous populations while carrying out the field work that became my dissertation. Dad joined me on my first research trip, but later I got to experience Nicaragua on my own. I got to listen to people's stories, hear about their purpose and life struggles, and learn about their needs. I hired a research assistant to help me gather even more interviews. We spoke to so many people. I felt that my work mattered.

But I was also very unsure of my next steps. When I first went to grad school, my goal was to finish my PhD, but I hadn't considered what would happen next, other than getting a high-paying job. I spent zero time thinking about my purpose. I put so much effort into assisting others and helping my dad finish his PhD that I never stopped to consider my ten-year plan or even what I would do after graduating. While I was a successful academic, I had no future goals. I didn't have the same motivation or drive, and I delayed finishing because I had no idea what to do after and didn't want a gap in my resume. I knew I didn't want to become a professor, and, despite some great experiences, I didn't see myself working at any of the places I interned at. The part I loved was connecting with people in the field. Plus, I still wanted to see the world, and none of my options at the time were pointing in that direction. The thing I did love doing, which was leading the Latino organizations, didn't feel like it could be a high-paying job—but I was wrong there too. I led huge organizations with hundreds of people, recruited workers and volunteers, planned events, brought in speakers, led my own talks, organized conferences, raised money, built partnerships with the other people of color groups (for example, Black Graduate Association for Scientists and Engineers) and so much more. At the time, I had no idea this was a skill in itself or that a lucrative career could be built around it. Plus I loved it—community is everything.

Because I didn't honor my skill set as something I could monetize, I went to my default of becoming obsessed with marriage. I had been with another Latino PhD student for years. Although we had zero chemistry or intimacy, we were really good friends. We were a fantastic team, especially when it came to organizing our Latino events, but had different values. We also cared deeply about politics and the world. People saw us as a power couple, and we were each other's champions. We supported one another's passion for helping others and for leadership positions. We also supported each other's research and careers.

But *apariencias* (how you seem to others on the outside) were super important to him. He hated if I cursed or if I became too passionate in moments. "Esther, a good woman doesn't do that." He hated if I argued with him over issues, especially in public, or if I pushed self-help and therapy. He represented everything I was fighting against: social constructs and obsession with what others thought and perceived. Everything was about molding to what was "right" before he would marry me. But, at the same time, that relationship dynamic was familiar and comfortable. I grew up around machismo men, so, for me, our relationship was what I understood as normal. He fit very well into all my circles, and we were both high-achieving Latinos with big dreams and intellectual curiosity. We also had an amazing community of Latinos. They were my family.

So, here I was in this position again, where losing him would mean losing the other people I loved dearly. It would mean giving up on those friends, those champions, those people I spent hours studying with or who took care of me when I got my wisdom teeth out. More than losing him, I would be losing my circle. Plus, my family loved him because they saw him as funny and charismatic, and he humored my little quirks.

But eventually, I built up the courage to leave him. I got tired of waiting for him to marry me, and the combination of my people-pleasing and perfectionism with his narcissistic and external validation tendencies meant the relationship wouldn't go anywhere anyway. It was just a bad combo. Plus, we were basically roommates with zero intimacy, best friends. I wanted more. I *knew* I could have more. I wanted someone to be with me because they couldn't live without me. Merely being a team was not enough anymore. Deep down, we knew that our values were not the same and we could never have the partnership I dreamed of or the one he imagined. Neither of us could be our authentic selves. He agreed that the relationship couldn't work long-term, but, like me, he was comfortable, and he didn't want to hurt me.

Looking back now, it's frustrating to see how much I still felt the need to seek the marriage check mark. Yet again, I spent years in a relationship that we both knew was wrong but looked great on paper. Yet again, I let external pressures and the opinions of others dictate my actions, no matter how much they clashed with what I felt inside.

The breakup was traumatic, and, as I predicted, it did come at the expense of losing my precious circle. When I lost my friends, it was definitely what hurt the most. I wanted my circle, my community, and I mourned that loss for years. We were all still part of the same groups, so I still had to see them and watch them hang out with my ex. It was a very lonely time.

Unlike my high school breakup, this time I used all my tool kits to avoid spiraling. I exercised. I dated. I engaged in my other circles. I was still sad but never hit rock bottom. It was hard to see then, but I've learned that your true community will never leave your side. Years later, I would rebuild those friendships on my own and create new ones. For either person, it's not worth staying in a just OK, partially satisfying relationship to preserve a circle of friends. Do what's right for you, and your true champions will come around.

After the breakup, I continued dating and making mistakes. I wasn't ready to communicate my needs and still didn't know how to do it in a positive way. After constantly fighting in my last relationship, fighting against all the molds he wanted to put me in, when I was finally free, I didn't know who I was. *Who was I?* I knew everything I didn't want to be, but I didn't know who I *did* want to be.

Finally, I enrolled in therapy, where I learned a lot about myself and how to voice my needs. With a bit more knowledge, I tried again to date my high school boyfriend and did everything I didn't do when I was younger. I thought maybe this was my chance to make things right. It was an interesting learning experience for me when I discovered that the previous failure had nothing to do with any mistakes I had made. This time, I said and did all the right things, but it still wasn't right. I now knew that I deserved more and that not everything was my fault—a huge realization for a high-achieving people pleaser.

I also learned for the first time about visualization and manifestation. I went to visit Sara, my late cousin's wife. I always admired her marriage to my cousin and the love they had for each other. He loved and respected her so much. I remember seeing them when I was six years old, wishing that one day I could have what they have. Who would have thought that, as an adult, I would be circling back, asking her for advice? I broke down in tears, telling her that I would never find what she had. She looked at me and said something that will stick with me forever: "If you believe that, then you won't ever find it." I had to be patient, trust that true partnership was out there for me, and believe that I deserved it. It gave me tremendous peace, and later I realized I should have been even *more* patient. Funny thing is, I find myself now saying these same phrases to others.

Finally, the time came to turn in my dissertation. When I finished my PhD, I thought I would feel amazing, but I was wrong. Here I was, sitting with a lollipop that said "PhinisheD" and both my diploma and Dad's, and all I wanted to do was cry and dig myself a hole to crawl into. I had reached the end. There was nothing left to achieve academically, and I still had no direction. What was I supposed to do now? Yes, I had reached my goal, but I had neglected to consider even one step beyond that point. Without a destination in mind, I could never be anything but lost. I continued therapy, but it wasn't what I needed. I had gained a lot of information, but it felt too passive and lacked a plan of action. What I needed was a coach. I don't mean to undermine therapy in any way. Therapy is essential (and became a must-have for me later), but it works best when combined with coaching.

Being there when Dad earned his PhD felt amazing, much more so than when I completed my own degree. I helped him a lot along the way and got Sonia involved during the last year. It was a real team effort, and I couldn't have done it without her. Sonia also lived with this burden, and it was a relief for both of us to see Dad reach that milestone.

I did, however, make one critical mistake. I didn't tell my advisor that I was helping my dad because I didn't want her to think I wasn't focused on my own work. When she found out that I had kept it from her, she was hurt, and I learned a valuable lesson about the importance of communication. Communicating what you're working on to others is important because, if they are the right people, they will cheer you on. However, I was so afraid they would use this information against me that I struggled in silence.

As I juggled two PhDs, the loss of a close community, and grief, I could have used the extra support. I didn't even share what I was doing with my inner circle until the end. When I finally informed my friends, they explained all the ways they could have helped me along the way. It's ironic that I spent so much time and energy helping others but couldn't see that others might also be there for me when I needed them most. I didn't know how to fill the empty hole created by finishing my PhD. I thought that by finishing and getting this huge check mark, all the answers would be waiting for me. For the first time in a long time, I had no achievement to strive for, and the path forward was unclear.

A FORCED ERROR

During grad school, I spent six months in Miami, caring for my sick grandmother. It was a relief to be outside of Berkeley, where everyone knew my previous relationship and I could mourn the community I lost. Although I was spending time with my grandmother during her final days, I was very lonely. While I was there, I spent long nights with my best friend, Mauricio, who I had known since middle school. I will always be so grateful to him. He always reminded me of who I was and gave me the courage to go after what I wanted. He was my center and my biggest champion in life. He is someone I will be friends with and close with until I die and if you are reading this, Mauricio, you can always count on me.

I also met someone new, a man named Nicolas, and we began a relationship. He was very committed and nothing like the other men I had dated. We shared a love for travel and helping others, and he was extremely romantic. He had a heart of gold, and we were both passionate about connecting with people. We both read the entire *Celestine Prophecy* series, and he offered me the intimacy and closeness I had craved for years.

After my grandmother passed away, I went back and forth between Berkeley and Miami. Because I didn't have any future plans, I explored all avenues I encountered. One avenue I could have pursued was working with diversity students, and I was offered a position in that area, but it didn't feel completely right yet. On top of that, we couldn't see any job opportunities for Nicolas. However, a sister university in Ecuador was looking for a visiting professor to teach master's students. The semesters would be short and intense, so I would only need to be there for short periods at a time. I accepted the job and moved to Miami to be closer to Nicolas, leaving for Ecuador several times a year to teach.

When I was home in Miami, I wanted to live with Nicolas, but my parents wouldn't allow it. He was also Nicaraguan and since our families were in the same social circle, I either had to be married or continue the commuter relationship. I tried to convince Nicolas that we should move to Berkeley together and test it out there and no one would know. I wanted us to break free from the pressures, do what we wanted, and be far away from our families. I didn't want to go back to Miami and feel caged again. I wanted to give our relationship a fair chance. I also, deep down, worried about him going from his mother's house to mine, but the pressure to get married was immense. Apparently, I wasn't as disconnected from the Miami dream of marriage as I had thought because when Nicolas made an amazing proposal in Cinderella's Castle at Disney,

I accepted.

This, of course, was a big mistake. I wish I had already developed the purpose exercise back then, which forms the basis of this book and gives readers the clarity they need. We would have seen that our legacies were different scales and that mine required sacrifices that he would be unwilling to make. We would have seen how much we were both impacted by people-pleasing. A better understanding of purpose and legacy would have saved us both a lot of stress, anxiety, and heartbreak.

The wedding was the party of the decade! It started off with amazing fun abroad with friends and family. There were fireworks, endless food and drink, side excursions, and tons of dancing. But things quickly became challenging. To his family, I was a threat. I was vocal and questioned things, refusing to accept the role of a "traditional" wife, and they were constantly downplaying my education and my career goals. Nicolas didn't express wanting someone traditional, but his family wanted it for him. And when his family pressured him, he would cave. Further, his friends represented the side of Miami I preferred to avoid. All men with fixed mindsets, married or seeking women who went straight from their parents' homes to their boyfriends' or husbands' and did *all* of the domestic duties: laundry, cooking, cleaning—everything. The thing is, this arrangement is great if you want it, but, behind doors, all these women were complaining about it. They didn't want to live like that, but they felt like they had to, and there was not one conversation about their dreams or goals.

That's what really got to me. Why were they just accepting this? Why weren't they communicating this to their partners and working together on a solution? I couldn't just sit and accept something I didn't want. Or maybe they were just complaining and venting because it was normalized. Either way, I wanted to be in a circle of ideas and growth, not one of gossip and complaining. I wanted positivity, not constant negativity. I had traveled the world, lived in diverse communities, and experienced the wonders of this planet, and suddenly I was right back where I started. Sure, I had earned a PhD, but I couldn't envision a path to genuine fulfillment in that environment, and I fell into a deep depression.

This was where you found me at the beginning of the book, staring into the ceiling fan. I was married and miserable.

Normally, I'm neat and organized but during this time, I lived like a slob. Our place was a mess, and I slept most of the day. I also gained a lot of weight. When I was home, I felt sad and lifeless. My vision post PhD was not what I expected, and I felt stuck. I would just sit there, frowning and emotionless. But whenever I returned to Ecuador, I would come back to life. Although I hadn't wanted an academic job, I loved teaching and the value I got as a professor. I felt like a real professional and that I was making a difference. I loved the time I spent in Ecuador but whenever I returned to Miami, the dark cloud of depression would smother me again and choke the life right out of me.

The supposed dream I was living—married life—didn't match what I had been sold. Marriage was supposed to be this amazing and fulfilling experience, an end goal for many people, but, for me, the product didn't match the description. I wanted a partnership, not chains. The marriage I had wasn't what I wanted, and I felt as if I was sold a false dream. At the same time, I felt guilty because I did agree to get married. No one in my family had ever been divorced, so discussing my situation was difficult. Whenever I brought it up, people would tell me that I was the one being difficult and to just work it out. So, I would just lie on the floor, staring at the ceiling, for most of the day. I tried to find hobbies and got into extreme couponing to get through it, but those were just band-aids. I thought that things might be better if we got out of Miami.

Around that time, a mentor from Berkeley reached out with an offer to run a diversity project. At the same time, I also applied for a job in Washington, DC, and I was accepted. I was torn between two choices. I had arrived at a critical fork in the road, and each path would lead to a very different future. Because of the government bureaucracy I would have to deal with, Dad didn't want me to take the DC job. He knew that world all too well. Sonia, on the other hand, said DC would open doors. She always steered me in the right direction, so I considered her advice and chose to go for the job in DC. While interviewing for that position, in a twist of fate, I met my future husband, Paul.

MY SPARK RETURNS

When I first noticed Paul in a crowded room, I thought, *I need to talk to that man.* I don't know why I felt that urge. I couldn't explain it, but I picked him out of a crowd of 200 people. We spoke, and

I found him very interesting. That was our first encounter. At the time, though, I just wanted to be friends and learn from him. Even if I had been single, I had been burned by Latino men, and I vowed that, even if my marriage failed, I would never be with one again. There was no way he would be the Latino man I visualized—the one who cooks, provides for children, and is romantic. But life proves you wrong…

Although I had already been introduced to synchronicities—the meaningful connections that suddenly pop up to provide opportunities that move our lives forward—through my own life experiences and *The Celestine Prophecy*, this was something truly **unmissable**. There was a mysterious and deep sense of knowing that I knew Paul on a spiritual level. My intuition sensed that this person was part of my intended destiny somehow.

Moving to DC was a total mess for my marriage. My sister got Nicolas a job, which was great for him, but the transition was difficult. However, the move changed something in me. I felt like I had goals again, and my spark returned. We had chosen this nice apartment, which I organized beautifully. I was no longer sleeping the days away. Instead, I thrummed with renewed energy and purpose. After getting the job in DC, I worked in international development, focusing on climate change, which was exactly where I needed to be. The job and experience were amazing. I was able to network and participate in a community of ideas, which was what I had wanted for so long. Nicolas, however, wasn't happy for me, and neither was his mom. Apparently, I was "ignoring my husband and not being a good wife."

"Never be afraid to make your voice heard for what you know is right."

The constant negativity was exhausting. I thought I had found my purpose, and they refused to celebrate it. The pressure was relentless, and I was so overwhelmed that I kept shutting down and never communicated how their behavior affected me. The noncommunication just exacerbated the issues and caused him enormous stress.

I had not let go of the social constructs imposed by my culture, so I pretended to the world that everything was fine. It was the way I dealt with it. Had I been courageous enough to open up about it then, things would have been different.

Nicolas also had a lot to deal with: my unhappiness, being in the middle of his family and me, and moving to a new place. Our marriage was exhausting for both of us, and I blamed myself constantly. I didn't feel the same way about him anymore—this had to be my fault. After all, I did take a vow. I blamed myself because I had accepted his proposal when I knew in my heart on our wedding day that it wasn't right. Deep down in his heart, he wanted a woman whom his family would love. He also wanted someone who was free, but not to my extent. He wanted a woman who had ideas but wanted to live in Miami and be close to his family and friends, someone who could blend. Again, our legacies didn't align. We just weren't aligned.

I had previously stopped therapy because my new insurance

didn't cover it. Finally, however, in this new job, I could start again. So, I restarted therapy and tried to unravel the mystery of my decisions. What was I doing wrong? I thought now that I could be myself, everything would work out. In therapy, I learned that I was gravitating toward the machismo personality, which matched that of the men I saw around me growing up and in my outer circles. I still hadn't been able to shake off the deeply ingrained cultural influences. I was still obsessed with the idea of marriage, and, instead of looking for a partner, I was seeking validation. I also struggled with communication. I thought, similar to the PhD, with the marriage check mark, I would have all the answers and it would bring me happiness. I mean, that's what I was sold. Once I understood the motivations behind my own unconscious actions, I could take responsibility for past choices and make better future decisions.

At that point, I knew one thing for certain: I wanted out of my marriage for the both of us. He also deserved to be happy. He later met someone amazing, who offered him what he really wanted and gave him the limits and boundaries he needed, and achieved happiness, which, in the end, was what I wanted for him.

BREAKING FAMILIAR PATTERNS

When I met Paul, I feared falling into the same trap again. I didn't know anything about him. Like I said, he was Latino too, and I thought I was simply repeating the same old pattern. I was still married, and I knew I had to tread carefully to avoid making a bad situation worse. I really only wanted to be friends, and I remembered

The Celestine Prophecy. There was a reason *why* I felt the need to talk to him, and there was information he needed to share with me.

I finally mustered the courage to approach Paul and invited him out with me and my friends. But he made an odd remark and dismissed the invitation. After that, I didn't want to talk to him again, as I figured I had misread the signal. But fate had other ideas.

During selection for the DC job, thousands of candidates went through a series of interviews—it was a grueling process. Out of all the people who applied, they only offered positions to around 200 applicants. Those who were successful got placed in various government agencies. As if fated, Paul and I both got selected, both got assigned to the same agency, and both ended up in the same department. What are the odds? He got placed right next to me, but he had dismissed me earlier, so I chose to ignore him.

However, with us working in such close quarters, avoiding each other was impossible, and we eventually became friends. In recent relationships, I had jumped right into romance with my partners and never built a foundation of friendship. But when it came to Paul, we were friends first. Actually, it was all I wanted at the time. At work, we visited each other's cubes and talked about our lives, our families, ideas, and everything else. We had a lot in common, and we learned a lot from each other. He also had stereotyped me as young and naive and was quickly proven wrong. We took lunches together and talked some more. Over the course of many months, we built a strong foundation of friendship. During this time, we never so much as shook hands. We didn't touch each other at all. We also never spoke about our relationships or hung out in the evenings.

Paul was married and had two kids. I, of course, was still married to Nicolas, so, in my mind, my friendship with Paul could only ever be just that: a friendship—and it was a beautiful one. A romantic relationship was completely out of the question, yet there was an energy between us that we couldn't deny. Sometimes when we were in deep conversation, our colleagues would try to talk to us, but they would often give up, saying, "You guys are in your bubble again," and leave us be. We recognized the connection we had, but so did the people around us.

One day, a group of four of us were sitting around talking. Paul and I had a vision of what we wanted for our fellowship. We told the others we thought we should do strategic planning for the agency's missions worldwide. We all had PhDs, and we all knew how to solve problems and think strategically. None of us had ever done anything like this before, but we knew the project would be useful and was what was needed. Our friends, however, weren't convinced, deciding that the idea was too difficult to execute.

Paul and I went ahead with it anyway and focused on marketing, hoping to get at least one mission on board. From his work as a professor and my work running various organizations, we were experienced at bringing people together. Granted, we didn't have any background in this specific niche, but we learned it all on the fly, and the program was a huge success. We really blew it out of the water.

Professionally, those years were some of my most fulfilling. As it turned out, Paul and I worked well together, so, after our first big win, we began traveling the world for work. We met so many people and helped countries with strategic development, impact storytelling, and more. The best part is that we cheered each other on. Being around a Latino man who admired and respected me and gave me all the credit in a room was rare to me. He had proven me wrong. I grew to respect him immensely and knew that regardless of anything, I would want this man as my friend and ally through life. We both loved our jobs: the work and the difference we were both making.

A BEGINNING AND AN END

Once we had proved ourselves with one mission, other countries brought us in to do the same for them. Naturally, the more we worked together and the more success we had, the closer we grew. During this time, we never became more than good friends. We still hadn't touched each other. No handshakes, no hugs, no physical contact whatsoever. Though, on one trip, I finally touched on a personal subject about his long-term dreams and legacy. It was there that it became clear how aligned we were. Soon, other realizations would strike us too.

As we stood in an elevator, saying goodbye for the Christmas break, we touched each other for the first time. It was just a hug, nothing more. Another guy was in the elevator too, and he looked at us as if we were crazy. I think he knew he had just witnessed something extraordinary. I didn't know what to make of it. We felt this electricity consume us. Why did this happen? Were we just friends, or was it something more? The situation was too confusing, so I cut off communication with Paul and spent Christmas with my husband and family.

I went home for Christmas with an open heart and willingness to work on my marriage. I was so energized by work and my friends that I promised to give it my best shot. But it was already broken and in disarray. I couldn't fix it, as much as I tried. Too much had happened. As people pleasers, we don't want to fail, and we want to fix everything. Plus, working it out would mean giving up my job and my new positive circle. Nicolas needed more time with me, which I couldn't give at that time. He wanted me to give up everything that mattered to me and that I was building for us, so we fought during that entire Christmas vacation. We were so miserable.

I tried to hide the fighting from my family. Looking back, I should have just let it blow up. Maybe, at that point, I could have communicated what I felt. Maybe our families could have helped us communicate. Instead, I was numb and emotionless. The situation was a disaster, and my anxiety was so high. It wasn't easy for either of us. It didn't get better after the holidays.

We coexisted in the same apartment, with not much communication. I still hadn't communicated with Paul, and I ignored all emails until he finally wrote to me directly, asking me what was wrong and if *he* had done anything wrong. A few weeks later, the darkness surrounding my home was too much to bear, so I contacted Paul and asked to meet outside of work—because he brought calm and light to me.

When we met for drinks, we were both super nervous and spent the whole evening talking nonstop. The situation was both awkward and romantic, and, over the course of the evening, tension built between us. At the end of the night, we were walking to the metro station, and I realized right then and there that he was the one, the man I had been looking for. In my therapy sessions, I had described my ideal partner. I had described Paul. Unbeknownst to me earlier, he was a part of my action plan, and I knew that now. Even so, I didn't know what to do with that information. We were both still in complicated situations, stuck in marriages we no longer wanted. But our connection was real, and we were the perfect example of what a healthy partnership should look like. However, I didn't want to be in an affair. I had been cheated on before, and I didn't want to do that to someone else.

When we arrived at the metro stop, it was time for the date to end, so I made my decision. I kissed him. I had to see if there was more to know. I also needed to understand where to place him in my life and to know what to do next. Paul was so shocked that he didn't move, didn't react at all. He was completely paralyzed. I put my hand on his chest, said goodnight, and went down the escalator, leaving him standing there with our first kiss lingering on his lips.

As I waited at the metro station, I decided I would do things right. I would be straightforward and honest. The kiss and that whole evening proved to me that other men existed. I wasn't sure what Paul felt, but it didn't matter at that moment. Finally, I could imagine a life where I felt safe, validated, and heard. I could be me. When I got home, I told my husband exactly what had happened. I explained that I had feelings for someone else and I thought we should separate. I made it clear that the marriage was over and told him I wanted to move out. "I know why you want out," he said. "It's because I've been having an affair with someone at work, isn't it? I haven't been giving you enough attention."

I could barely believe it. Clearly, our relationship wasn't working, and this only confirmed what I already knew. We had both hurt each other, and it was broken beyond repair. Whether Paul and I ended up together didn't matter because now I understood what a healthy partnership felt like. I knew what I wanted, whether that be with Paul or someone else. The partners we pick, past, present, and future, are our responsibility, and the time had come for me to start making better choices.

A SERIES OF DEVASTATING EVENTS

The aftermath of my decision was a disaster. I was prepared to meet some resistance, but I could not have imagined the magnitude of the backlash. I would experience several setbacks before I could move on with my life.

Friends, and Nicolas, kept telling me how wrong Paul was for me and how it was just a fling. They clouded my mind with statistics on affairs. I mean, they weren't wrong. Traditionally, affairs don't last, and the people involved are usually running around to escape their problems, which, admittedly, Paul and I were doing. In my heart, though, I knew that ours wasn't a cliché situation, but the words of others clouded my perspective.

I also told my parents I no longer wanted to be in the marriage. They tried all their tactics to talk me out of it and said that I needed to think about my decision more carefully, that I was ruining my life and the family name, and that I would regret my decision. They saw me as just being "difficult," but all they had ever seen was the image of perfection I kept up, doing my best never to show my stress and anxiety.

An incident abroad added to the stress of a messy divorce. I was in Ecuador for a few weeks, working and teaching. One night, I was walking with Julian, one of my students, and a car slowly approached. Four guys with guns jumped out of the vehicle and quickly approached us. It didn't seem like a random mugging because the men looked professional, like well-dressed mafia guys. Until then, Paul had been with me in Ecuador, walking with me every night, but only for a few days for work. The appearance of these men on the same day that he left wasn't a coincidence. They had been watching me.

Julian and I exchanged an uncertain look. What did these men want with us? Money, perhaps. But something felt off. I couldn't say why exactly, but I thought they wanted to take me. I had read all the U.S. government warnings about travel to Quito. Most of the time, though, the official information is exaggerated and warns of the worst-case scenarios, but, unfortunately, at this moment, it was spot-on. I felt that I was about to become the victim of an express kidnapping. As the men approached, I could see their tension growing. It was happening.

Julian looked at me. "Run," he said. For once in my life, I didn't overthink it, and I just ran. Even though the men had guns, I took off running, zigzagging to avoid getting shot, and screaming for help. I waved frantically at the cars on the street, but no one stopped to help. No one wanted to get involved in the situation. Finally, I made it to the residence where I was staying and breathlessly explained what had happened. They sent a group to look for Julian, but he and the armed men were gone. I was panicking, worried that the men might come back for me and certain that something horrible had happened to Julian.

I was distressed, and I needed support. I needed Paul, but he was back in California with his kids, and he couldn't help me then. If he couldn't be there when I needed him most, how could I ever rely on him to be there for me? I thought about the warnings my parents had given me about him. Following the incident, I shut Paul out. Nicolas, of course, helped me get back home and reestablished himself in my life.

Julian did eventually turn up. The incident *was* an express kidnapping. The kidnappers had taken all of his money and his computer and forced him to withdraw more cash from the ATM before releasing him (I had no words, so a month later, I sent him a new computer). Thankfully, no one was physically hurt. However, the trauma of the event would stay with me for some time.

A GLIMPSE OF THE FUTURE

When I paralyzed Paul with a kiss on our first date, I didn't know what was going through his head. I later learned that the kiss had provoked an out-of-body experience that had left him too stunned to react.

In his vision, an enormous book appeared before him and when it opened, the pages flipped, one after another. On those pages, he saw us sitting on a beach. He saw us walking and holding hands. He saw us pushing a baby stroller. Page after page, our shared future flashed before his eyes. Paul was in love. However, he was a people pleaser as well. He had spent years in a marriage, trying to be everything for the family, and he didn't attend to his own needs. He feared losing his kids, whom he loved more than life itself. He didn't want to hurt them.

After the incident in Ecuador, I continued to shut him out. For me, it didn't matter what had happened between us. Paul needed to be true to himself and do what made sense for him. Even though we weren't speaking at the time, he did start his own separation process. He came to the conclusion that the situation was not fair for him or her. It was time to take a chance to be happy, and he was prepared to be solo.

The traumatic event in Ecuador shook me, and I experienced a month of darkness, attending therapy to deal with PTSD. Gradually, over the course of months, as I came to terms with what had happened and with therapy, I started to become myself again. I had let that one big event pull me back into my old life, giving Nicolas hope that wasn't there, which wasn't fair. The time had come to finally put an end to it. My parents, infuriated and ashamed, stopped talking to me, which turned out to be the ultimate test. How much did I really want to be free? Was I willing to lose my family? Was I willing to lose it all? Yes, I was. I remember being firm with them on the phone when discussing my marriage, saying, "No, it's not what I want." But they felt I was overreacting.

Although the entire divorce process would take a long time to complete, I finally started proceedings for the both of us. I cried daily. I never wanted to hurt Nicolas, and I cared for him deeply. He had a huge heart, and he didn't deserve this. Every day, I had to give myself permission to accept that I didn't deserve this either and, in the end, me leaving would be better for everyone.

Slowly, with time, I let Paul back into my life, and we figured out a way to make our long-distance relationship work. We took things day by day. He had resumed his tenured professorship and was trying his best to juggle his own complicated divorce, being present for his kids, and growing our future together. We met each other over breaks and weekends whenever we could, but it was slow and gradual. I had a lot of healing that needed to happen and darkness to overcome. During this time, my sister was my rock and one of my largest supporters. She didn't judge my actions and was there when I needed her the most.

As Paul and I got to know each other more and more, I shared with him stories about my childhood and my extended family. One night, when Paul was visiting me, I spent the entire evening telling him all about one of my favorite cousins. She was a ray of sunshine in our family, vibrant and creative, but had been struggling lately. The next morning, I was about to reach out to her to share everything that had happened to me. I wanted her to know that my life was also kind of a disaster and thought that maybe we could support each other. Just then, about 30 minutes before my alarm went off, I got the call that she had passed. It was devastating. We all wished we could have done more to keep her safe and healthy. I hope she knows that she is never forgotten.

My parents still weren't talking to me, which made the situation even more difficult. When I saw them at my cousin's funeral in Miami, they were cold with me. Her funeral impacted me greatly. I felt that the formality of the ceremony and the tone of the speeches missed the opportunity to celebrate her life, and I felt so upset by that. She was this amazing person, an amazing human—why were we not celebrating her? We had been so close as kids, but lately we had grown distant over misunderstandings. She was so young, and her untimely passing really made me see that our time on Earth is limited and I could not waste mine. I understood that I needed to take action.

I also needed to know if my parents were going to be part of my life with Paul.

A few months after I fell pregnant, I reached out to them. Did they or did they not want to be part of their grandchild's life? I had come to terms with it either way. I had found the man I manifested and I had to believe that if they really loved me, they would come around. And they did. They loved me beyond belief. It was just really hard for them. They also agreed to give Paul a chance. We flew to Miami, and Mom and Dad met with Paul. *They loved him.* And more than that, they saw the calm he brought me and the spark he had reawakened in me.

On the day I had my sonogram and saw my daughter for the first time, my divorce was finalized. The day was filled with darkness and light. I was free to move on. On top of that, I had my family back and would soon give birth to a beautiful daughter. It did come at a cost, though. Nicolas told our mutual friends about my affair, and I lost many of them. At the time, I didn't have the heart to tell many of them the entire narrative, that it was the both of us, so I let them believe I was the monster.

Nicolas and I eventually spoke years later and forgave each other. I gave him an annulment later and although I didn't agree with it, I let him and his mother put the one-sided story in there so he could marry the woman of his dreams and live the happy life they have now. It was my way of saying "I'm sorry."

"I knew what I wanted, what needed to happen, and I was prepared to fight for it."

THE AMERICAN DREAM

Paul and I reached a point at which we had to decide where we wanted to live. He was back living in California, and I worked in DC. Paul was a tenured professor and a department chair with twelve years on the job, so it made sense for us to settle in California and not derail his comfortable career. But something didn't feel right. Settling in California felt too much like the white picket fence American dream—a dream for some perhaps, but not for me. Besides, Paul's own divorce had been super complicated. His kids were having a hard time, and the co-parenting arrangement with his ex was a real challenge. Compared to Nicolas and me, they had so many more years behind them and so much more history. Long-term in DC was out of the question because, at the time, Nicolas still lived there, and it would be best for everyone if we went somewhere else. Clearly, we needed somewhere new, a fresh start. So, we moved to Nicaragua as part of the diplomatic corps.

These years were a time of personal and professional growth. Working as a diplomat, I continued to travel the world for work and after our time in Nicaragua, we moved to Jamaica and later the Dominican Republic. During our time in Jamaica, our son, Maximo, was born. We had practically achieved the American dream: two Latinos with PhDs, well-paying and prestigious jobs, kids, nice house.

Through our jobs, we had all of our housing, private schooling, and medical expenses paid for. Wherever we were, we always lived in the best neighborhoods. By all measures, we were successful. We had lives that many would envy. We were living the American dream. However, I lacked one important ingredient that makes a fulfilling life: alignment.

In some ways, my job was very satisfying. For instance, one week, I would be wearing my best suits, facilitating conversations with governments and huge international organizations, and finding ways to make a positive and lasting difference in communities. The next week, I would be in the field with my work boots and mosquito repellent, speaking with locals to understand their needs and the constraints they face. I was at the forefront of facilitating transformative change, and I got to see communities develop. This was why I had gotten into international development in the first place, and the work itself was rewarding. However, the bureaucracy and the work environment soon killed any joy or satisfaction.

The organization was designed in a way that, in my line of work, we were all competing against each other for promotions and recognition, which created a difficult work environment (the opinions expressed here are mine and mine only and do not represent the views of the U.S. government). As much as Human Resources (HR) in Washington tried to tell us we should promote a "one team" spirit, we weren't just colleagues or friends; we were also rivals, opponents, and, in some cases, enemies. Of course, there are always exceptions, but they were hard to find.

Over time, I've learned that these issues weren't unique to my organization. Any monster bureaucracy suffers from similar problems, and people start to get jaded, burned out, and forget why they joined in the first place. On top of everything else, we had to deal with the political pressures that come with the job, which sucked much of the joy out of the work, at least for me. Fundamentally, we represented the organization and were not free to be truly creative, innovative, or collaborative. To be fair, I knew what I signed up for and had been warned of the pros and cons.

Although I had found a job where I could make a meaningful difference, I had not found my purpose, and I gradually grew more and more miserable in the role. Also, as a woman of color, I often faced micro- and macro-aggressions, bullying from White men and women, and threats when I spoke up about local staff and their rights. However, my accomplishments were stellar, and I kept climbing the ladder. I earned so many awards that my entire wall was filled. I also championed causes worth fighting for. Leading a dedicated team, I successfully introduced recycling initiatives at the embassy, overcoming tremendous pushback. I quickly discovered that facing challenges alone often invites scrutiny. However, shared initiatives backed by a group of passionate individuals could ignite substantial change. The triumphant accomplishment of our recycling battle was indeed a glorious victory. Remember, I have my great grandfather's blood, so, like Dr. Benjamín Zeledón, I was determined to make the organization better from the inside.

From the outside, I'm sure it looked like I should have been blissfully happy. According to all the check marks I had been brought up to believe in, I had reached the pinnacle of success. So, why wasn't I satisfied? Why couldn't I shake the constant and growing feeling that I was in the wrong place, doing the wrong thing? I felt guilty for feeling this way—so many people around the world worked their entire lives for a fraction of what I had. Why couldn't I just be grateful for what I had? Also, what option did I have? Could I just quit my job? Where would I go? I felt the burden of taking a financial risk and didn't want to put the well-being of my kids in danger. But as I started to pay closer attention, I realized that, other than a few exceptions, the people around me were largely miserable, invested in the system, accepting injustices, and just counting the days. I could also never be one of those paycheck players or quiet quitters. I give 100 percent to the job and cause.

I was determined not to live out a slow death, unaligned, unfulfilled, constantly stressed and anxious. I began to see my situation as a stepping stone, the short-term sacrifice I was making in preparation for my leap forward into a life of purpose. I needed to find the compass that would point me in the right direction and the road map that would help me get there. While in my current situation, I decided I would make the best of it—and I did. I taught Zumba to local staff, made friends with drivers, hosted dinners, got to know the countries I was in, made new friends, and maximized the experience with an open heart.

THE POWER OF PLANNING

Let me take you back to my pregnancy with my daughter. At that time, I had moved back to Miami to be close to Mom so she could help during the pregnancy. It was also a time when the U.S. had no paid maternity leave. Paul was still closing out his other responsibilities and trying to be present for his older kids as much as possible, so he couldn't be there all the time. I, of course, had romanticized pregnancy. In my mind, I would have an endless glow. I would have all kinds of food cravings, and I would have this amazing water birth. My reality could not have been more different.

I felt horrifically sick almost every day of my pregnancy. My hormone levels fluctuated like crazy, and my fluid levels were always low. Despite only being able to eat a few things, I gained one hundred pounds. For context, I'm a petite woman, barely 5′2″. Worse, there were complications, so I was concerned when I went into labor early. When my water broke, I was only thirty-two and a half weeks pregnant. I called the hospital to find out what I should do. They didn't seem concerned and said I should relax and only come in when the contractions started, but I knew something wasn't right. I was so early—why weren't they concerned? Regardless, I followed their instructions and kept calling back.

I called Paul, and he was on the next plane from California to Miami. He arrived early in the morning, and we immediately went to the hospital. The staff was so condescending and tried to convince me I wasn't in labor and that my water hadn't broken, which I knew wasn't true. Instead of actually examining me, they put me on a monitor and assured me that everything was fine. Certain that they would be sending me home any minute, they didn't even assign me a proper maternity room. Instead, they stuck me in a small and crowded triage room, where I would eventually give birth.

Twenty-four hours had passed since I felt my water break, and they still hadn't performed a sonogram. I kept saying that something wasn't right, but I clearly wasn't being loud enough, and the staff didn't listen. When Mom arrived at the hospital, she, Paul, and I decided that it was time to demand a sonogram. After hours of pushing them, the doctors reluctantly agreed.

After the sonogram, no one communicated anything to us. When

I returned to my room, they put me on an IV, and I suddenly began to have monstrous contractions. They had induced me without my knowledge. I was in horrific pain and didn't know why. It wasn't until Paul noticed that the IV bag read "Pitocin" that we understood what was happening. At one point, the nurses came in and asked me to stop making noise because I was scaring the other patients. Later, as the contractions grew stronger and stronger, I tried to get up from the bed and instead fell on Paul, and, as we learned later, caused major damage to his knees. I was treated like shit, and it was a terrible experience.

Eventually, the doctor entered the room, a concerned look on her face. "This baby needs to come out *now*," she said. "It's in huge distress." Even with the complications, she insisted that I give birth vaginally. To help the baby come out, Mom and Paul had to sandwich me—they literally squeezed my legs to my body like I was a sandwich. I didn't understand what was happening. Why wouldn't they do a C-section? Why, after all the waiting, was it now an emergency? During the birth, we saw that my daughter had the umbilical cord wrapped around her neck four times and wasn't getting enough oxygen.

Eventually, Xilonem (See-LO-nem, a beautiful Mayan warrior goddess from Central America) was born, but we didn't know if she would survive. She was purple, and her Apgar score was low. To add to this, they had to tear out my placenta manually. This hurt more than the birth itself, and, again, I was so confused. This was not covered in our Lamaze classes.

The whole time, the medical staff were screaming at me like I had done something wrong. They treated me like a clueless teenager. Originally, I had called the doctors helpline, and the staff had directed me to this hospital. Now, the doctor was yelling at me for going to the wrong hospital.

"You should have known better," she said. They didn't have a ward equipped to deal with my daughter's condition. Even though I explained that my doctor's team had sent us there, I was still in the wrong. I spent the days after feeling traumatized. I didn't speak up or advocate for my needs. I let them bully me. Finally, when I could no longer take the abuse, I spoke back. Once I made them understand the reality of the situation they had caused, they didn't know what to say. I had to exert my education and experience and voice that my treatment was wrong and that they had jeopardized my daughter's life. It wasn't until then that I started to be treated like a human, which was so wrong on so many levels. The worst part is that my education or the fact that I had followed the process didn't matter. All they saw was what they thought was a young-looking brown girl. I got the same treatment that my mother received and so many countless women of color face every day.

They rushed Xilonem to another hospital in something that looked like a spaceship, but they left me right where I was. I thought that my daughter was going to die, and I was stuck there without having held her. My body went into a kind of shock from having her so suddenly taken away from me, and my mind began to grieve. The whole experience was one terrible shock after another.

Xilonem survived. We had originally planned to give her a much softer name but with the odds so heavily stacked against her survival, naming her after a warrior goddess was so much more appropriate. She stayed in the hospital for weeks before being released, and that time felt eternal. We didn't know exactly what was wrong with her. They did all these tests, checking her for meningitis and so many other things. At one point, from her forehead to her heels, she had eight needles in her. However, once she'd had time to deswell and recover from the initial birth trauma, she made a breakthrough. At the same time, I had people, who had been through something similar, reach out to me, and they gave me the advice and information I needed. My community came through. It was amazing. I could have sued the hospital, but I didn't. I just wanted to put the whole experience behind me.

A year and a half passed before we realized that something was wrong.

Xilonem wasn't talking, and her behavior was concerning. Similar to the birthing process, many doctors pushed me to wait until she was older, and many discouraged us from trying to address what they thought was a nonissue. We were "exaggerating." It wasn't until a medical doctor came to visit the embassy and was willing to sit and listen to me and my daughter for an hour that things changed.

I will never forget her. She agreed that I needed to look into it and helped me start the process. After much investigation and numerous studies, we received an explanation. During her difficult birth, Xilonem had lost oxygen to her brain stem, and a lot of her issues related to inflammation in her neck. We could have avoided all of this with a C-section. Recovery was possible, but she would need a lot of therapy and additional help along the way. Therefore, until Xilonem got better, following my purpose would have to be put on hold. I couldn't take any risks that might interfere with her recovery. The good news was that the odds were in her favor: she had a 95-percent chance of overcoming most of her limitations if she received intensive interventions before the age of five.

My second question was: how long would the therapeutic process take? The amazing therapist, referred to us by the embassy doctor, that we worked with in Jamaica said about five years. Five years! My heart sank a little. I knew I couldn't stay in my job forever, miserable and unaligned, but the insurance coverage was amazing. I needed to give Xilo (her nickname) the best chance for success, so I accepted the timeline, the money, and the insurance.

Five years seemed like an eternity, but at least now I had an exit date, and I could bear the weight a little better. I wanted to go back to the experience I'd had when I first met Paul, traveling and doing strategic planning—but it would have to wait. Xilonem was two at the time, so she would be seven when I exited. We also had piles of medical expenses and Paul's child support to deal with, but the timeline was set.

I put measures in place to prepare for my eventual career or position change. All of the money I saved by not having to pay rent, I put aside for Xilonem. We started her on a comprehensive set of therapies that, frankly, also included a lot of training for me and for Paul. We learned about occupational therapy, speech therapy, and behavioral therapy, equipping ourselves with the knowledge needed to guide Xilonem through her five-year recovery and beyond. Every spare moment we had, we focused on her. We also hired a specialized teacher, who accompanied her once she began attending school.

Although the search for my alignment was on hold, I could still plan for the future and try to make the transition as smooth as possible when the time arrived. I also realized that although this was on hold for me, it did fill part of my purpose—making a vision for her possible. So, for now, Xilonem was my priority, and I was going to do everything in my power to get her mainstreamed and help her thrive throughout her life.

As time went on, I found myself repeating the same mistakes my parents had made with me. I was so scarred by the near-death experience of Xilonem's birth that I felt the constant need to protect her, and I realized that I was treating her as the sick child who, above all, just needed to survive. I started seeing a therapist, who helped me see that, in fact, Xilo was incredibly strong. Her own determination, some strength inside her, had helped her survive. We also saw that, even at a very young age, she was so determined and so dedicated to her work. We changed the narrative so that all of us could see her as the limitless powerhouse that we watched her become.

We also learned that the best thing for her was to have a sibling. At first, we looked into adopting a baby. I always wanted to help a kid in need, so we started the initial scoping, but the amount of money and bureaucracy was overwhelming. It shouldn't be that way, but we didn't have the money, and, between Xilo and work, my time was super limited. So, we went the pregnancy route.

The thought of being pregnant again scared me, so I spoke to several specialists before trying. Luckily, we were living in Jamaica, and, armed with the wisdom of experience, I chose to take extra precautions this time around. Throughout the pregnancy, I had a home doctor, who monitored me and the baby to make sure we were both healthy. I had the best care and doctors in Jamaica. That doctor even became our close friend. At the end of the pregnancy, I returned to Miami, where the doctors told me that, due to my previous experience, I would likely have another premature baby. This was compounded by the high level of stress I had in my job and position. My dedication to the job was being questioned. I had extra work piled on me, and I was being blocked from taking advantage of the rights and benefits the job would have afforded me. Despite my precautions, thanks to this added stress and anxiety, my pregnancy was even worse than the first time. I was so sick the entire time, and my workspace was right next to the microwave, where fish was heated every morning.

At least in terms of dealing with the hospital and the doctors, I was prepared this time. I got a new team of doctors and researched them thoroughly. I knew all the hospitals, risks, and plans of action. I knew how to listen to my body. I understood the precautions I could take, and I was armed with information and care from Jamaica.

When I went into labor, the hospital sent me home three times, but I persisted. I knew I would give birth that weekend, so I sat there until they finally took me in. Even then, they wanted to discharge me right away, but I had learned from my previous experience, and I wasn't going to let them push me out the door. I demanded a sonogram and shots for the baby's lungs, and I kept demanding until the doctor agreed. My pushing shouldn't have been necessary, but it was absolutely justified. Right after the sonogram, they rushed me for an emergency C-section, and Maximo was born. From that experience, I learned that you can advocate firmly and get your needs met. Never be afraid to make your voice heard for what you know is right.

My two hospital experiences illustrate why planning is important. When I went into labor the second time, I suspected that the medical staff would turn me away, but I knew what I wanted, what *needed* to happen, and I was prepared to fight for it. I had a plan of action and the determination to see it through. As a result, despite being born just as early as Xilo, Maximo was born at a healthy four and a half pounds, with strong lungs and a solid Apgar score. He was out of the hospital in two weeks. I am proud of that moment. My son is not only alive, but he is happy and healthy as well. I also researched and got the best care. Did it come easy? No. Did I have to be firm, make noise, and be clear about expectations? Absolutely.

ONE STEP AT A TIME

I was both devastated and relieved to leave Jamaica. In the years we spent there, we developed an amazing community of people we could trust—they were family. We also had the best medical care, and Paul even had two surgeries in-country and got care for things he had been dealing with for a long time. Xilonem had also received the best treatment plans and care. Even so, I still wanted to leave that position. I was ready to move on and feel more aligned professionally. With Xilonem more advanced in her treatment, I could think about myself more. I also understood that I was ready to fight for the things and people I cared about. No more witnessing other people getting bullied, and no more just putting my head down and working. I put in my best work, won awards, and found joy in teaching Zumba and mentoring the local staff and community for free, but I also became much more vocal. I built an amazing community and found meaning in my work. Jamaica will always be one of the best places we have lived, and we made the most amazing friends and network, which we have to this day.

When we moved from Jamaica to the Dominican Republic, we brought Xilonem's specialists with us. I didn't want to start over again with someone new and risk derailing her progress. Of course, many of the things I did for my daughter were expensive, and I experienced a lot of resistance from others, including my family. They questioned how I could spend so much money on teachers and specialized programs. Even worse, they would ask: "Why did she spend so much time in therapies, and why didn't you just let her be a kid?" To them, her struggles were "just a phase," something she would outgrow with time. But I had science on my side. I understood that early intervention would mean a lifetime of benefit for her. I was seeing the value of making a short-term sacrifice for long-term gain, and it was absolutely a trade-off I was willing to make. People were also questioning how much money I was spending on specialists—but I didn't care. They were focused on the short-term, but I had a long-term vision. I had a strategy, which involved working with dozens of specialists, and we were constantly celebrating successes. And here's the thing: it was working. Trust your gut, *always*.

"I had a plan of action and the determination to see it through."

By the time Xilonem started kindergarten, she had become much more independent, and people noticed the change. They began to wonder if maybe there was a method to my madness. Her change and growth has been truly spectacular. Now she's fully independent and mainstreamed, a top student and athlete, who has visited twenty-nine countries so far, is fluently bilingual, and dreams of owning a chain of luxury hotels. Are there still things she is working on? Absolutely. But, today, nobody questions the choices I made. In fact, many parents ask me for advice and resources, finding it difficult to believe how far she has come. Even her psycho-development specialist congratulated us many times and reminded us that many parents don't stick to the plan. Often, as many of the critics suggested, they hope it will just get better on its own, and they wait too long to properly intervene. I also understand the attrition in terms of keeping up with therapies. With the diagnosis, care, and treatment plans, it can be overwhelming, expensive, and hard to navigate. Also, it means putting other priorities on hold and waiting a long time for a sign of hope.

I selected to go to the Dominican Republic for my next assignment to work with an amazing leader whom I had worked with before. He was a champion for people of color and modeled all qualities of a true leader. After a time, I rose to a leadership position, only to discover that the situation in the office was dire. My boss informed me that we might have to shut down the entire unit because climate change was no longer a political priority. I was inheriting a dying portfolio and a disheartened team. With all the changes, the move had been rough on Xilonem, and now I was being told I might need to consider alternative countries. I was done with just putting my head down and accepting fate. Remember, the five-year timeline was close to ending.

"The environment office isn't going to survive," my boss said. "You may want to consider other plans."

"That's option one," I said. "What's option two? How can we turn this around?"

"I don't see how we can," he said. "It isn't a priority globally… However, there is one interesting region—the border between the Dominican Republic and Haiti. The staff here don't have an appetite for it, but it's where there's the most need for development. If you can find a way to run with it, go ahead." To this day, I'm still thankful for him, the opportunity he gave me, and him believing in me.

The task before me was monumental. Not only did I have personal reasons for wanting to make this work, but I was also leading a tremendously talented team, whose jobs were at stake.

This was my chance to showcase my talents and rejuvenate the skills I had to put on pause during my time in Jamaica. How was I going to revive the office, resurrect the entire mission organization, and put us back on the map? I had to think strategically, which is what I love doing.

First, I applied for seed money to tour the region. At the time, I knew nothing about the Dominican Republic-Haiti border, so I had a lot to learn. I also needed a team across offices and technical sectors so, from scratch, we could develop a shared mission, vision, and purpose. Without champions and buy-in, this whole effort would be doomed to die. It was time to put to the test the skills Paul and I had learned years before in strategic planning to craft a plan for my team and for the whole organization to create sustainable and positive impact.

I created the group from across all offices, and the people I selected brought in so many skill sets that many didn't even know they had. Together, we came up with a plan and once I received funding, I visited the border for approximately a week every month, learning what I could from all the relevant actors: communities, local government, schools, orphanages, churches, parent-teacher organizations, local businesses—anyone who could provide useful intel. We discussed what others had tried in the past and attempted to discover why those things failed. I also asked what people would like to see done differently. Once I understood what local communities wanted and needed on the border, I met with the national government and private sector to understand their priorities.

We collected a massive amount of data from a tremendously

diverse range of sources. When I analyzed all of the collated information, I discovered a major theme: there was a huge disconnect and a lack of cooperation between all the relevant actors. For example, the community might apply for money to build a clinic, which they would erect with volunteer help, but the government would neglect to assign a doctor or nurse. Without medical staff, a clinic was just an empty building that would end up being converted into a community center or something else. Similarly, money to build schools was often wasted, as no teachers would be assigned. Sometimes, church groups and volunteers came along and built something without consulting the community at all. Understandably, the people were frustrated and felt that their leaders couldn't be trusted.

The disconnect observed between the different groups on the border highlighted the importance of listening. Before you can truly help someone, you must first understand their needs. When those offering aid listen and those in need speak up and communicate with each other, a shared vision emerges. That's the secret sauce: bringing together all the relevant players to identify common goals and purpose and, together, hashing out win-win solutions. Professionally, addressing communication issues such as these became my superpower because it aligned with my purpose. Working on the border was where I gained my most important insights, honed my most critical skills, and tested so many of the techniques you will learn throughout this book.

Then I had to put everything into action. Communication breakdown was the biggest problem, so I gathered all the relevant parties in a room together to talk, listen, and understand one another's perspectives, dreams, and goals. Then I pushed them to identify the barriers to achieving their goals and, eventually, to jointly identify how they could break through those barriers. I can't emphasize enough how different this approach was from the traditional way of carrying out development work. As the donor, we would typically come to communities like this as "experts," who would identify what we saw as the greatest need, and any consultation with the community was really just to tell them what we would be funding. The communities always accepted the donor funding but as soon as the money ran out, there was little to no lasting impact. Without the genuine buy-in from the community, those activities were doomed to be short-lived. The community-focused, community-led approach I implemented in the border region was a revolutionary attempt to make the local community's wants and needs the nexus of development.

With consensus, I next applied for funding to implement the shared vision that emerged during these discussions. Then I demonstrated the success of the locally led approach, scaled it, and raised more money. Many people believe that fundraising for development or NGOs (non-governmental organizations) is all about selling. But, in truth, it's more about being crystal clear on your mission, vision, and purpose and finding the right fit with funding sources. If people resonate with your cause and feel a genuine connection and alignment, they'll come forward with the funds. For us, the key was to understand this, be clear about our goals, and hold on tight to them. Eventually, we went from an office operating with a lean budget to raising nearly US$100 million for both in-country and regional programs. But it didn't happen overnight. With the support of amazing leaders and a team that trusted me and believed in the mission, vision, and purpose, I built that success one step at a time.

Like I said, I had a great team behind me, and I know that I stretched them in ways that sometimes felt uncomfortable to them. The massive growth in our portfolio came with new responsibilities but also secured funding for their positions and created opportunities for growth. I was able to help many of them move up the ladder or shift into different positions or technical areas, according to their own goals and aspirations. I coached them on how to interview, develop their skills, and elevate themselves professionally. We discussed their purpose, their dreams, and their goals, and I empowered them to work toward their objectives. We made our vision a reality. I learned so much from them too. I felt that I was doing what I used to do before when I was in middle school, high school, and throughout my life but now in a professional environment. Once again, I was coaching, and I loved seeing my best people thrive.

As the team grew, new members brought fresh perspectives, and the diversity of opinions strengthened our group. We worked with communities to create things they needed rather than some impractical dream sold to them by a cocky donor or disconnected organization. We leveraged the private sector, and we gained respect from the government, made a name for ourselves in Washington, and made real, lasting change in communities—the work paid off.

Those years were amazing. We were innovative; morale was high in the organization, and we had so much fun. We would do Zumba, go to each other's houses, do happy hours, host themed dinner parties, and I made some amazing friends that I still have to this day. At that moment, I felt I was thriving. It was a time when all the stars aligned at work: great bosses and leadership, amazing team, huge impact, support, and community. I would celebrate birthdays with the friends I had made in the communities I served, taking their tours and fishing with them. I admired their passion and love for their work, and it felt amazing to make their purpose and dreams a reality. I was connected, impactful, and valued. I loved my job and the work.

The role, the impact, and everything that came with it during those few years were extremely rewarding.

TICKTOCK, TICKTOCK

Those wins came after a rough start. When I first arrived in the Dominican Republic, things didn't start out smoothly. At first, the job came with its share of frustrations. Although I had an amazing army of champions in the beginning, I also had the opposite. Some people outside of my team didn't understand my motivations and thought I had ulterior motives for doing what I did. I was questioning the status quo and threatening the system. There were so many naysayers ... which is common when you're trailblazing. I learned that questioning the system comes at a personal cost. I was subjected to incredible scrutiny, as my personal finances were investigated, and I was interrogated multiple times. As I mentioned, at times, the system could be adversarial and toxic, and I think others often saw the changes I brought as a threat to them. One great thing that came out of this period, though, was that I learned firsthand about change management. It became a passion of mine, and I eventually earned a certificate in change management. I began to be more strategic, learning more about the roots of the resistance and how to find win-win situations.

I also learned that not everyone wants to be helped. When I saw someone who was lost or struggling within the organization, my instinct was to offer assistance, invite them to come and work with me, and coach them. But if they weren't ready to receive that sort of help, they would misinterpret my intentions and reject the offer, which made me question myself and my abilities. Impostor syndrome would kick in. However, I soon grew to understand that not everyone is ready to move forward, discover their purpose, and strive for their goals. I could only help those who wanted to be helped. As a coach, this was a hard reality to accept. But it also helped me become a stronger manager and leader. I learned to pick my battles and only fight the ones where I had others behind me.

Although I had dozens of awards, I rarely received recognition for some of my most important work, which was empowering others, helping people advance in the organization, giving communities and local staff a voice, and creating change in the local system. To me, the results I got, the ones not highlighted in organizational metrics, mattered—they just didn't matter as much to the organization at that time. That's misalignment.

On top of which, very few people of color held the position

I was in. Worldwide, only about 2 percent were Latinos, and the statistics were dim for other ethnic groups too. Women were also a minority in leadership roles, so I had to work twice as hard and make twice as much noise to have a seat at the table. Again, I am forever grateful for my two male mentors of color, who gave me the feedback and courage I needed to do it. I became much more assertive and confident, fueled by the success of my projects. And I can tell you without a hint of doubt that, throughout my journey, it has been the Black community that has not only extended their support but also left a lasting imprint on my heart. It's a community I'll forever hold dear. They're more than just people I've met along the way; they're a family I choose every single day.

But I worked ridiculous hours—fifteen-hour days—to manage my projects and my team and still keep up with my kids' therapy calendars, my household help, and diplomatic events on many evenings. I felt responsible for all the communities, my team, my colleagues, and the work. I felt the ethical responsibility to keep things moving. The thing is, my team growth strategy included more staff and more help for the team, but our hiring process was super delayed, and everyone across the board was overstretched. So, I took a lot of the brunt to keep true to my promises. It was another key lesson I learned later: add buffer time to your deadlines and objectives because, in the end, you can't control outside variables that could delay your best-laid plans. All those hours away from my family, I began to ask: What, in the end, was my impact? What was it for? And what was it costing me? The combination of long hours at work, having to manage staff at home, and all the therapies were starting to weigh on my and Paul's relationship. Our marriage had hit a hard part, and I started to feel suffocated. I was yearning for and seeking joy and connection in my life.

Further, within the organization, I had nowhere I wanted to grow. I was a director of a large unit, with a wall full of awards, but my impact still felt small. I know it's a matter of perspective and that my work had already impacted many people. Still, I was never able to quiet that little voice inside me that kept telling me I was meant for more. In my mind, I was yet to fulfill my true legacy, be truly aligned, and live my purpose. As happens in the diplomatic service, people transitioned out, and my biggest champions left. What once was an amazing place, filled with light and energy, was gone. At this point, what I had to do became clear.

Although I had created a community, the vibe wasn't the same anymore. Now, there were additional layers of micro- and macro-aggressions, and it was happening throughout the organization, not just to me. I took the hits for everyone else, and there was no outlet for me. There was no protection, no security, and voicing dissent became unsafe. If I couldn't speak out against injustices, fight for our beneficiaries and staff, and help people pursue their own mission, vision, and purpose, then what was left for me? All I saw around me were the fixed mindsets of people unwilling to grow and change. It was back to darkness and to so many colleagues drinking their sorrows away on weekends. Plus, the thought of us leaving was negatively affecting my daughter. I took some time off with her to have the space to make the best decision for me and the family. More on this later.

While I had made my exit plan, I hadn't planned beyond my exit. I had no idea what life would look like beyond that point. I couldn't imagine it, so how could I plan for it? Realizing this was a pivotal moment because I finally had to sit down and give my alignment and living my purpose some serious thought.

WOMEN IN LEADERSHIP

My situation was one that many high-achieving women in leadership and executive positions will be familiar with: having to face severe pressures between work and family, feeling like you have to work twice as hard to get even close to the recognition of male counterparts, and shouldering the weight of helping provide for the family while sacrificing your own purpose. For underrepresented groups and women of color, these pressures are only amplified. Add to all of this, systemic racism, snide remarks from colleagues and supervisors, and the constant, exhausting scrutiny from those hoping to catch you being in some way inappropriate. It's unfair, infuriating, and disheartening. There's also the unspoken rule that you pick up as you start climbing the career ladder as a woman: never, and I mean never, volunteer for logistics or party planning. If you do, you've just made your climb that much steeper and given everyone else an easy excuse to slot you into administrative roles. This was a tough one for me because I'm always looking to lend a hand, but I learned to channel that urge through my volunteer groups instead. A word of advice—please, don't pass that duty on to another woman in the group.

We also live in constant fear of using our voice and losing everything we have built. My friend, Helen, and I began our development careers together. She was a kind and remarkable person but also a vocal advocate for change. Because of that, she was constantly overworked and punished with scrutiny, and she often talked about quitting. One day at work, shockingly, she suffered an aneurysm, and we lost her. When I got the news, my heart just plummeted. I couldn't help but wonder, if she'd managed to leave when she first wanted to, would she still be with us today? If her voice had been welcomed instead of seen as disloyalty, might she have lived a longer, happier life?

When writing this book, I spent three days, overthinking and sleepless, worried about the consequences of being brutally honest. The day I almost deleted this entire section, I got a call from Fred, a friend I had met a few months back, and he asked if we could ride together to an event and talk. It was odd because Fred never called me, and we never rode together to events, but I agreed. *It must be important*, I thought. When I got in the car, Fred told me his wife was being bullied at work, and it was affecting the family. It was a story that resembled mine word for word, a story I had never told him about. I exited the car like I had been hit by lightning. Two days later, it happened again. Three days later, I could barely believe it, but it happened again—practically the same story repeated to me by a completely different person. That's what you call synchronicity. It was life's gentle reminder to me that we're not alone in our struggles and that I had the obligation to share it with all of you so we can stop it together.

And that's the thing: women in leadership and executive positions are expected to just soldier on. Show any sign that any of these pressures are getting to you, and suddenly you're just not meant to lead. You're not ready. We're supposed to stay silent, remain fearful, and keep our heads down. How many women have pushed through some of the worst moments in their lives for fear of showing weakness?

Previously, I had another pregnancy I haven't mentioned yet. They were twins. Paul and I were terrified but also so happy. I loved the idea of having twins. But then there were complications, and I lost one of them. It was early on. The doctors said that, while unfortunate, it should give the other a better chance of survival. So, I soldiered on, didn't really take any time for myself, and kept working. Paul and I had a strategic planning trip scheduled in Asia, and it seemed like great timing. We arrived, met the amazing people at the office, and got to work planning our big event.

The night before our high-level event, the unspeakable happened. I started to feel really bad, and, sparing you the details, I lost the baby. Paul was devastated, and we both cried the whole night. But, in the morning, the show had to go on. I got dressed, went to work, gave an amazing presentation, and facilitated a room of over one hundred participants. It's tempting to say, "Wow, she's so strong." But the truth is that I needed to grieve, and my body needed to rest. Why couldn't I just let go? Paul could have handled the presentation perfectly well on his own, but I couldn't fathom having my colleagues think that I couldn't handle it.

That pressure to soldier on is immense.

"Did it come easy? No. Did I have to be firm, make noise, and be clear about expectations? Absolutely."

TIME TO GO

My contract in the Dominican Republic was coming to an end, and I had reached a melting point. I either had to dedicate another year, or four years, and move to a new country, or quit. I was hyperventilating at the thought. In just ten years, I would receive my pension, and I could retire. It wasn't *that* long. *Maybe I should just ride it out?* Quitting then meant that I would lose my pension, lifetime health insurance, and many other perks. Besides, I had to think of my daughter and her needs. Sure, she was doing much better, but that didn't mean she wouldn't still need help. On top of that, Paul's kids were in college, which wasn't cheap. I also had a full staff working for me, including a driver and a teacher, so I would have to phase out dependency on those people. I had already funded our driver's college education, and I felt very invested in their lives. The choice that had seemed so clear almost five years ago was now clouded in doubt. I felt the pressure of their lives and livelihoods—they depended on me. I was also scared for my team, not wanting to leave them to the wolves and without a replacement for a while. Further, I believed in the work. Basically, I was thinking of everyone but myself. The pressure to make the right decision was crushing. Luckily, I had my best friend, Rita, to count on. She came over daily in the evenings after her shifts, and we would talk about life, struggles, dreams. She had hers too.

The transition would be difficult. I had to account for all the people who depended on me but also for all the people I depended on. To make my crazy work hours feasible, I had grown accustomed to having everything and everyone I needed to make life manageable. At the same time, I was paying some of my family's (and extended family's) expenses, so I didn't just have to phase out my dependence but also other people's reliance on me. As an extreme people pleaser, having to sever some of these ties caused me so much anxiety. I had to take inventory of all the dependencies in my life and begin phasing them out. The time, energy, and money I had been giving to others, I needed to invest in my own future and business.

So, I made a plan. I knew that change would still be difficult for Xilo, and I needed to prepare her for that. I took time off to dedicate to her well-being and transition, but I needed that time to heal as well. I did inner work—therapy—and, once I was ready, signed up for coaching and made a two-year plan. With all the uncertainty before us, I wasn't ready for anything longer, so I started with two years. I wanted to ensure that Paul and I would be solid and in a place where we could navigate this together. In navigating his family, his children, and grief, we had already been through so much together, but that's his story to tell. We got through it with extensive therapy and, later, coaching because I wanted to make sure we were both ready for this. I also worked to fortify myself because I knew that actually leaving my position would provoke a lot of resistance and manipulation. I knew leaving on my own terms would not be accepted. I knew challenges would come with this decision, and I had to be so confident in my purpose and alignment and have my resilience toolbox ready.

Even after preparing myself as well as I could, I still hesitated to pull the trigger and resign. I got the pressures I anticipated from others, being told that my whole team was depending on me to steer the ship and I'd be abandoning them if I left. People kept telling me that I would be crazy to resign. I had a dream job that only 1 percent of people who apply ever get, and I would never find another job this good. I was also told that every job sucked and I was naive to believe there was a "dream job." Again, this was everyone else projecting what they had been told and what they had convinced themselves of. At the time, there were very few women in leadership and almost no women of color. I had broken the glass ceiling, and I was an example to others who aspired to rise within the organization. How could I leave when I was at the top of my game? Pressure came from all angles.

People guilted me, saying they would be sad if I left because they had all invested so much in me. My colleagues and supervisors, knowing how much I cared about my team, told me that I was abandoning them. My family reminded me that I had built a great future for my kids and I would be foolish to throw it away. My friends argued that I would regret giving up my dream job—what would I do? But I drew strength from the inner work I had done. I constantly told myself, *What do you mean? I have so much to offer, skills beyond this job. I believe in myself. The little voice inside—she knows I can.*

Of course, I also received many micro- and macro-aggressions before resigning. Here's the thing: when you're doing what people want and not rocking the boat, loopholes in your favor can always be found. However, when you push against the status quo and voice your own wants, needs, and opinions, all of sudden, people use the same rules against you to block your path and threaten you. My resignation and departure were inconveniencing the powers that be, and, suddenly, I was thrown an obscure rule that would require me to pay back thousands of dollars unless I stayed until the end of the year or didn't resign. They wanted to coerce me into staying on because it made their lives easier.

As women and people of color, this is the type of bullying we face, and we don't talk about it enough. Of course, you can't even argue with these types of people because, suddenly, you have this rule shoved in your face. No one told me about the rule before, and even the human resource specialists were unfamiliar with it. If I had known about the rule before, I could have planned things out differently. But it was my payment for pushing back—I was backed into a corner, and there was nothing I could do. There were also other ways they could make our lives difficult. A local staff member once confided in me about the subtle punishments she faced at work. She described how her travel reimbursements were consistently held up, and her boss tactically skipped over her when it came to doling out praise.

Sadly, I am not the first or last person to experience these types of issues. Most people are forced to accept whatever conditions are placed on them because, financially, they can't do anything different. Everyone was sure I would also just put my head down and stay in the job until leadership found it convenient for me to go. But I knew that more time meant more opportunities for scrutiny, and I wasn't going to take it anymore. It hurt most knowing that I was one of their top performers and had just secured all these wins for them, and none of that mattered. I was at my limit. I was done with the yo-yo, where I had amazing bosses, colleagues, and experiences and then, in a short period, the opposite. It was terrible.

With Paul's support, I wrote a fat check and bought my freedom. At this point, it had become too much for my family too. That was the line. Plus, if I could raise almost US$100 million for a government organization, what could I achieve and do for the world if I explored my capabilities on my own terms? What could I achieve with the freedom to truly spread my wings and fly? What could I achieve with a clearly defined alignment that allowed me to live my purpose, and a goal to match? There really was only one way to find out.

FINDING MY PURPOSE, LOSING MY SHIT

When I was young, I was fascinated with meteorology and would watch the Weather Channel all day long. I loved watching meteorologist Brian Norcross and the guests he had on his show. I remember being motivated by their knowledge, inspired by their confidence, and comforted by their calm presence. Their whole job was to help millions of people through some of the scariest weather events imaginable. I was awestruck, inspired, and moved at the same time. Right then and there, I understood my purpose.

At age twelve, I imagined myself on the covers of *Time* and *National Geographic*. I didn't just want to be in magazines for the sake of it. I wanted to be there because I had inspired people to reach their goals and live their potential. I imagined myself as a respected thought leader, traveling the world and helping people achieve their dreams. The positive impact I would make in the lives of the people I helped would be enormous. *How much better would the world be if everyone was aligned, living their potential?* I thought.

I've always had exceptional empathy for people whom society often labels as problematic or bad. When I saw people suffering from depression or gravitating toward crime and violence, I sensed an emptiness inside them, as if they had given up on their dreams. In my mind, those who were struggling needed help overcoming trauma, finding their own purpose and path, and developing their own solutions rather than trying to live someone else's ideals. They needed versatile tools, not strict instructions. My purpose was to gift these tools to the people who needed them most. It's so frustrating to look back now and see that I knew my purpose way back then when I was twelve years old, watching the Weather Channel, but I ignored it over the years and pushed it aside to pursue other goals. Now, so many years later, it felt so good to be coming around to my purpose again. Going to college, getting my PhD, working as a diplomat—I had certainly taken the scenic route to get there, but now I had arrived at a place of clarity. My purpose was clear.

On a trip to Miami, I explained everything to my parents, and I ended up having a major meltdown. Although I had hinted for years, we had never had a conversation about how they treated me growing up and how it affected me throughout my life. We discussed how, growing up, they put Sonia on a pedestal, expecting her to achieve great things, whereas I was the weak and sickly child. Going to college and getting married were their only goals for me. But once my parents realized I was smart, suddenly I was going to be a doctor.

I told my parents that they had always seen me as a crazy dreamer, fighting against all the injustices I saw in the world, but they would tell me to keep my head down and not make any noise. I tried to tell them that by this point in my career, as a seasoned professional, I still felt like I had nothing meaningful to show for all the years behind me. It may sound strange since the impact was huge, but that's how I felt. Sure, I had a lofty title and had touched a lot of people with my work, but I hadn't made the global impact I dreamed of to the millions of other people who needed it. I tried to explain this to my parents, and, once again, they looked at me like I was crazy.

"That's nonsense," Dad said. "You've helped so many people. Thousands."

"That's not my purpose!" I blurted out, feeling the blood rush to my head. They didn't understand. To them, I was the girl who helped everyone. If you need something, call Esther. Errands, shopping, travel, college applications, government services paperwork, money, customer service—if you need anything, Esther is your girl. They thought that helping people with daily tasks or short-term, mini projects was my entire purpose and that I found joy in just doing that. But it wasn't true. I was meant for so much more, and the realization that my parents didn't understand me pushed me to breaking point.

Everyone present would agree that I completely lost my shit. The explosive reaction was totally out of character for me. Usually, I'm calm, levelheaded, and well-mannered, but, this time, my frustration was too much to contain. I realized that the people closest to me, the people who had raised me, knew next to nothing about who I really was or, worse yet, my potential. To this day, they find it shocking that I'm an extrovert. They still see me as a shy ten-year-old and probably always will. I had helped a lot of people, yes, but I wasn't anywhere near the scale of impact I knew I could have. My ideas weren't global. I hadn't created a *movement.*

I need to believe again that I can have more, I thought. *I can't be afraid of sacrificing comfort to follow my dream. I have to at least try.*

"I'm going to do this," I said. "I'm going to follow my dream." That conversation with my family removed any remaining doubt that resigning was absolutely the right move.

Years later, I discovered my Gene Keys profile. When I read it, it blew my mind. It laid out for me my hologenetic profile. Reading it through, I realized that I have a deeper sense of purpose coursing through my veins. It's a part of me. This is just a sample of what it says: "Your inner purpose is to … bring something totally new to the world … You are ahead of your era … You need to go deep within yourself to sense this wave and then have the courage to surf it out into the world."[3]

Are you ready to surf with me?

LETTING GO OF THE AMERICAN DREAM

Much of my whole experience made me think about the American dream. By all measures, I had what the majority of people worldwide want: prosperity, freedom, and democracy. It turns out that the American dream isn't about a particular place but, rather, a universal concept. I lived in a big house in a safe neighborhood and had a decent-paying job. I got my weeks of paid vacation. I had achieved the great American dream!

But at what price?

The American dream has been built on the backs of immigrants and people of color who, ironically, are among the least likely to feel that they have achieved it. The stats say that Latinos in the U.S. are almost 10 percent less likely to believe that they have achieved the American dream compared to their White counterparts. For Blacks, the difference is a staggering 24 percent. It's easy to bypass what statistics say, but those gaps are significant. Nearly one third of Americans are Black or Latino, and less than half of them feel that today they have the ability to enjoy financial stability, safety, and a little bit of leisure. Overall, 83 percent of Latinos think the American dream *is* within reach, making them big believers.[4] But the reality is that massive gaps persist for Black and Latino populations in terms of education, earnings, and health compared to other groups, and their progress toward the indicators of the American dream has at best been stagnant for decades.[5] Similar statistics exist in other countries: Canada, United Kingdom, Australia, and let's not forget Latin America, and more…

There is an entire library on systemic racism and differences in opportunity, which explains these data, but the impact comes down to this: **millions of people are conditioned to strive for a definition of success that they might not ever reach.**

The American dream is built on an ideal of material prosperity based on the philosophy that hard work, paying your dues, and believing in the system will get you there.

For me, the emptiness of having achieved the American dream was overwhelming.

Nobody tells you that prosperity might cost you your soul. Nobody tells you that moving up the ladder and living in the nice neighborhood means often hiding your authentic self. It became super clear that wanting to follow my purpose, believing that I could live life on my own terms, and looking for ways to thrive outside "the system" identified me as a problem—to my colleagues, many friends, and my family.

But, around the world, the U.S. is no longer perceived as it was, in large part because the American dream hasn't lived up to its potential. Time has shown that the search for material prosperity has created deep inequality, a disregard for mental and emotional health, and an environment ripe for mass shootings. The U.S. is no longer on the list of the top ten countries in terms of quality of life.[6]

Further, although called the American dream, the concept transcends borders and continents. I can tell you from my own experience of being in all corners of the world that the desire for these check marks is universal.

So, worldwide, people are redefining the elements of the American dream. Prosperity has to include emotional and physical well-being, not just financial stability. Freedom also means the freedom to live as your authentic self without judgment.

For me, letting go of the American dream has also meant letting go of my parents' dreams. Realizing that I value purpose over the perception of safety and that living my nontraditional life on my own terms is my choice to make has brought me peace. I've created the opportunity to thrive in the way that best suits me. So, when I say that I seek to help you make your dreams come true, I mean YOUR dreams—not those imposed on you by an improbable ideal. I'm talking about following those that will leave you feeling fulfilled as you live out your purpose every day. It means also having the courage to break free from our comfort zones and the systems that give us a false sense of security.

A LONG WALK TO THE EXIT

Once I finally decided to quit my job, Paul and I found a two-bedroom apartment with a view of the ocean. At the time, we were living in a five-bedroom house, so the move would be a major downsize, but we would be free. We had done lots of planning and calculating, and, with Paul's income, we could just afford to make it work without sacrificing the things that really mattered to us.

I handed in my resignation. The diplomatic service isn't a regular job that you can just walk away from, so the exit process was far from smooth and took two months to complete. Also, they didn't tell me that I could have kept my life insurance and some other benefits, so I lost them in the end. But this was just another reminder of the environment I was leaving and that my decision was the right one. Finally, after a drawn-out exit period, I was free—and I was so thankful.

Freedom felt amazing. After years of stifling bureaucracy and a toxic atmosphere, I could finally breathe again. In the months that followed my exit, I woke up every morning and thanked Paul for helping me gain my freedom. I felt so alive. I saw a future of endless possibilities, and nothing could hold me back. I also connected with a grad school friend who'd left a government job to leap into the world of entrepreneurship. Not only did he root for me big-time, but he also melted away any worries I had about what the future might hold. Forever grateful for his words.

After taking such a big leap and landing on my feet, I've noticed a domino effect among my circles and champions. My success has inspired the people around me to prioritize their purpose, make career changes, and follow their dreams. They can see that what I did works, and it compels them to take similar action—and they're happy. For me, that's the best part of all of this: showing people the brightest path and watching them walk it with purpose. No joke, I can name at least five people who resigned within a year to follow their dreams and freedom. *Same happened after I got divorced. Notice the trend…?*

And that's MY purpose: To be the trailblazer. To help high

achievers embark on their limitless journeys, surpass the boundaries that hold them back, and embrace and nourish the extraordinary within. All the ups and downs in my life have brought me to this point, where my thoughts, visions, actions, and impact are aligned with my purpose. That feeling is magical.

THE LIMITLESS LIFE

I wish my twelve-year-old self could see me today. That girl who dreamed of confidence and making a difference in people's lives would be so thrilled to see that my work helps thousands and thousands all over the world every day. But even more, I wish that my sixteen-year-old self could see me now, that girl stuck in the pit of depression, feeling that the future looked bleak, and questioning whether she had anything good to give. She would be amazed to see me full of peace, direction, purpose, drive, love, energy, optimism, and alignment. I see her now during my hypnotherapy sessions and tell her, "We did it." I know I will always be a high achiever, but these are my check marks now.

I wake up every day full of gratitude and fire. I'm thankful that every new dawn is a chance to further my legacy and that I get to do it with an ultra-supportive partner by my side. I thank him every day for also believing in me. I'm even more thankful that I had the courage to believe in myself and the vision I had for a life of MORE. And I'm thankful for the genuine community of champions, who have supported, encouraged, and inspired me every step of the way. On your own journey, not everyone will support you, but those who do, those who are there when you need them, they are gold. I see you. I appreciate you. I hold you in my heart.

> "That's the secret sauce: bringing together all the relevant players to identify common goals and purpose and hashing out win-win solutions."

But the most incredible transformation has been this FIRE and voice inside me. I spent so much of my life nurturing a little spark, protecting it, fanning it, and keeping it safe from forces that sought to extinguish it. But now, full of everything I need to thrive, that spark has ignited my soul. Lighting that fire is what I mean when I say that I want you to become LIMITLESS. It's the feeling that my impact in the world can be as large as my imagination. It's the understanding that my capacity to learn, to grow, to make a difference has no boundaries and that any barriers have solutions.

That superpower of feeling limitless has changed nearly every aspect of my life for the better. At home, I am so much more present. I get to attend almost every performance at my kids' school now, a rare occurrence when I was working fifteen-hour days. Just that seemingly small change has made a huge difference to both Xilo and Max, who value family time above all else. For Paul and me, it has meant a new era in our relationship, where we are partners, collaborators, cheerleaders, parents. It's the relationship I know he and I always dreamed about, the one where we lift each other up and together we are so much more than we are individually. We talk about this often, and our eyes fill with tears of joy because we can't believe how happy we are and that we found each other. They're also tears of redemption because we have proven wrong all the naysayers and social constructs that stacked the odds against us as a couple. They're tears of courage, a celebration for having listened to our inner voices, which told us we were meant for more. The tears are an explosion of happiness and light. It's magical.

The flexibility I now have has also allowed us to make something Paul and I bonded over in some of our first conversations a reality: a desire to live overseas and travel with our family as much as possible. Paul and I are expert travelers, and we go everywhere together. The family comes along on work trips whenever possible and every January, we make our travel plans for the whole year. Europe, Asia, Oceania, Latin America, the U.S.—we go everywhere. Travel teaches our kids about diversity and empathy, and, much like my trip to Nicaragua as a teen, helps them see beyond themselves and their worries. For us, travel is a source of human connection and self-care. We love being amazed by the exotic and, at the same time, feeling the commonality of struggles, aspirations, and dreams everywhere in the world. And everywhere we go, we love to eat. The life we lead could not have been possible without the decision and action plan to begin living my purpose. Travel is now also where I can share my story and coach others. I have clients all across the world and speak in venues far and wide. It's a dream.

You might not believe it, but my health has improved significantly. Just before I resigned, I had my annual physical. Suffice to say, I was a mess. My body chemistry was all out of whack; my sleep patterns were irregular, and they found several cysts I'd never had before. The doctor looked at me and said, "A few more months of this, and you would have been in the hospital." I made the change right on time. The body shows your stress before the mind knows what's happening, and the extreme pressure I had been under had begun to harm me from the inside. I shudder to think how my physical deterioration could have played out had I stayed in a situation that was so wrong for me. Today, I sleep like a baby; the cysts have disappeared, and I have more energy than ever. I feel amazing.

Also, my relationships improved, and I built a sense of community all around the world. I found new circles of amazing entrepreneurs, coaches, and creators. I made close friends in Australia, Zimbabwe, the United Kingdom, France, Haiti, Dominican Republic, and more. And, unexpectedly, Mom and I became closer than ever. Our relationship transformed into one of positive energy, enthusiasm, ideas, and support—something I yearned for my entire life.

Rather than frustration and anxiety, my work has become a source of fulfillment and alignment. My consulting work not only respects my limits and boundaries, but the work itself also focuses on helping communities and organizations align their actions to their mission, vision, and purpose—directly aligned with my own purpose. Naysayers will always be around, but, these days, when they show up or start to threaten my peace, I shut it down right from the get-go. I know what's important now, and I won't compromise who I am ever again. I know my worth and impact, and I am unstoppable. I have a legacy to keep building.

But even more, I have been able to undertake my own entrepreneurial journey, opening my own business and building a team, directly seeking out high achievers who, like me, have been weighed down by social constructs, cultural expectations, and external pressures. I've started a global call to action to all the high achievers who have reached every check mark, chased every goal put before them, earned every gold star along the way, and still feel that there's more. They still hear that voice inside them, telling them that they have a higher purpose still waiting for them. I'm here to tell them—to tell YOU—that it's within your reach. I am living proof that, regardless of the struggles you've faced and the barriers put in your way, you have an inner compass guiding you toward purpose. You can create the road map to guide you on your journey, and you already have the tool kit to keep you on your path to a limitless life.

PART TWO: HIGH PERFORMING MINDSET

Now that you've walked with me through my journey, it's time for you to examine *your* journey thus far and decide where you want to go. You've seen the highs and lows, the trials, the triumphs, and the transformation. Now, I invite you to grab the wheel, program your GPS, and hit the gas on your own journey to craft your limitless life.

In the following sections, I will guide you step-by-step through the process, sharing practical strategies and insights that will empower you to create a life that resonates with your deepest passions and goals. Remember, this isn't just about the destination. It's about the journey—your journey. So, let's get started. Here's to your extraordinary adventure of creating your own limitless life.

Let's do this!

MINDSET CAN BE YOUR OWN WORST ENEMY

So where do we start? With our minds.

As you have learned from my story, I have made many, many mistakes and had moments of "failure." Before we continue, I want to emphasize how I refer to failure. Failure is an event, NOT YOU. High achievers often internalize failure as an inherent characteristic or as part of their identity rather than an event. This is a key difference between fixed and growth mindset.

OK, so what do I mean by that…?

Previously, I believed that I wasn't born with superior abilities or intelligence and that my capabilities were set in stone—they couldn't be changed or improved upon. This belief started when I was a child, and I was stuck in a fixed mindset.

What Is a Fixed Mindset?

A fixed mindset, especially in the context of high achievers, is believing that abilities and intelligence are innate and cannot be developed. It is also the belief that when failure occurs, it reflects your identity and inherent abilities. Thus, someone with a fixed mindset avoids taking on new challenges, going against the status quo, or pursuing their purpose because they feel the need to be "perfect" to the outside world or keep up *apariencias*. Taking risks could reveal limitations or a lack of talent. Those with fixed mindsets may also give up easily when faced with obstacles, as they believe that if something is difficult for them, it is because they simply don't have the ability to do it. They also fear disappointing others, especially people close to them.

Also, this mindset tends to be fueled by the belief that success is based on the external definitions of success: certifications, recognition, and check marks only. While these aspects are great, they aren't the only results worth focusing on.

I was with one of my clients, Betty, at a workshop, and she was only mentioning her identity as a public figure. She had a hard time seeing herself any other way. We took a step back and focused on her skills and abilities instead of her position. I reminded her that she is a master at connecting people, a successful entrepreneur, and someone who makes things happen. I turned to her and said, "You are so much more than what you think." She messaged me the following day, saying she had never thought of herself that way. She was so fixated on her last role that she hadn't unpacked her other skills and other things she could do.

Even when we recognize our other skills, it's scary to start something new or see ourselves differently because it can lead to not being amazing at it—*at first*. The fixed mindset is tricky because it can cause stagnation in your personal and professional growth and, ultimately, make finding fulfillment difficult. It causes us to avoid the push that will lead to constructive criticism, feedback, and vulnerability, leading to a lack of motivation or resilience when faced with obstacles, as well as procrastination around improving.

Now, you may be thinking, *What? I don't get it.* High achievers get amazing results, and I look up to all of them. It's true—high achievers are great at achieving goals and the things they set their minds to. However, as in my case, many of these pursuits are "external" and not linked to what they really want. High achievers are driven by a desire to excel, but their mindsets can greatly impact the way they approach challenges and setbacks on their journeys to success.

It took me a while to realize that success was more than a result of inherent talent. Effort and practice are also big contributors and, in some ways, even more important than talent. But my limited, fixed mindset held me back from taking risks, and I was scared a lot. I realize now that this was one of the reasons why it took me so long to leave my job. I feared failure and didn't want to "lose it all." Even when I rationally knew I had huge abilities and had proven it, I was tested again with the fixed mentality when someone I worked with questioned my character. Immediately, I went back to blaming myself and seeing it as my failure, rather than as an event to learn from. I turned into a hermit and decided to stop taking risks. I repeated that pattern so many times, like the entire disaster of my daughter's birth. I questioned my abilities, blamed myself, and thought I wasn't capable of a better outcome.

What Is a Growth Mindset?

A growth mindset, on the other hand, is the belief that your abilities and intelligence can be developed and improved through effort and practice. High achievers with growth mindsets view challenges and failures as opportunities for learning and growth. They understand that success is a result of hard work, effort, and determination, and they're more likely to take risks and persevere in the face of setbacks. They also tend to be more open to feedback, using it as an opportunity to improve themselves. Please note that when I refer to feedback, I mean the type that's constructive, not the kind that's given to put you down or crush your spirit.

With a growth mindset, failure is seen as a natural part of the learning process and not as a reflection of a high achiever's abilities. They learn from failure and see it as a stepping stone to success. With this mindset, high achievers become more resilient and persistent, leading to a much more positive attitude toward change. They adapt easily and are open to new experiences and learning opportunities. To me, my daughter is the ultimate example of a growth mindset. She has always worked her butt off, knowing and believing in her ability to learn and grow. I believed she could, and so did she.

If you're a high achiever, you can have any goal you want. There's nothing you can't do, and everyone looks up to you for everything. But I know that, deep inside, you have a little voice telling you that you want more or different and you—and you alone—are keeping yourself from doing what YOU want.

If you're here, I'm willing to bet there's something else you want out of life—maybe even something you've almost never talked about to other people. It's what that little voice inside your head keeps nagging you about. It's that feeling inside of you that, even when you're celebrating successes, wants more, or something a little different, or maybe even completely different. And you don't even want to express it. Because how could you? You feel you should be grateful for what you have. You should be content with all your successes. And people may not understand it. People depend on you, and you don't want to disappoint them. You've worked so hard. How could you risk losing what you've built? Your mind is stopping you.

But guess what? You can do it. As a high achiever, you're thinking, *I can't do that. I'm not an expert.* This was me when I first started building my social media presence. I was terrified, felt awkward, hated my voice, and I didn't like the way I looked on camera. I thought about giving up completely. But I kept at it—I knew my message had to get out! With time and practice, I got so much better, and I'm still getting better. You can break whatever imaginary ceiling you've placed on your current growth path. Yes, you're scared, but the thing is, you do have the power to improve.

You've seen it in your own life. If you were to go back and see my first videos, you would see how far I've come…

With a growth mindset, we embrace challenges and failure as opportunities for growth. We perceive failure as a stepping stone to success and are more resilient and persistent in the process. Further, under this mindset, constructive criticism and feedback are valued. It is the belief in the power of tenacity—you are capable of developing abilities and skills, regardless of natural talent. It's having a positive attitude toward change and adapting easily. It is being open to new experiences and learning opportunities.

"We made our vision a reality."

Once upon a time, you had that mindset. As a child, you dreamed big and made goals, and, if anything, it was hard to imagine what could possibly get in your way. But then, social pressures kicked in, and we were made aware of our imperfections. Despite learning to be great at so many things, we forgot that growth has ups and downs all the way to the top. Imagine being able to merge your childlike confidence with the resources, skills, and experience you have now. You would be limitless!

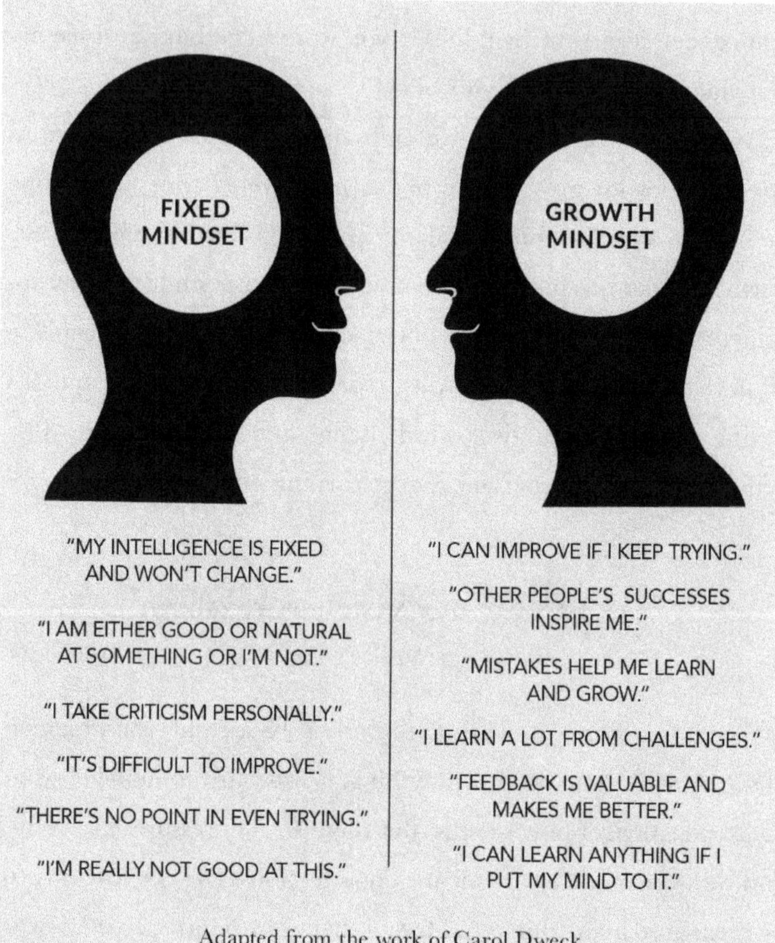

FIXED MINDSET
GROWTH MINDSET
"MY INTELLIGENCE IS FIXED AND WON'T CHANGE."
"I AM EITHER GOOD OR NATURAL AT SOMETHING OR I'M NOT."
"I TAKE CRITICISM PERSONALLY."
"IT'S DIFFICULT TO IMPROVE."
"THERE'S NO POINT IN EVEN TRYING."
"I'M REALLY NOT GOOD AT THIS."
"I CAN IMPROVE IF I KEEP TRYING."
"OTHER PEOPLE'S SUCCESSES INSPIRE ME."
"MISTAKES HELP ME LEARN AND GROW."
"I LEARN A LOT FROM CHALLENGES."
"FEEDBACK IS VALUABLE AND MAKES ME BETTER."
"I CAN LEARN ANYTHING IF I PUT MY MIND TO IT."

Adapted from the work of Carol Dweck

The other tricky part is that our purpose (which I will get into more later) is not linear, and it doesn't have set check marks. Most things we chase have a sequence, almost like a guidebook or checklist: the "right" school, the degree, the steady job, the "ideal" partner. But these are almost never the things our little voice inside tells us about. For the things we really want, a life of fulfillment, we have to stretch outside of the steps and check marks and, ultimately, our comfort zones. Very likely, nobody will have a road map. We might not know anyone who has done it before. We may be the first. First in our families. First in our field. We're trailblazers, and we have to create our own road maps.

Yes, it's uncomfortable. We often think we don't have control over our mindset. However, what we do have control over is how we approach it every day. It's a daily practice, like anything else. Over time, you develop a growth mindset about creating a growth mindset. With practice and taking it step-by-step, adopting a growth mindset becomes more comfortable.

IT'S THE PITS

Sometimes, a whole series of things hit you all at once. It usually starts with feeling like you have no time. You're overwhelmed by your list of things to do, and the demands on your time are relentless. From the outside, it looks like you have it all together. You've taken care of the kids, helped your family, and at work you're meeting all your deliverables and KPIs. But you feel the pressure for more time. You need more time for friends, family, partners, and for the things you love. Slowly, self-doubt creeps in, and you start to drown in it, thinking there's no way you can actually get it all done, keep everyone happy, and still have time for yourself. Soon, the feeling grows, and, as you start to question your ability more generally, the impostor syndrome sets in. You're just waiting to be discovered as a fraud. So, you freeze. Procrastination becomes your go-to coping mechanism, and you put off your big dreams and stick to the simplest, safest things, at which you're almost guaranteed to succeed. It's a terrible place to be, and I can't tell you how many brilliant, successful, and good-hearted people feel this way.

They are literally in the PITs. Procrastination, impostor syndrome, and time overwhelm, have taken over. Oof! It feels like so much, so let's break down the PITs.

Procrastination

This may sound counterintuitive, especially for high achievers, but, in fact, many achievers and people in general suffer from procrastination. It's not laziness, but rather a symptom of something larger. It's one of the biggest obstacles faced by my clients with high-paying, high-profile jobs. Heck, I suffered through it when writing this book.

Procrastination can stem from a variety of reasons but most often from both fear and a lack of emotional regulation. Let's start with fear. If we are constantly held to this crazy, high standard and suffer from perfectionism, we freeze at the start of something new. We start avoiding a task because it seems so big and challenging, and we're afraid of failing. So, we put it off. Procrastination can also stem from a need for emotional regulation. So, what does that mean? With no end in sight, our bodies and minds need some gratification. Add some time overwhelm as our tasks and responsibilities stack up, and we just shut down. If we are constantly chasing goals that don't feel like our own and don't fulfill our inner purpose, we feel unregulated and seek something to bring back a sense of balance.

That's where procrastination comes in. We start to bake, shop, watch our favorite shows, socialize, or find little pieces of our purpose to bring some life into us. We find ways to fill that void inside.

Procrastination is definitely one of the biggest pain points my clients come to me with. To the people super close to them, it seems like they "just have a lot going on right now." So, one of the most common things I hear is, "I just need to get organized." But procrastination is much more complex than that. It's how we react to past trauma, and it's a go-to strategy to avoid feeling like we might fail.

One of my clients, Laura, was an executive at a Fortune 500 company. She had the title everyone dreamed of and a high salary. When she came to me, she didn't want anyone to know she was my client. She was part of the company's leadership team and had a reputation to uphold, and she didn't want anyone knowing she was seeking help. But she was drowning and felt that her life was spinning out of control. She made everything worse by killing time on small tasks—aka procrastination.

First, we mapped all her projects, tasks, and timelines. We then created a color coded calendar and did a time audit. Laura started to realize several recurring patterns at work. She also realized a lot stemmed from fear of failure. She was constantly being questioned, and she was constantly being dumped with other people's workloads.

When she received another big initiative to lead, she felt the world on her shoulders and all the voices of people questioning her abilities. So, she would default to the tasks she was comfortable with and procrastinate on all the large projects. It was overwhelming to even begin and deal with one more layer of scrutiny. We worked together on dividing those big projects into sequences of small tasks, celebrating the small wins, and creating systems to prevent overwhelm altogether. We integrated her new toolbox into a daily practice. It took time and persistence and some strategic choices around what tasks she would and would not accept in the future. But Laura was able, with purpose, systems, and strategy, to overcome both her procrastination and feelings of overwhelm. Better yet, she started to translate this into advancing her own dreams.

It's also worth saying: your procrastination activities can be great motivators. Later, we'll get into how we can give ourselves our favorite procrastination activities as rewards for reaching milestones.

Impostor Syndrome

Impostor syndrome is a phenomenon where people, despite achieving all the check marks and climbing all the ladders, feel like frauds. They feel they aren't good enough yet and need more training, titles, and certifications. They also often feel guilty, believing that they don't deserve all the recognition they have received.

Again, this may sound super counterintuitive for high achievers. Haven't they literally accomplished *everything*? Two things are really important here. Firstly, high achievers are their own worst critics. They're the first to see what went wrong and what they could have done better. This goes hand in hand with the perception that failure is an inherent trait, so high achievers tend to minimize the value of their successes. Secondly, impostor syndrome pushes high achievers to constantly seek the next success. *I just need one more thing, and I'll have credibility. I'll feel better when I win the next award.* It's a never-ending quest to defeat the impostor syndrome by overwhelming it with success. But no matter what you achieve, it's never enough. That feeling of not enough stems from chasing what's not internal.

Now, you may be like, "Esther, that's confusing because you just told me I can have more, break any ceiling I want." This still holds true. Just make sure "more" is what you want, not what others want or what you feel you "should" do. Example—I could have continued in the diplomatic service and maybe one day could have become an ambassador, but that wasn't the "more" I wanted or that was internal to me. I would have still felt like I was constantly struggling to prove myself, and the impostor syndrome would always be there.

A big part of impostor syndrome is also tied to needing a sense of belonging. In the professional world, a significant part of your success is determined by your network, your alliances, and your contacts. Here, impostor syndrome also gets in the way, adding pressure to be accepted and casting self-doubt on social interactions, making you feel like you don't belong. It starts a very unhealthy dialogue in your mind: *Look at that person next to me. They're so much better than me. I can't do this. I'm not good enough.*

Here's an example of my own self-doubt in action. Before I interviewed for the job in DC where I met Paul, I flew to Puerto Rico, where fate proceeded to work its mysterious magic. There, I ran into a group of my graduate school friends. Remarkably, a lot of them were on the same advisory board for diversity and tropical studies I was currently on. They were also applying for a particular government fellowship that we had all discussed during graduate school. Years ago, it was my dream fellowship, but, as life went on, I had forgotten about it. Looking back, this was another clear example of synchronicity—my energy calling out to those who had an important message or lesson for me.

As we sat in the Jacuzzi, sipping fruity rum drinks, my friends tried to persuade me to submit an application to the fellowship. "How could you not apply?" they asked. "We always talked about getting this fellowship and going to DC."

I thought about how I had struggled to decide what to do after finishing my PhD and feeling lost. "There's no point in me applying," I said. "It's a waste of time. I won't get it."

"You've been working, and you've finished your PhD," they said. "You'll get it." These were my champions—the people who believed in me even when I didn't believe in myself.

I still wasn't convinced. Applications closed *the next day*, so I barely had time to apply for the fellowship even if I wanted to. I also had nothing to lose. So, I got out of the Jacuzzi and submitted my application. And just as my friends predicted, I got the fellowship.

If I had listened to my impostor voice, I would never have submitted that application. Thankfully, my friends yelled louder than the impostor!

Most of the time, the high achiever will internalize instances of success and connect them to luck or their contacts—which isn't true. Success, in fact, consists of two phases: the first is connections and opportunity, but the second is hard work and hustle. These impossible external standards and the generalization that success is all the first phase keep us from celebrating our wins and achievements.

Now, of course, these two phases are *not* created equal for everyone. Thus, in the first phase—connections and opportunity—discrimination and additional hurdles create barriers for Latinos (like me), women in leadership, and other marginalized and underrepresented groups and races, making them more susceptible to impostor syndrome and getting in the way of internalizing accomplishments.

For many marginalized groups and people of color, impostor syndrome also stems from the significantly higher level of scrutiny placed upon them. While others who make constant mistakes, use blunt language, and fail to produce are given seemingly endless second chances, people like my client, Laura, get no forgiveness. Every move is overanalyzed, and any misstep, no matter how small, unleashes reactions that are disproportionate and sometimes explosive. The higher she climbs, the greater the scrutiny. When the feedback is shared, it's very direct, sometimes condescending, and almost never constructive. What's the natural reaction to feeling like you are constantly under a microscope? Stress. A need to be perfect. A growing feeling that maybe there's something wrong with you; maybe you don't belong there—impostor syndrome.

Let me share an example from another one of my clients. Emma was a Yale graduate, top of her class, and one of the few people from her childhood neighborhood who was able to get out. She had a great job, had written several books, and was on the radio.

Everyone in her circle looked up to her. By all common standards, she was successful. But, on the inside, she struggled with impostor syndrome.

Emma drowned in self-doubt daily and was constantly comparing herself to others who were more successful than her. She saw every criticism she faced as an indication of her own failures and flaws. She would internalize all feedback as a reflection of not being good enough, believing she had failed her public. Worse yet, she was suffering in silence because she felt alone and like no one could understand.

This is a big part of impostor syndrome: feeling that your struggles are fundamentally unlike others—feeling alone, different, and, at the same time, that you are burdensome and not special. Emma felt she couldn't share her struggles with anyone because so many counted on her. She also felt that she was letting them down or somehow it would ruin her reputation. Sound familiar? I'm here to tell you that you are not alone. Through my program, we were able to create strategies for Emma to overcome impostor syndrome and, more importantly, have a system in place to prevent big lows when it would creep up again.

Time Overwhelm

Time stress, overwhelm, burnout. You know that feeling when you're lying in bed and your mind won't stop spinning? Or when your heart is racing and you're so tired and dizzy and feel like you don't have enough time in the day? I know that feeling too. For many people, this is where the PITs starts—having so many tasks and responsibilities and being the one everyone counts on. So much gets piled on that, even if you had some control with time management, it becomes too much and leads to overwhelm and burnout. Further, because you need to be the best—a superstar—and prove yourself to others, you take on more than you can handle in your personal and professional lives. In many ways, this is the root of the problem: we take on things that don't serve us but, rather, fill the needs of others, leading to high levels of stress and workloads associated with burnout. The result? More stress, emotional exhaustion, and physical and mental health problems. We give away so much of our time to small tasks that serve others that we end up putting ourselves and our goals second (third, fourth...) and disconnect further from our own purpose.

Driven by FOMO

Let's delve into the life of Rosa, a high-ranking executive at a bustling corporation in the private sector. Rosa is the epitome of success, as viewed through the conventional lens. She's constantly on the move, zipping from one event to the next, one city to another. Her life is a whirlwind of projects, friends, social events, and high-stakes meetings. However, beneath this flurry of activity, there's an undercurrent of constant pressure. Rosa is perpetually overscheduled, and her life is stretched thin, like a rubber band on the verge of snapping. Despite being physically present at countless events and gatherings, her mind often seems far away, unable to fully engage in the moment.

Driven by a deep-seated fear of missing out (FOMO), Rosa

finds it challenging to prioritize her commitments, so she's unable to find time for the things that matter to her. Consequently, she is perpetually caught in a vortex of busyness, but without any clear direction. She gave away all her time to others' priorities, and the projects close to her heart lay untouched, collecting dust. Rosa's life is a classic example of being caught in a cycle of unending hustle without a clear compass. It's a hectic and overwhelming dance, where the music never seems to stop. Her story illustrates the struggle many high achievers face in being time poor, seeking balance, direction, and true fulfillment in the midst of ceaseless busyness.

POP OUT OF THE PITS

So, I just bombarded you with the PITs. Now what? Too often, the people who work with me focus on fixing the PITs. *I just need to stop procrastinating. I just need to feel more confident in my abilities. I just need to get organized.* But by themselves, those attempts almost always fail. No matter how many times you tell yourself you're going to get up and start getting things done, the motivation inevitably fades, and you're back to scrolling on Instagram (or whatever your favorite procrastination tool is). The planner you bought sits unused, and you feel just as bad about yourself as you did before. Well, as it turns out, the PITs have root causes, fundamental issues and "whys" that drive you to feeling overwhelmed and down on yourself. We need to POP you out of the PITs. To do this, we must take control of the root causes and get you back on track and thriving.

Here are the three big things you need to get ahold of to start feeling like people respect your time, that you are moving in a positive direction, and that you are prioritizing your goals and needs:

- **P**eople-Pleasing
- **O**verthinking
- **P**erfectionism

Let's dive deeper into each element of POP.

People-Pleasing

If I had to choose the one category that I constantly battle with the most, it would be people-pleasing. I'm that person who responds to WhatsApp messages and texts immediately. I'm that friend who will drive in the middle of the night to help you. I'm that mentor and coach who will get on the phone at 1 a.m. when someone needs me. For each of us, people-pleasing looks a little different, but the essence is the same: giving up a piece of ourselves for the pleasure, comfort, approval, or satisfaction of others. Now, these actions in moderation are great—they make you a caring and generous person—but when people-pleasing starts to implode your life or makes you feel like you aren't being authentic, it's a problem. For me, people-pleasing has always been about being there for everyone to solve their problems.

"What could I achieve with the freedom to truly spread my wings and fly?"

I will give you an example. There was one week where I felt so tired, and I decided to pull out my time aligner. I felt really off because, usually, I have all my time accounted for, but there was something that was making me tired. I started to tally everything—not just my goals, projects, and logistics but also how many times people asked for things. By the end of the week, I realized what was wrong and why I was always *so* tired. I had fifty-seven requests from other people in just one week. *Yes*, fifty-seven! These ranged from, "Can you review my CV/resume?" to, "Can you edit this one phrase for me?" to, "Can you help me sell my dinner table?" to, "Can you book a doctor's appointment for me?" The thing is, these little requests add up, and I was getting at least eight requests a day. I was doing all these little requests in between my other things, either through WhatsApp, text, or chat, and I was putting the needs and demands of others before my own and even my family.

I mean, no wonder I was so tired. I had no boundaries, was always available, and didn't exert any assertiveness or even push back. I lived in fear of causing disappointment, not even knowing if I *would* disappoint others by not being there. I became so accustomed to being everyone's fixer that I put myself, my projects, and my dreams last.

This realization was a harsh wake-up call. I became resentful and started to feel taken advantage of—but I also had to take some responsibility for the situation. I wasn't communicating how much effort it took or that I had other things going on, and I wasn't expressing to anyone that my time was valuable. And I had done all these things since I was a teenager. Everyone just assumed I loved helping with everything, and it didn't occur to anyone that I might have other priorities. That's the thing with people-pleasing. I do love helping others, but I don't have the time, energy, or desire to spend all day, every day doing it, especially when it means sacrificing my own goals.

Let's look at a client example. Katia was a mature woman with four grown children, whom she loved more than anything. Now that she was an empty nester, she and her husband, David, were trying to reconnect as a couple. They wanted to travel more and had embarked on a fitness journey together.

One day, after a visit to the local animal shelter, Katia walked out with two dogs she had adopted. It wasn't her plan, but she couldn't say no to those big eyes. The dogs brought a new love and energy into the house and when Katia felt stressed, they helped her re-center to what really mattered.

To those around her, Katia was the dog lady. *She loves dogs*, they thought. *All dogs, all the time.* So, friends and family started asking her to dog sit. They all saw it as a win-win. They got a service they needed, and—guess what!—Katia got more dog time. But here's the thing: Katia loved *her* dogs and hated dog sitting for others. However, the urge to people please was strong with her, and she couldn't figure out how to tell them without hurting their feelings. She didn't want the friendships to end or even be damaged, so she would give in and dog sit every weekend. It was hard because even though she hated dog sitting, she loved feeling useful and helpful. She tried to communicate in a roundabout way to her friends that she was tired, but the message wasn't going through. She felt trapped and frustrated, and even David was starting to complain that he felt a bit neglected.

With my support, Katia worked on first being honest with herself and then learned how to be honest with others without hurting their feelings. It took some time for her to even admit that she didn't like dog sitting, and her fear of hurting others' feelings tied back to so many experiences in her past. But, slowly, she made progress. She did this by communicating before dog sitting requests were made that she was now prioritizing other things. By setting clear expectations from the beginning, people-pleasing can be avoided. We worked on creating scripts for texts, emails, and phone calls, and we talked through several what-if scenarios. Slowly, Katia figured out what responses felt comfortable, especially when she needed to convey a message without hurting others' feelings.

If, however, you're in this situation and you continue to give in and give in and stay silent, you will gradually become more and more resentful and frustrated, angry that others persist in taking advantage of you. Eventually, you will snap, and it will be ugly. I have definitely been that person who snaps, and it's not pretty. This leads to a mindset of: *Every time I communicate my desire to stop people-pleasing, people react negatively, so I'm just going to stay quiet.* But, in reality, people reacted negatively not so much because you snapped, but because you caught them completely off guard. Suddenly, they feel that they have been lied to all this time, and they ask themselves, *What else has she been hiding?* This is the irony of people-pleasing: you do it because you don't want to hurt others' feelings but by being dishonest, you are probably hurting them more.

It's also worth saying that a big part of taking control of people-pleasing involves retraining the people around you, those who are constantly demanding your time and energy. They are used to you being at their beck and call, and they firmly believe that your purpose in life, your passion, your joy comes from helping them with their issues. So, when you start to take control of your life and time, there may be pushback. People may be genuinely confused and offended, and they will do their best to persuade, encourage, and guilt you into solving their problem "just this one last time."

Thus, a big part of my work with clients also includes developing strategies and techniques to manage the pushback in ways that allow you to stay true to yourself and keep you moving toward the goals that are meaningful to you. At the end of the day, you can't really help others if you're drowning, angry, and resentful. By creating those boundaries, you put yourself in a position to more effectively make a difference in the lives of others.

Now for the O.

Overthinking

So, you know that feeling when you overthink everything? You spin and spin and think of every single outcome, especially everything that could go wrong. Yes, I know it too. A few years ago, when I started my Instagram, I would spin and spin every day, wanting to post something. I had a million ideas but struggled to commit to any of them. I would spend hours and hours agonizing and when I finally created my post, I would end up taking it down and second-guessing whether it was any good.

Even something as simple as buying a plane ticket a few months in advance would send me spinning. I would spin and spin inside my head, wondering when the best time to buy was and whether I was making the wrong decision. And those are fairly small things, so you can imagine how hard it was to leave my 9–5 job to start my own business. Major overthinking for months.

The thing is, I thought this kind of behavior was normal. I come from a family of overthinkers. My parents would delay making decisions on whether to sell or buy a home for years, and they put off signing a will for almost a decade for fear of making a mistake. It takes them half an hour to figure out what to order at a restaurant. I understand now that their big life decisions had consequences for so many people, and they have also lived with the fear of hurting others. But growing up in this environment, I also came to believe that analysis paralysis was an inherent part of making any decision.

Maybe the pattern is familiar to you. When needing to make a decision, you think of the top five potential outcomes and since you're a high-achieving people pleaser, you mentally inflate the value and likelihood of the negative possibilities. Failure is awful, and anything that isn't complete success is, by definition, failure. So, you start to imagine all the possible paths that could derail the success of your decision, no matter how distant the actual likelihood might be. It becomes a cycle of indecision because no choice guarantees success, and every option seems to have too great a risk of failure.

This is the paralysis I lived in while I was quitting my job. I was in paralysis because I was constantly weighing all the pros and cons and second-guessing my decision. I was terrified of losing everything I had built, worried that my kids might be left without health insurance, scared of feeling like a burden again. I was even terrified of changing my LinkedIn to reflect who I wanted to be. Those who sought me for coaching knew me as a coach but to the rest of the world, I was an international development professional. Also, all the voices from the outside—friends, family, colleagues—telling me that I was making a huge mistake by giving up my pension added to my never-ending overthinking. Even in the process of writing this book, I've spiraled into overthinking so many times, worried about who might be offended or whether some information was too personal to share. The struggle is real.

But overthinking goes a step further… It's also the process of doubting yourself and feeling insecure when a friend doesn't write back right away or when someone makes a snarky remark. It's the constant back and forth in your head that you did something wrong. The harshest critic is yourself.

For high achievers, overthinking might be especially deep when the decision is about choosing what *not* to do: leaving a job, refusing to walk other people's dogs, turning down social engagements. We are the ones who stick it out to the end. We always show up; we help others, and we're there for everyone. Overthinking has ties to people-pleasing, and both of them, if uncontrolled, can take you straight to the PITs.

If not moderated, overthinking can also lead to a cycle of worrying that's overwhelming and playing on repeat—in other words, rumination. *The New York Times* published a great article called "How to Stop Ruminating" where it highlighted that if your rumination is to the point where you are distracted from what's important, it's something that should be addressed first in therapy.[1]

Perfectionism

Oof! Now on to the topic of perfectionism. As a high-achieving perfectionist, I'm always pushing myself to be the best in everything I do, but this chase and relentless pursuit of perfection also leads to feelings of inadequacy, procrastination, and even burnout. We put tremendous pressure on ourselves to always perform, to always be perfect, and when something goes wrong and we turn out to be human like everyone else, it leads us straight to the PITs—procrastination, impostor syndrome, and time overwhelm. For the same reasons, perfectionism makes us risk-averse.

To make matters worse, to those around us, perfection becomes an expectation, and, as high achievers, we're constantly being held to this unattainable standard. We're praised for being masters of our arts. We create either the picture-perfect family structure or career, go to the top schools, or have the best jobs. In many positive ways, we become role models, as we reach the goals that many aspire to. But, over time, we start to feel that our entire worth and identity is defined by being "perfect."

We saw this earlier with my past relationships. I had created this perfect scenario in my mind that represented what life had to be or look like. When reality turned out to be different, I was completely devastated. I saw failure as *me* and not an event.

"Failure is an event, not you. Change failure from "I failed" to "it failed.""

I felt inadequate and filled myself with self-doubt, blaming myself for everything. I couldn't separate myself from the event. I was defined by my success or failure. I translated any little doubt or insecurity in my mind to a sense of failure as a person, partner, professional, or parent. This is the mindset I would carry forward, so the next time I wanted to start a project or got stuck on a task, I would immediately fill with fear and self-doubt.

Perfectionism also shows up in different ways ... Gus is a dedicated entrepreneur. He was incredibly meticulous, painstakingly focusing on every single word in his business documents. From proposals to emails, every piece of communication had to be flawless. Gus had an unwavering commitment to perfection. He would redraft, edit, and revise until every phrase was just right, every comma was in its perfect place. His documents were indeed impeccable, but this fixation on perfection was a double-edged sword.

The thing is, he would also get praise for it. His clients loved that his documents were flawless. While his perfectionism resulted in faultless work, it also became a barrier to growing his business. The considerable time and energy Gus poured into refining every detail meant that he had little left for other essential aspects of his enterprise. Client acquisition, a critical area that required his attention, was being sidelined. Gus's relentless pursuit of perfection was, in fact, a roadblock on his path to success. Perfectionism had become a deterrent rather than a driving force, preventing progress instead of propelling it.

Together, we put time bounds on tasks and also thought about percentages of perfectionism he would give to each task. Not every document needed 100 percent. Some, he learned, could be as low as 20 percent. I also helped him communicate expectations with his clients up front, asking which items needed perfectionism and which didn't. Example script to clients—"Given our tight deadline, out of the five items we need to push through this week, which ones do you need perfect with amazing quality and which ones do you feel can be second or third tier?" Asking these questions reduced anxiety and allowed Gus to still get praise for the documents that required more attention and care, freeing up his time and allowing him to propel his business. It all comes down to clear expectations.

The roots of procrastination can also be found in perfectionism. There's this fallacy that procrastination comes from being lazy or neglectful, but it's often really a problem with self-regulation. It's a mind block and fear of not being able to meet one's perfectionist standard or not having the time to do it at the expected level of perfectionism. This leads to stagnation and avoidance of the task altogether—procrastination. Negative reinforcement makes this whole cycle worse. If you feel you'll be judged or criticized, you'll tend to freeze and avoid the task. If you don't think you'll be able to complete the task perfectly, you choose instead to avoid it completely.

Jamal struggled horrifically with the opinions of others. Having been praised his entire life for being perfect, a hard worker, and ambitious, he struggled so much with self-doubt because his identity, his image of himself, was based on the feedback he got from others. Whenever he had a setback or somehow didn't live up to this perceived expectation, he worried first and foremost about what other people would think of him, and he would freeze. We spent a lot of time talking about his heroes, both those he admired as a child and those he admired now. It was a big realization for him to understand that the qualities that drew him to his heroes were about the loves, passions, and common interests they shared, but it was never about them being perfect. If your heroes aren't perfect—and they never are—maybe it's OK to be a little gentler with yourself.

Along those same lines, it's also important to understand that the concept of perfection itself is a fallacy. All humans are inherently imperfect yet perfect in their own ways, including our heroes and mentors. They make mistakes, and they have their insecurities. The edited, airbrushed versions of celebrities' lives we see on social media are designed to hide their imperfections and vulnerabilities.

So, every time you're looking to the side and comparing yourself to others, remember that they're also suffering and not showing you the complete picture.

Yet, the hardest thing is to accept our own imperfections and humanity. We identify ourselves as "fixers," and everyone looks up to us since we are "perfect." This also results in us being very hesitant to get help. But guess what? We all need help—we can't do this alone. We need therapists and coaches to guide us. We need community. We're humans, who need to get out of our heads. We've created a strong facade, and we keep reinforcing that facade. By pushing perfectionism, we're also harming the next generation by creating an expectation of an impossible standard and perpetuating the glorification of "suffering in silence."

Not everything needs to be perfect. Once I accepted that I didn't need to be the perfect coworker, friend, spouse, or family member, I stopped making my bed. I hate making my bed, and it feels like a completely futile thing to do. So, I stopped. It seems like a small act of rebellion, but, for me, having a messy bed every day became the symbol of freedom. It was the sign that I could let go of the things that live in my head.

CODE-SWITCHING

"Esther, you have to ROOOUND your VOOOWELS and open your mouth when you speak." That was the critique I got from a trusted mentor in graduate school after a run-through of a presentation I had to give. I was a little confused at first. I thought I would get pointers on the substance of my presentation or, at the very least, tips on how to make my presentation more engaging. But, instead, I was made to understand that if I wanted to be taken seriously as a researcher, I should learn to speak standard American English. Basically, sound more "White."

I have often been condescendingly told, "You sound like J.Lo" and have always been very confused. I have the utmost love for J.Lo, and I couldn't understand—*What's wrong with the way she sounds?* At the time, I was focused on being a high achiever, and I took the feedback from my mentor in the helpful spirit in which it was intended.

So, I did what millions of Latino, Black, and immigrant kids worldwide do to get ahead: I developed my "customer service" voice. I learned when and where to adopt my non-regional, rounded-vowel, Spanglish-free accent. At first, I felt stupid faking the accent. It's not who I am. But here's the obnoxious thing: it works. If I have to call the phone company or my credit card company, it's a fact that, 100 percent of the time, I get better, more polite, faster service when I use my customer service voice. So, you get used to it, and your customer service voice becomes a tool in your arsenal to make your life easier.

More formally, the customer service voice is called code-switching. As a general definition, code-switching is switching between one particular language or dialect to another, depending on the environment or social position we find ourselves in.

From a cultural-linguistic point of view, code-switching can be something beautiful and powerful. The multitude of ways that people code-switch shows the blending of cultures over time, and, especially for those of us who have lived an immigrant experience, it represents the refusal of people, proud of their roots, to fully relinquish their home languages, customs, and cultures. However, customer service code-switching holds none of that for me. As I reflect back on that moment after my presentation, I feel so deeply offended and angry at myself for not having had the presence of mind to defend my identity.

As a high achiever, I learned from an early age how to reach the check marks of success. There was a lot of hard work and tenacity, a lot of putting off fun to get my work done. All those sacrifices were tough, but, over time, I realized that what cost me the most were the times when I changed who I appeared to be in order to fit in and get ahead. And it wasn't just how I spoke. This also translated to my polished suit, flat-ironed hair, short nails, subtle glasses… the list goes on.

I remember an incident at work when I was in the diplomatic service. A group of us had a little "breakfast club" in the cafeteria a few times a week, which would often turn into Paul and I mentoring and coaching some of our less experienced colleagues. I relaxed my code-switching during those times, and I thought I could be myself. One day, a young woman, new to the group, interrupted me as I was speaking. "Ohmygod wait… Are you speaking English? Where are you from? I can barely understand what you're saying! Are you sure (while staring at my badge) you're American?" It was an awkward moment, clearly ridiculous, and completely uncalled for. But it's just one example of the types of aggressions I and so many others face on a daily basis.

Worse is that this wasn't the first (or second, or third…) time this had happened to either Paul or me. We once had embassy security guards surround us, hands on their holsters, because they thought we had snuck into the embassy. I froze and babbled something in Spanish as they became more agitated. Paul said, "Esther, speak to them in American," and as soon as I did, their demeanor changed completely. They dropped their hands and visibly relaxed. They apologized profusely. We didn't look like we belonged, and speaking to them in our common, native language just made it worse… *Sigh.* So, we code-switch.

However, code-switching is draining—it takes a toll on your energy and emotional state—and it doesn't just translate to verbal speech but also writing. Long workdays and code-switching, combined with having to maintain a smile all day, was exhausting. After ten-plus hours, my brain would get foggy, and I would make occasional mistakes in my emails and verbal communication, defaulting to writing and speaking in Spanglish.

The thing is, as high achievers, people are waiting for us to make mistakes. The next day, I would be flooded with super harsh critiques and told that I was unprofessional or that my writing had a "tone." What many people don't realize is that while we are tired from the workday like everyone else, we are *extra* tired because we have to constantly watch what we say and how we write to ASSIMILATE, ultimately, to make others feel comfortable. And that, my friends, is why we need breaks and why we are exhausted. I say this for all the readers who are nodding their heads right now in agreement but also to all my non-people-of-color readers to help them understand.

"For me, the emptiness of having achieved the American dream was overwhelming."

The accumulated spiritual and emotional cost of code-switching wears us down over time. A huge part of finding and living your purpose is living authentically and as soon as you become fully cognizant of who you are on the inside, it becomes increasingly difficult not to have the real you reflected in all aspects of your life. Today, I code-switch much, much less, but it's still ingrained in me, and I know it will take additional time to remove it from my tool kit.

I now allow my colleagues, my clients, and, yes, customer service workers to hear my Miaminess, with some Spanglish thrown in. In my business, you'll hear the real me as much as possible. However, when I'm on the phone, I do still slip sometimes and when I do, Paul pokes his head into the room, genuinely confused, wondering if someone else is there. But in presentations, I know that my customer service voice is still there, super present. In those moments, I give myself kindness and compassion. I have been code-switching for so long now that it has become a part of the authentic me.

I hope, with time, we can all hear the real us and not encourage others to change to fit the mold. However, I also have to say that I fully support those who do code-switch. Trust me, I get it. It makes life much easier. I'm here for you regardless, and I SEE you.

HYPER-SCRUTINY

Ever feel that if you make one mistake you receive much harsher feedback than others? Ever feel that others can get away with making a billion mistakes but if you make one, they won't let you live it down? Ever feel that you get dumped on way more and tested as you climb the ladder? This is very common for people pleasers and perfectionists but especially true for high achievers. I can't even begin to tell you how often in my life, and in the lives of my clients, this comes up. Because of their successes and accomplishments, high achievers are subjected to hyper-scrutiny.

Hyper-scrutiny refers to an intense or excessive examination or observation of someone or something. In the context of a person, it often means their actions, decisions, and performance are constantly being watched, tested, analyzed, and critiqued at a high level of detail.

Let's look at a case from my personal journey. Imagine me, Esther, in a new team. By now, you won't be surprised that I hit the ground running, performing at an excellent level right off the bat. I was fostering a positive team dynamic, mentoring staff, and even helping secure significant wins for our team. But as I began to gain more visibility within the organization, my performance became the subject of heightened scrutiny. I started feeling a sense of unease, the looming shadow of expectation hanging over me. It felt like everyone was waiting for me to make a single slip, one tiny mistake. Sure enough, in exhaustion, I made an error, and it was magnified to become an enormous issue. Despite my numerous recent successes and the fact that I was juggling multiple projects simultaneously, all anyone could talk about was my mistake. Criticism overflowed from the incident and even reached as far as my personal social media page and past assignments. Strikingly, other team members who weren't pulling their weight went unnoticed, their inadequacies accepted as the norm. Yet for me, there was zero room for error or forgiveness. Sound familiar?

Paul has told me several times about one of his greatest mentors, a grad school professor of his that later became a colleague. He was a huge sports fan, and all his stories and analogies were somehow related to sports and athletes. When discussing high performance athletes, this mentor would often say that, to the fans, "They are only as good as their last play." Fans are fickle and expect perfection. One mistake, and even the best athletes are forcefully ejected off the pedestal. I felt the same at work. One mistake, and, suddenly, none of the wins mattered.

There's also an expectation that high achievers should be role models and leaders in their industries and circles. While there's a lot of positive in that, it also means that their words and actions are watched very closely and analyzed. Their outward success breeds jealousy among family and coworkers, which manifests as extreme scrutiny and analysis of every choice, decision, word, and output. For some high achievers, this becomes so intense that they become quiet quitters, where they stop giving their full effort or going the extra mile and instead do the bare minimum to avoid drawing attention or criticism, either from their families or in their professional lives. It's a type of protection mechanism. Imagine that—excessive, undue hyper-scrutiny can turn a high achiever into a low performer. The alternative, like in my case, is no better. You become a highly anxious workaholic.

To give you perspective, I want you to think about how some celebrities and public figures receive so much media attention when they wear one different outfit or say anything even remotely controversial. Selena Gomez, Meghan Markle, Michelle Obama, Rebel Wilson, Oprah, Kim Kardashian, Cristiano Ronaldo, and countless others live under this microscope daily. People take anything they say and purposely misconstrue it, twisting their words, or even a momentary glance caught by the paparazzi, to ridicule them or make a viral meme, while so many others are untouched and can say anything. "Oh… that's just Don being Don." But it makes sense. The success of high achievers is often hated, envied, threatened, and judged by those who perceive themselves as less successful. They feel the need or obligation to voice any imperfections or faults, either to justify their own current state or for general public awareness. Small minds uplift themselves by tearing others down. Unfortunately, this puts a lot of pressure on all of us and amplifies perfectionism and lack of trust. It leads to a whole cycle of PIT, POP, and the paralyzing fear of not wanting to make a single mistake. From here, it's a downward spiral. Trust me, I've been in that PIT, that dark hole, many times.

I read a great quote from Katherine Schwarzenegger Pratt in a *New York Times* article that sums up the situation nicely. She talks about how her mother cautioned her about the "'never-ending' trap of correcting the record," which I completely understand. You want so badly to call out the lies, clear your name, and show how your success isn't about taking all the glory. But all that does is further feed the negativity and, in the eyes of the haters, only justifies their false opinion of you. "I see what people say," Schwarzenegger Pratt adds, "but I just know that it's so far from reality."[2]

NAYSAYERS

Meet Sofia. Like many, Sofia had dreams and aspirations that extended beyond the confines of her traditional Latina family. She wanted to create a vibrant social media presence to share her thoughts, express her creativity, and connect with a broader community. But every step she took toward this goal was met with criticism from her family. Sofia's mother would scrutinize each picture, dissecting her appearance, and her cousin would overanalyze the meaning behind each quote. The barrage of judgment from her family members was exhausting and demoralizing. It felt like every post she made was a trigger for a storm of unwanted opinions and endless phone calls. The constant criticism began to take its toll on Sofia. The fear of judgment, the worry about what her family would say next, started to paralyze her. She began to censor herself, her creativity stifled, her voice suppressed. She found herself in a constant state of anxiety—a feeling all too familiar in immigrant families, where cultural expectations can often clash with personal aspirations.

Naysayers are individuals who habitually express negativity or skepticism about ideas, plans, projects, or ambitions. They tend to discourage us from pursuing our goals or dreams, often highlighting potential problems or obstacles in a pessimistic way. In reality, their negativity says a lot about them and what they suffer from: fear, jealousy, lack of understanding, and resistance to change. But especially coming from those close to them, the negativity takes a toll on people like Sofia.

Naysayers often create doubt and uncertainty that lead to a lack of action or progress by the person being targeted. The first step is recognizing that their projections are based on their own fears and limits, not yours. It's hard in the moment to be so rational but once I helped Sofia see those statements as standalone thoughts based on others' own insecurities and not about her, she was able to start moving forward. I could relate to Sofia because my life, although filled with many champions, has also been filled with roughly double the number of naysayers. It helps to remember what a fellow coach once told me: "Naysayers are just confused fans."

COLLECTIVE SOLIDARITY

In my journey, whether in international development or as an entrepreneur, I've consistently found collective solidarity to be my greatest asset in the face of hyper-scrutiny. During my tenure as a diplomat in international development, I consciously sought to build a tight-knit group of champions, where we could mutually support each other. Within the challenging environment of intense scrutiny, we acted as each other's supportive pillars, constantly reminding ourselves of the transformative impact we were making and acknowledging the actions of others for what they were: unjust. We served as each other's buffers, sounding boards, and beacons of encouragement when the pressures threatened to overwhelm.

As we explore the concept of collective solidarity, it's really important to draw a clear distinction between two types of support: group support and champions. While both are valuable in their unique ways, they serve different roles in our journey. Group support provides a shared space for collaboration, venting, and mutual encouragement. This network is made up of individuals you work with, connect with regularly, and even unwind with after a tough week. They share your experiences, understand your challenges, and are there to celebrate your wins. However, most of the time, this is merely temporary support.

On the other hand, champions are those few individuals who truly know your core values and strengths—they stand by you through thick and thin. They are the ones who check in on you in moments of crisis. They understand that you, like everyone, can make mistakes and face tough situations, but they know these instances don't define you. They see your worth and potential, and they believe in you unconditionally. They stand up for you, defend you, and provide the emotional backing you need when things go awry. For instance, during a difficult time, when I faced a heavy accusation, it was my champions who came forward. Despite the severity of the situation, they checked in on me, providing support, validation, and hope.

In contrast, some of the individuals who were part of my group support, who I had spent countless Friday and Saturday nights with, sharing frustrations over drinks, remained distant and silent. This experience made me realize the crucial difference between group support and true champions. It also made me reexamine where I put my time and energy.

Without a doubt, the concept of champions extends well into the realm of family dynamics. We often consider family as a built-in support system. They are, after all, our first point of contact with the world, the fundamental building blocks of our identity. But, just like in professional circles, families also have their share of naysayers, silent observers, and dedicated champions. When shit hits the fan, it's not always the entire family that shelters you from the downpour. Sometimes, it's just a select few—the champions. These individuals rise above petty squabbles, long-standing disagreements, or societal norms. They stand by you, not out of obligation, but because they genuinely believe in you and your potential. Their faith is unshaken by rumors, mistakes, or stumbles. They're behind you, even when you choose the out of the ordinary, follow the path less taken, and seek something different from everyone else around you.

Whether it's a sibling who defends your unconventional career choices, a grandparent who quietly slips you a much needed word of encouragement, or a cousin who reaches out during challenging times, these champions are the family members who hold up the mirror to remind you of your strength when you're feeling your weakest.

Understanding the difference between general support and these champions is just as crucial in our personal lives as it is professionally. It guides us toward nurturing deeper connections with those who truly have our backs, and it helps us confidently ignore all the others, who are often naysayers. Honestly, if they're not your champions, who gives a F#%& what Tia Leah, Primo Juan, Aunt Jane, or Uncle Rob think. Their perception and data are limited and a reflection of their own fears. It's time to let go of the fallacy that everyone needs to be a champion. You only need a handful to be your steady rocks that you can anchor to in rough waters. They're the lighthouses guiding you back when you veer off course or start to give up. In the narrative of our lives, they're the unsung heroes, who help us rise, time and time again, to face our challenges and embrace our limitless potential.

Therefore, as we navigate our lives and careers, we need to recognize and value both these forms of support but never confuse one for the other. Champions aren't merely a part of your support group. They're your unwavering advocates, your pillar of strength during storms, and your cheerleaders in every victory. These people and the time you invest in them are a priority.

When I embarked on my entrepreneurial journey, I was moving into unfamiliar waters, and it was far from smooth sailing. From putting myself out there on social media to facing criticism, it was a rough voyage. Yet, it was the steadfast anchor of my support networks that kept me grounded, giving me the strength to keep pushing forward.

As I've progressed in my life and career, I've come to appreciate and purposely seek out mentors and coaches who offer not just guidance but also a community. I remember searching for a group coaching program aimed at female entrepreneurs, knowing that I wanted a great coach and a vibrant community. My patience was rewarded. I found an amazing coach, and I discovered a wonderful cohort of women, each embarking on their own entrepreneurial journeys. These experiences underscored the value of collective solidarity. It served as an anchor, providing me the much needed support, camaraderie, and shared strength that enabled me to thrive, even under the most intense scrutiny.

THE ROOT OF EXHAUSTION

What happens when you live in the vicious cycle of PITs and POPs? Gradually, over time, over years, sometimes decades, it wears you down to the point of exhaustion. This isn't just your average version of being tired or busy or overwhelmed. This isn't the spiritual deficit that a trip to Jamaica or taking up yoga will cure. Not even close.

The word "exhaustion" literally means "to have one's strength drawn out," and this comes closer to approximating the feeling. A recent study shows that 25 percent of Americans are so stressed they can't function. They're paralyzed by "the impacts of uncontrollable stressors."[3] While work stress is widespread in many countries, the "U.S., Canada, and countries in East Asia" have the most stressed workers in the world—and others aren't far behind. "48 per cent of Australians reported high levels of stress at work, making them the second most stressed-out workers in the world."[4]

You've given your all, but it doesn't feel like enough. You feel like a runner in a race, where, no matter how hard you run, there's always a pothole, a banana peel, or an angry dog trying to derail you, and you just can't anymore. You're exhausted.

The first time I felt massive exhaustion was when I was a student in college. I worked several jobs, still helped my family, and had enormous pressure to achieve. But I was falling behind, barely treading water. Remember, I had to work to catch up academically and also pay both my parents and my tuition contribution. The stress made me feel not just tired, but drained.

Take that situation and press repeat several times throughout my life. As I look back on my studies, my career, and my relationships, I know that exhaustion and overwhelm have impaired my thinking, affected my moods, blurred my memory, and ruined my focus and productivity. I felt that if I voiced my exhaustion, I would be burdening others. If I communicated my need for balance in my life, I wouldn't be taken seriously as a professional or given a seat at the table. If I took a break, others would judge me. If I sought therapy or coaching, I was acting elitist and privileged. If I was vulnerable, I would let down all the people who looked up to me. On top of all that, the voices saying, *Life isn't fair* or, *You should be so grateful for what you have* always swam through my head. Plus, why did I deserve a break when everyone around me was still struggling?

I know I'm not alone in feeling this way. We all need a break. As I said, not just a rest, but a real break from the pressure, to let our souls recharge and center on the things that really matter to us. We need to work to change the narrative that rest and self-care are weak. Exhaustion shouldn't have to be the norm.

THERAPY AND COACHING—TWO POWERFUL TOOLS

Let's dive into the complex world of therapy and coaching, especially from the perspective of an immigrant and, in my case, a Latina. The misconceptions are many, often reduced to the blunt statement that therapy is for "locos," the deranged or mentally unstable. And coaching? That's an entirely alien concept and, as I've been repeatedly told, something for "privileged elites." But these narrow views hold us back from true growth and self-understanding.

In many cultures, therapy is seen as a last resort, something only for people grappling with insurmountable issues or a crisis. But this viewpoint couldn't be further from the truth. Everyone can benefit from therapy. Therapy serves as a personal mirror, reflecting your life story and providing the space to unpack the experiences that have shaped you. It's a path to better understanding yourself, your reactions, your tools, and the lens through which you perceive the world. It reveals vulnerabilities and areas that need attention, providing insights into your own behavior patterns that you might not have discerned yourself.

My journey with therapy opened my eyes to my own struggles with setting limits and boundaries, issues I was completely oblivious to until my sessions started. It threw light onto my underlying anxiety, the unhealthy tendency to overwork, and the resultant exhaustion. It also helped me understand how I functioned as a partner. Only after acknowledging these issues was I ready to step into coaching.

Coaching is about creating an action plan for your future, challenging limiting beliefs, and putting you on the path toward your goals. A coach is a guiding hand, holding you accountable, pushing you to strategize, and always propelling you forward. It's about unlearning and relearning and giving you the clear path forward.

Like therapy, coaching is for everyone. In one of my favorite TED talks, Dr. Atul Gawande says, "You are never done, everybody needs a coach."[5] If the greatest athletes in the world all have coaches, helping them to be better, so should we. Dr. Gawande highlights the importance and the impact of coaching in the medical field, saying, "I saw a team transformed because of coaching. And I saw at least one life saved because of it."[6]

Despite the transformative power of therapy and coaching, another hurdle presents itself: the expectation of free services. As I embarked on my journey as an entrepreneur, I encountered countless people asking for free coaching. However, excellent coaching requires understanding people, intensive preparation, careful listening, and thoughtful unpacking. It demands time, energy, and a wealth of knowledge—it's not a commodity that can be handed out freely without undermining its value.

In our society, we need to start acknowledging the worth of intangible skills and services. In many jobs, technical skills are valued far more than soft skills, such as facilitation, networking, coaching, and mentoring. However, these are the very skills often missing in our workforce. Until we begin valuing and compensating for these skills, the narrative won't change. Therapy and coaching are not signs of weakness or luxury indulgences. They're critical tools for personal growth and professional development. I still can't get my parents to sign up for therapy or coaching, but I know that stops with me. My kids do both, and it's high time we all acknowledge the value of therapy and coaching and let our generations heal, thrive, and approach their limitless potential.

Why not use every tool at our disposal to unlock the most powerful, limitless versions of ourselves? As far as tools go, therapy and coaching are as effective as they come.

"Freedom felt amazing."

STEP INTO POWER

Looking back, I understand why I was always "coaching." I wanted more for others and more for myself. I wanted people and communities to have the freedom to discover who they really were and go after it while taking care of themselves. I want people to be limitless, while being free of exhaustion, anxiety, and overwhelm. We can take breaks and recharge from the heaviness of life. We can create a better situation for the next generation and leave an impact. We can slay all our goals, while being fulfilled. I'm not saying it won't take a lot of work and hustle, but we can align our hustle and make time for the things that matter.

And guess what? You can get there. You don't have to stay stuck in the vicious cycle, where the PITs and the POPs feed off each other to keep you questioning your self-worth, stalling your big plans, and generally keeping you playing small. Instead of feeling drained and exhausted, you and others can live in POWER. Living in POWER allows you to adopt a growth mindset and gives you back control of your life.

So, what's POWER?

- **P**urpose
- **O**rganization
- **W**ork-life integration
- **E**njoyment
- **R**esilience

Let's dig into Purpose.

PURPOSE

Everything starts with purpose. Beyond helping you understand WHAT you feel you're meant to do with your life, the process of discovering your purpose gives you the WHY. And knowing your WHY is essential. Knowing your purpose gives you the constant reminder of your ultimate objective, which keeps you going when life puts challenges before you. If you're clear on your purpose, you'll be able to kick PITs and POPs, especially overthinking.

There was a shocking study conducted in the United States that found that **80 percent of people don't have a clear sense of purpose.**[7] Imagine that! Only 20 percent of Americans—and probably close to that percentage worldwide—strongly agree that their purpose in life is clear. To me, it's not that surprising.

After a long career as an international development professional, trained to help countries, communities, and organizations accelerate their development, I frequently observed that beneficiaries were never asked some very key questions: "What do *you* want? What is your objective as a household, organization, community, nation?" Instead, after researching the context, development practitioners would bring in their ideas and then request proposals to fund it. "Consultations" with communities were more about telling them what would be done with the money than actually soliciting their ideas or input. It was a very paternalistic model, where we knew what they needed and what was good for them better than they did. We had beautiful strategic documents that showed, for example, that if we provided schooling, there would be more trained workers. Economic growth would accelerate, and everything would be great. We imagined a causal chain of events that would lead to joy, harmony, peace, and prosperity. We created, in effect, a series of check marks and told beneficiaries that if they met them all, they would be successful. But we never asked them what success looked like to them, what they saw as their greatest needs, or their purpose. It may come as no surprise to you that the single greatest challenge in international development is the sustainability of impact. As soon as the donor money is gone, the project falls apart if people aren't invested in the process and outcomes don't align with their values.

The same is true with people. We grow up with the weight of expectations always pushing us in a particular direction, with lots of check marks along the way to measure our progress. Thus, it's no surprise at all that the overwhelming majority of people reach adulthood without a strong sense of purpose. They feel caged and suffocated. They've never been asked or given a real opportunity to pursue their purpose, fully supported and free from judgment or expectation. Stress, overwhelm, and burnout result from a fundamental misalignment. But does it have to be this way?

In the international development world, we see an encouraging shift emerging. Donors are becoming painfully aware that hundreds of millions of donation dollars are having little lasting effect, and they're beginning to recognize the need to alter their approach. This burgeoning transformation is a movement known as "localization." This aims to bring local voices to the forefront and fund the causes these communities deem most important. It sounds simple, but it requires a fundamental shift in the way bureaucracies and technical experts go about their business. I was fortunate to be part of this transformative initiative, hired independently to help spread this approach within a major donor agency.

As promising as this movement has been, it has its challenges. Many communities, having tailored their activities according to external expectations for so long, struggled to define their own mission and vision. They've functioned for years under a paradigm of "any money is good money," and being introspective and collaborative proved challenging. They were unaccustomed to evaluating their real needs and calculating the actual value of their time. Meanwhile, development practitioners grappled with learning how to truly listen to communities and collaborate effectively. The shift from a check-mark-driven approach to a more inclusive, community-centered methodology was also challenging for a behemoth bureaucracy with relatively rigid policies and procedures. But despite these hurdles, the movement toward localization marked a crucial step forward, a step toward a more equitable and effective development strategy. Even early results suggest that the localization model yields better and more lasting results than traditional methods. Because the work aligns with the needs and purpose of the community, there's a level of buy-in never seen before, and the work takes on a life of its own, beyond the donor funds. Purpose brings lasting change.

This experience underscored for me the immense work that still needs to be done at an individual level to make such a movement sustainable. It highlighted the critical need for individuals to be able to identify their own mission and purpose. For a cause to have a lasting and meaningful impact, the individuals involved must possess a deep understanding of their motivations and aspirations. The localization movement isn't just about restructuring the external landscape—it's about reshaping our internal landscapes too, for enduring, meaningful change. Also, it's important to say: this doesn't just apply to international development but is relevant to government, education, health care, public relations, technology and so many other industries and sectors.

So, how do we apply localization to ourselves as individuals? At first, this may seem daunting. We're taught to see life as a series of check marks, such as getting a degree, a job, buying a home, getting married, and so on. We're taught that these are the main goals that matter and that they're sufficient to bring us happiness and fulfillment. Those awkward questions we get from family during the holidays all come from the check marks: "Have you finished school yet?" "When are you going to get married?" "What, no babies yet?" We're never asked about our dreams and aspirations. And I can guarantee you, sitting at Thanksgiving dinner, nobody ever asked, "Esther, are you happy?" It's no wonder there are so many movies made about dreading the holidays. Wouldn't the holidays be so much better if we were asked different questions? "Are you doing what you love?" "Do you feel like you're making a difference in people's lives?" "Are you making enough time for yourself?"

As life continues, we start to question everything and the lives we've created because we don't know if we've done it for ourselves or to appease those who have been pushing check marks on us our whole lives. We experience a "midlife crisis," as some people call it, but I like to refer to it as a "midlife awakening." It's when you're forced to start looking within—if you haven't already—and you realize that your life is short and you're either going to take action now and live with fulfillment or just give up that dream. It's that moment when you realize that you can't keep up the misalignment and that you've already given away too much of your time, energy, and soul to people and things that just drain you.

I once did an experiment where I did the same purpose exercise for first and fourth graders. I wasn't sure that it would be a very interesting conversation. After all, how much could kids so young have to say about life and purpose? Let me tell you—never underestimate what's going on inside your kids' heads. They have thoughts and feelings much more complex and profound than we can imagine, and, more and more, I'm convinced that it's our job as parents to help them express what's going on inside of them.

Doing the purpose exercise with the kids gave me a very unexpected result. What I found was that first graders were much more clear and open about their purpose. They could answer most of the questions and were still free of the majority of social constructs. This meant they answered the questions honestly and unfiltered, without the voices of their parents, teachers, television, or society telling them what they should believe. A perfect example was a seven-year-old who drew a complex scenario depicting conflict between nations and suggested an innovative solution to enhance their communication for dispute resolution. Another provided a surprisingly well-developed and articulated vision of a world free of pollutants and fueled completely by solar energy. However, by the time the students were in fourth grade, the questions and answers were already clouded by their parents and societal wants. While the first graders gave a huge variety of answers about purpose and what the world needs to be a better place, the fourth graders gave much more generic answers, really just variants of the same answer.

Now, not all societal and external expectations are "bad." The answers the fourth graders gave were all positive and kind. Some social expectations are beneficial, such as ethical and professional behavior, and they're necessary to a well-functioning society. But so many social constructs, norms, and customs, and, thus, the goals that get passed on to us end up serving as limiting factors, constraints that interfere with positive growth. It's not a matter of whether they're good or bad but, rather, if they're aligned with you and something *you* want. In many ways, that's the difference between a goal and a check mark: a real goal is yours and comes from you but when it comes from outside, it's just a check mark.

The benefit of purpose extends to more than identifying goals and direction. With purpose, you can help reframe overthinking. If you're clear with the direction you want to go and the filter through which you see the world, decisions come to you much more quickly because you're able to zero in on what matters. You can shut down the spinning that comes with any major (or minor!) decision. It will be helpful to eventually state your purpose into a phrase, something simple, clear, and meaningful. As you approach any situation or decision, you'll revisit your purpose phrase, asking yourself targeted questions, such as, *Is this aligned with me? Does this advance my purpose?*

Further, having clarity on your purpose helps with focus. What do I mean by that? Well, high achievers are frequently brimming with ideas and enthusiasm, drawn toward new opportunities and the thrill of setting and reaching ambitious goals. They excel at problem-solving, often producing an abundance of potential solutions and pathways for any given scenario. I definitely fall into this category. However, this gift can also become a challenge. The excitement of limitless possibilities can sometimes lead to a lack of focus, resulting in scattered time management, difficulty with prioritization, and a lot of half-started projects that don't get the follow-through needed to succeed.

In the face of such dynamism, understanding one's purpose serves as an invaluable anchor. This clear sense of purpose can act as a filter for opportunities, helping high achievers discern which ideas, paths, or solutions align with their overarching goals and intrinsic values. By anchoring their initiatives to their purpose, high achievers can prioritize projects that contribute to their long-term legacy and provide everyday fulfillment. It provides a direction, a compass to navigate the sea of possibilities.

Clarity of purpose also means you'll choose not to pursue some of your ideas and initiatives—at least not immediately. Purpose provides you a lens to prioritize your goals over time more efficiently, allowing you to channel your energy and talents to those activities that best push forward your ultimate legacy. This doesn't mean that all your other ideas just die. Instead, it means that you share them with others aligned to your vision or you identify a point in the future where you could revisit your other ideas. So, a purpose-led approach can transform your abundant energy and ideas from potential chaos into a focused force for achieving meaningful success. Further, taking the steps to live your purpose brings you authenticity. Authenticity is your shield and your beacon, guiding you away from the shadows of impostor syndrome toward the illumination of your true self.

We love the chasing and the hustle, but our hustle needs to be aligned to avoid burnout.

Your hustle needs to be aligned to your purpose—you have to keep focused on it. It's no surprise that the Center for Creative Leadership labeled purpose as the number one component of well-being.[8] As a high achiever, I know it's not realistic for me to tell you to slow down or that you need to find ways to do less. I love being active and working hard, but I've said it before, and I'll say it again: the killer is misalignment—when your actions don't match your purpose. Misalignment is when you're doing 200 things, fixing everyone else and moving their ideas but not putting your own into action. If it's your purpose, it's not work, and you'll love doing it every day, even when it's hard. You'll stick with those ideas and push through overthinking and self-doubt. The well-being comes from knowing that your hustle is making a difference to you and the world.

Understanding your purpose also helps bring some peace about your life in a larger sense. High achievers, like my husband, Paul, often ask themselves questions like, *What have I done with my life? Has any of it been meaningful? Has any of it been for me?* It's a line of questioning that can bring both panic and sadness. But as you understand and define the elements of your purpose, you'll see how you've tried to push your purpose and eliminate what no longer serves you in your everyday life, even if only partially and subconsciously. Your purpose is part of you and, even though you may not have nurtured it as much as you would have wanted to, you also haven't completely erased or forgotten it. When you know it's for you, you'll push through moments of self-doubt and the impostor syndrome. Look! You have a gift, and you have value. You've had it since you were a kid. I can tell you that the first grader in you definitely had purpose, and that first grader lives on in you. With your purpose, you can celebrate every day.

Your Life Is Your Legacy

Back in the 1940s, Dr. Harold Ehrensperger, a professor emeritus at Boston University, returned from an international trip. He had spent time in the South Pacific, Africa, Latin America, and India, becoming friends with Mahatma Gandhi along the way. Upon his return, he spoke to his students about the need for a radical mindset shift, stressing that we must move away from war talk and advocate conscientiously for peace around the world. He told the students that they must bring the new change. In an exchange with Gandhi, he asked him for a message to take back home to his people. Gandhi replied, "My life is my message." Ehrensperger wrote a book about his time in India called *Change of Heart* and suggested that one's life must also be their message.

I wholeheartedly agree with this powerful message. I believe that *your life* is your legacy. How you live, what you stand for, and what you give to others.

An Amazing Friend

At the beginning of my five-year exit plan, I met Rita, a hairdresser who quickly became my best friend. When we first met, I asked her about her hopes and dreams. As it turned out, she had several important goals. She wanted to go back to school, start her own business, change the relationship she had with her husband, and travel the world. To me, she confided these hopes and dreams that she hadn't shared with anyone else. So, I helped her. But more importantly, we helped each other. She was my champion, and I was hers.

What's crazy is that she was someone so unexpected, so outside our typical circle, to whom we opened our home and our family. That's why it's so important to be open to the opportunities the universe places before you. She brought light, joy, and positivity and was a beacon of light to us in some of our darkest moments, as we were to her. We always felt her energy and always uplifted each other. As in other parts of my life, I knew that meeting her was no accident and that she came into my life for a reason—synchronicity.

After getting to know me and seeing my relationship with Paul, Rita took the leap and started making big changes in her life. She understood that she wanted and deserved something different, something more. She traveled with us to different parts of the Dominican Republic and really started to live her best life. We had so much fun, and we even designed swimsuits together as part of a business plan. We got to know her amazing daughter and visited her at her home and met her pet turtles. My kids treated her as family, and I trusted her with my life. She was someone I could call at any time of the day or night, and she was my greatest, truest champion in some of the lowest moments I've shared with you.

But when Rita began suffering from frequent migraines, she saw a doctor, who informed her she needed surgery. The procedure was relatively simple but costly, so another neighbor and I helped her fundraise. We rallied our network and raised the money needed for the operation. The surgery was scheduled to go ahead on a Friday afternoon. Everything would be fine.

On the day before the surgery, Rita came to my house, and we agreed that her daughter would stay with me for the weekend so she wouldn't have to stay at home by herself. She could also help me entertain the kids. Win-win, we both thought.

"I'll see you Monday," Rita said, and I had no reason to doubt it.

Right after the surgery, we were told that the procedure went well and Rita was going to be fine. But all of a sudden, her daughter told me she had to leave. At first, I thought she was just going to hang out with her friends. "Where are you going?" I asked.

"The hospital called," she said. "Mom's in a coma."

"Go," I said. "Call me when you know something." That feeling of dread started to well inside me.

Within two hours, I received that phone call. Rita had passed away. Complications, they said, and she didn't make it. I couldn't understand it. She had just started really living her life, following her passions, and realizing her dreams. She was still young and had so much left to do. We were going to start a business together when I left my job. That was our plan.

"You're going to come and work with me," I had said to her. "We're going to do this together." We were both excited for the future. From the beginning, she was my advocate, my coach, my best friend. She was *everything.* I can't really put into words the devastation I felt.

After Rita's death, I felt a lot of guilt. The surgery was supposed to repair an aneurysm, but instead she went into a coma and bled out. Because I helped fundraise for the operation, I questioned my part in her death. Should I have taken her to other specialists? Should I have learned more about the surgery? Should I have persuaded her daughter to be there with her sooner? All of these questions and more spun through my head in a whirlwind of uncertainty and guilt. I struggled to make sense of it all, while wallowing in profound grief.

Rita's funeral didn't help me process her passing. It just made things worse. In Latino culture, we don't tend to celebrate the person who has died. Instead, we focus on ourselves, discussing how fragile life is. "It could be any one of you in that box," said a guy at her grave site, and I felt a visceral reaction. I used to tolerate the tradition because it was a part of my culture. Who was I to question it? But at Rita's funeral, when everyone made it all about them, I was furious. Why was no one talking about what an amazing person she was? Rita served the community, her family, and left anyone she met feeling warmth, love, and positivity. While I was at the funeral, not a single person she had helped stood up to celebrate *her*. It was all about *them*.

I was struck by a massive epiphany. Her eulogy was all about sending her into the afterlife and warning everyone to be "good people" rather than a celebration of Rita's life. I realized how few people actually knew her deeply. The eulogy didn't mention what dreams she had, what sparked her drive, what made her tick, what made her laugh. People knew *about* her, but only a handful knew what mattered inside of her heart. I realized then and there that I wouldn't leave her legacy untold, nor would I neglect mine. I knew

I had to trailblaze my own way and if I didn't succeed, I would die trying.

> "The body shows your stress before the mind knows what's happening."

Rita's death made me question my decision to quit my job and start a business. It felt as if everyone was against me—my colleagues, my friends, my family—and now the person with whom I was going to take this journey was gone. Was it a sign that I shouldn't do this? If I proceeded down the path we had planned, I would be venturing on alone. Paul, of course, would support me every step of the way, but I hadn't had the same in-depth conversations with him. I had shared almost everything with Rita. She was to be my partner in this, the other half of the operation, and now she was gone, leaving a gaping hole in our plans and my soul. How could I do this without her? After her death, I spiraled, and I had a hard time getting out of bed. My kids worried about me, and, to be honest, I barely remember those days. I still showed up to work, hiding my pain, but I quickly enrolled in therapy, which helped me start moving forward.

At the same time, my employer was putting a lot of pressure on me to make a decision about quitting. They demanded that I give them an answer by a certain date—or else!—but I told them I would prefer to take my time. I learned the value of setting boundaries and not being coerced into making a choice or taking an action. You've seen by now how it all played out. They bullied me every step to the exit, making threats and trying to manipulate me into staying. Why would I want to stay with an organization that treated me that way?

Paul and I sat down and discussed our options. Rita's passing clouded my thinking, and I continued to question if I was making the right choice. But I wasn't just doing it for me anymore. I was doing it for her, too. Her legacy was in my hands. After our discussion, we decided that we wouldn't stay a moment longer. The time had come to leave.

Synchronicity

You've seen already, several times in my life, where a chance encounter or a random event turned out to be incredibly meaningful in ways that weren't really random at all. These synchronicities have helped me recognise when I'm on the right track. It's like a wink or a nod from the universe.

The term "synchronicity" was first used in this sense by pioneering analytical psychologist Dr. Carl Jung back in the 1920s. Jung defined synchronicity as, " ... a meaningful coincidence of two or more events, where something other than the probability of chance is involved."[9]

In fact, two-thirds of therapists believe synchronicities can help their clients during therapy.[10] I have certainly found this in my coaching practice too. For me, synchronicities have always helped me find a deeper meaning and led me to my purpose. I believe that by listening to our intuition, observing the synchronicities in our lives, and radiating the energy that draws synchronicities to us, we make great strides on the path to our greatest legacies.

Embracing the concept of synchronicity is like tuning in to the frequency of your life's purpose. When you're clear about your purpose, synchronicities present themselves as affirmations from the universe, providing gentle nudges to keep you on course. My life is peppered with the confetti of such instances, often surfacing just before pivotal changes or decisions, serving as a much needed validation of my inner voice.

One such instance happened in 2017, when my husband, Paul, was contemplating leaving his job in diplomatic service. Despite being miserable and feeling out of alignment with his true purpose, he was apprehensive about leaving, mainly due to financial worries. The risk felt too big. He didn't want to place an additional burden on me, and his innate desire to please others was adding to his stress. The situation was further complicated by the agency wanting to send him to Frankfurt and me to the Dominican Republic, a typical circumstance in diplomatic service, where families often find themselves torn apart. It's a sacrifice many wore as a badge of honor and a practice I found deeply distressing.

Seeking respite from the tense situation, I persuaded Paul to accompany me on a trip to Panama, which happened to coincide with his birthday. While celebrating at a bar, we chatted with a stranger named Henry. With no knowledge of our situation, he shared stories about his financial ups and downs and his career as an aircraft runway engineer and designer. Eventually, most of the others in our group filtered out, and it was just us and Henry. Suddenly, a pensive look came across his face as he looked Paul straight in the eye and said, "You know, if there's one thing I've learned in my life, it's this: it's only a risk if you don't have the skill and experience. If you have the skills and the experience, the only risk is not doing it." *WHAT?* It was like he had seen into Paul's soul and perfectly understood his dilemma. Inspired by this chance encounter, Paul returned home and quit his job, never regretting the decision, and he's now making a greater impact than ever before.

Synchronicity struck again in 2018 when Paul was battling depression due to estrangement from his oldest child. On a trip to Machu Picchu, an unexpected conversation with Tom, an octogenarian stranger on our train ride back to the city, proved pivotal. Tom, thoroughly unaware of Paul's struggles, shared his own experience with estranged children and advised us to, "Let go and just trust, be happy they're happy. Life is too short, there are others who need and want you, and you're missing out on amazing moments." Following this serendipitous meeting, Paul sought therapy and embarked on the difficult journey toward self-forgiveness.

These instances are more than mere coincidences. They're examples of synchronicity at play. We didn't just happen upon them—we invited them into our lives and welcomed their wisdom. This open invitation to the universe allows for the possibility of synchronicities, subtly guiding us in our journeys and affirming our alignment with our purpose.

As I found myself drafting the chapters of this book, I felt the need to reach out to Nicolas. His response was warm, providing me with updates about his life, which now includes a new baby and an overall sense of contentment. Our conversation was brief, and I mentioned that I would be incorporating aspects of our shared past into this book. He was supportive, encouraging me to narrate my version of the story, assuring me he would never attempt to silence my voice.

Before this, our last conversation had been an argument over our annulment, during which I called him a hypocrite. His lack of alignment with the church was apparent to me, so I couldn't understand why he was choosing to take an action that was so incongruous with his own beliefs, especially for the sake of someone else. I argued that erasing our past was impossible, that it had shaped us into the individuals we had become. To my surprise, he informed me that my words that day had deeply impacted him. The sentiments I had voiced had provoked a reflection in him that ultimately led to his decision not to go through with the annulment. I had been oblivious to the fact that my candidness could have such a profound influence. It was a different kind of synchronicity—one where I felt a pull and took proactive steps, making synchronicity happen. In that moment, I felt as if our narrative had come full circle, and it gave me what I needed for the writing process.

WHAT IS YOUR LEGACY?

In our society, there can be a misconception about what legacy truly means. It's not simply about fulfilling the expectations of your parents or being a good parent, sibling, daughter, or son. It's not contingent on whether or not you have children or whether you've been featured in a magazine. At its core, legacy is about your unique impact on the world. It's about the actions you've taken that have influenced others, the values you've upheld, and the example you've set for those around you. Your legacy is the imprint you leave on the world, which can be as simple as a kind gesture that changes someone's day or as monumental as a life-altering invention. Each one of us has the power to shape our own legacy, independent of societal expectations and pressures.

So, how do we know what our impact is? What *is* your legacy? What do you want to be remembered for? What do you want people to say about you? If you don't know, don't worry—I'm here to help. I'm going to guide you through an exercise to help you unpack this. That's what this exercise does—it digs deep into your heart and soul and helps you rediscover what truly matters to you and why. What's more, it puts it into action. I call it the Obituary Exercise. It may sound a little morbid, but, believe me, it's actually all about living fully NOW!

Before we begin, I want to let you know that the "purpose" process is going to be uncomfortable. Like I said, we're going to dig into questions like legacy and what you want to be remembered for. We're going to go deep into who YOU are. But I promise you once the uncomfortable settles, you'll feel energized, inspired, and ready to take action.

So, are you ready to take the next step in defining your legacy?

OBITUARY EXERCISE

Now it's time to follow each step of the Obituary Exercise to define your legacy and determine what you want to be remembered for, starting with step one:

1. Close your eyes and imagine it's your funeral (in present time). You died last night.

Who is there? What do those present say about you? This should be as honest as possible. Based on your life as you have actually lived it up to now, what would people really say about you?

Take your time to imagine it vividly, and write down the details.

....

....

....

....

....

....

....

....

....

....

Now, you may want to fight me on this, but I urge you to really push through. Most people don't change their lives until someone really close to them passes away or they have a near-death experience themselves that awakens them to start living. Don't wait until that moment. I've had clients in retirement just starting to find happiness, but you don't have to wait that long. Before you move on to the next section, go back to that question and really put yourself in that moment. Make sure you were honest, thought about the reality of your life up to now, and answered as thoroughly as possible. Once you're ready, let's continue.

2. Now take time to reflect on what people said about you.

Once you have gone through your honest, specific statements, how do you feel about them? Pretend you're floating and viewing everyone from above. You get to hear all their side conversations about you as well. Is it what you want to hear? Are they saying anything alluding to dreams and possibilities that haven't been reached yet? Did they even know about your dreams?

Disclaimer:
I'm a huge proponent of not caring about what others think. This isn't an exercise to get into the depths of what other people think about you but more to stretch you and to observe the legacy and impact you're leaving. Funerals are usually a place where people celebrate lives and avoid gossiping.

So, do you feel fully satisfied with what people are saying about you? Is it how your life should be spoken about? Do you feel there's something missing? Is there something cringeworthy or frustrating in what they're saying?

I'll give you an example. Remember that major meltdown I mentioned earlier, where I exploded at my dad? Dad was telling me, "But, Esther, you've helped thousands and thousands of people." That, for me, was cringe. I don't want to help thousands. I want to help millions. It hit me to my core to understand that those closest to me had so little understanding of who I was, what I wanted, and the scope of my dreams. This leads us to the next question.

3. What do you want people to remember you for?

Close your eyes and imagine your funeral again, but this time imagine what you would want people to say about you. Imagine you've lived a full, long life. If it helps, imagine that you had almost unlimited resources at your disposal, allowing you to take any path you chose in life. Write down all the details. Be very, very specific. What stories are they telling? What are they feeling inside that hasn't been said out loud about you? How are they describing your life? How are they describing your characteristics? How are they describing your *impact*? Refrain from generic statements like, "He/she was a good parent..." or, "He/she accomplished a lot..." Be as specific as possible. Remember, this is a celebration of your life.

4. Reflect on "the gap."

Is there a gap between the two visualizations? Is there a gap between what people said about you and what you'd like people to say about you? Write down the differences.

"Carve your name on hearts, not tombstones.
A legacy is etched into the minds of others
and the stories they share about you."
—Shannon L. Alder

If you feel super confused and uncomfortable at this point, don't worry. Even if you're someone who thinks of purpose all the time, there should be a clear difference between what was said and what you want to be said. This feeling is completely normal—it's what we want to feel. Later, we'll channel this discomfort into action. This gap is an indication of what's missing to go from A to B.

If you're struggling with this exercise and visualizing your untimely passing, another question you can ask is this: if you had unlimited resources and time, what single problem would you solve for the world? This will unlock in your mind what you would do with your life if you were limitless. With this in mind, try starting this section over…

FROM A TO B: UPGRADE YOUR LEGACY

Once you've clearly identified your legacy, it's important that you don't just leave it sitting there in the "someday" pile. I always insist with my clients that we make a plan to include the legacy right now in their lives.

My mantra is: *The time to upgrade your legacy is now.*

If you really want to stand for something in this world and leave a legacy for others, then it must be in your life plan. Some people feel that they are too late, missed the boat, or are too old to create a legacy. That's BS! As the Chinese proverb reminds us, "The best time to plant a tree was 20 years ago. The second best time is now." Your legacy isn't always something you have to do. It's something you are.

So, are there parts of your legacy that you need to change or upgrade? Be specific. For example, I realized after the meltdown with my dad that I needed to scale my impact and extend my reach. I needed to get out there and make my voice known and heard.

....

....

....

....

....

....

What is one thing you can implement in your current life, no matter how small, that would help build your legacy? Small actions add up to big changes. For example, my first action was to follow accounts of speakers whom I admired and watch videos on how to create greater reach on social media.

If you're uncomfortable with the legacy exercise, you're not alone. Louis came to me looking for help in his career. He was ambitious and smart, still early in his career, but not a newbie. Impeccably dressed, his image and presentation mattered to him, but, beneath a businesslike exterior, I could tell he had a heart of gold.

He said that he wanted to elevate himself professionally and get promoted. Louis also said that he wanted me to help get rid of his empathy since he felt it was holding him back. He believed that, in order to get ahead, he had to be an unsympathetic hard-ass. More on this in a later section.

Louis was very uncomfortable with the legacy exercise, and he defaulted immediately to very generic answers, for example, "Good son and good citizen." I encouraged him to dig deeper and be super detailed. When we finally got down to what he really wanted, that's when he burst and realized he wanted so much more than just a promotion. He broke down because there was so much he hadn't even touched yet. He wanted to be known as a leader in his field. He wanted to be giving speeches as a thought leader in his space. Specifically, he wanted to uplift youth and establish a charitable foundation. His A to B gap was wide, but he had taken the first step by being clear on who he wanted to be. Even though it felt super overwhelming at the time, that breakthrough was a great moment to be celebrated. Just that one realization that his legacy was so much bigger gave Louis so much clarity and the courage to start taking small steps.

YOUR LEGACY HELPS YOU LIVE YOUR LIFE ON PURPOSE

So many people today worry about their life purpose. They search and search and search. Countless books and articles are written to help people find that elusive purpose and many people think that if they just found "it," everything would be OK. Their lives would magically work out roses, and nothing would bother them because their mission would be number one.

Now, don't get me wrong, I totally understand this thinking. I have contemplated my life's purpose more than most, and I've done some crazy and wild things in pursuit of living my dreams. But what I've discovered, and what I want to share with you, is this: without knowing your real legacy, your purpose can be easily confused with your strengths, or what you're good at. It's a common mistake that people make when searching for their life's purpose.

> "Every time you're looking to the side and comparing yourself to others, remember that they're also suffering and not showing you the complete picture."

YOUR PURPOSE ISN'T WHAT YOU LOVE

When I tell people that discovering your purpose isn't about finding what you love and doing it at the expense of all other things, they often look at me puzzled. After all, that's what we've been told:

"Follow your bliss. Do what you love, and the money will follow," among other things. Even corporations focus on this type of thinking without questioning it. Doing what you love is part of your purpose, but it's certainly not the only factor.

Let me give you a personal example. During my post-sophomore research trip to Costa Rica, I finally decided to pursue my passion for dancing. I spent hours every night learning merengue and salsa with my friends and, by the end of the summer, became a professional. I loved dancing so much, and learning it from my friend, Carlos, a Costa Rican local, in nature under the stars, felt like a dream come true. Dancing calmed me and reduced my anxiety, and doing it every night made me feel free.

Not only did I love salsa dancing, but I was good at it, and I started dancing competitively. Through grad school, I competed and enjoyed the time with my fellow dancers. Sure, it gave me pleasure, but it didn't become my career. It wasn't "the thing" I wanted to give to the world or teach. It was the thing I did for pleasure. When I stopped dancing as often, people would ask me, "Do you miss dancing?" Although I missed the thrill of competing, I wasn't thinking much about it or longing for a deeper relationship with competitive dance. Dancing wasn't my purpose.

Instead of focusing on just the things you love, think about what draws you to those things. With salsa dancing, I loved the harmony of feeling like a system, almost a new organism, that moved together. Over time, I also came to see my work in environmental science much the same way. The study of natural systems and how they interact and depend on each other is almost like a dance. Although I was great at both salsa dancing and environmental science, neither was my purpose.

Once I understood that my legacy was to help millions of people discover and live their purpose, it all made sense. My real, deeper strength was the ability to see people, communities, teams, and entire countries as systems and to lead those systems to achieve the greatness within them. The things I love—dancing, environmental science—gave me tools to achieve my legacy without themselves defining my purpose.

That's why the singular focus on "doing what you love" can be bad stand-alone advice. I love salsa dancing, and I love travel deals, but I'm not destined to be either a dancer or a travel agent. Sure, many people make incredible careers around what they love, but you'll soon see when you do the Purpose Sun—my formula for discovering your purpose—that they probably had the same compatibility in other categories too. For the record, when I did the Purpose Sun exercise myself, salsa dancing didn't even appear until way at the end! That's when I knew that doing what you love isn't the only ingredient to a sustainable and pleasurable life map. As you'll soon see, your purpose is an intersection of your natural traits, your learned skills, what you've overcome, *and* your passion.

"Your purpose is part of you and, even though you may not have nurtured it as much as you would have wanted to, you also haven't completely erased or forgotten it."

YOUR PURPOSE ISN'T WHAT OTHERS SAY

If I had done what my dad wanted me to do, I would be a physician—but I would have been a miserable physician. I admire and respect medical doctors, but I also know that being a medical doctor isn't for me. Dad thought I would make a great doctor because I'm smart and can cope with pressure. I also work well in a scheduled environment and like to problem solve, but those traits are transferable to many careers. So, your purpose isn't best seen through the lens of other people, as others may have incorrect assumptions about you and unfulfilled dreams of their own that bias their opinions. Or they may think you'd make a good medical doctor or engineer or lawyer because then you'd be financially independent and, therefore, "successful" by society's standards. But I've learned that the check marks of stability don't equal happiness. Plus, it's a very limited way of thinking. In today's world, the pathways to financial independence and career success are infinite.

For some people, this may be the hardest part to accept. Many high achievers have built their own personal value on the basis of what others think, so going against the grain—against the positive reinforcement they've received their whole lives—can seem like too much. It helps to go back to those fundamental traits that people see in you: smart, ambitious, organized, problem solver, calm under fire, and so on. Even if you choose a life path different from what those around you approve of, you're still all those things. Recognize that those characteristics will carry you forward, no matter what. By choosing the path that builds your legacy and advances your purpose, you're making the best use of your talents and skills.

Victoria is a trained pharmacist, but she was feeling uninspired and frustrated in her career. She had so many other things she was interested in pursuing: blog writing, learning to invest, and about twenty other side projects. I instantly knew that she would be overwhelmed if she tried to do them all and that she wasn't really clear on her ultimate zone—the place where her skill set could be cross-trained into other areas and fully utilized.

We worked together on dividing up what skills she had, what she really felt helped others, and what the world needed right now, and she crystallized her plethora of exciting ideas into two well-planned and possible ideas. These were the ideas she could start moving on right away, building toward her legacy and beginning to live her purpose.

DISCOVER YOUR PURPOSE—THE PURPOSE SUN EXERCISE

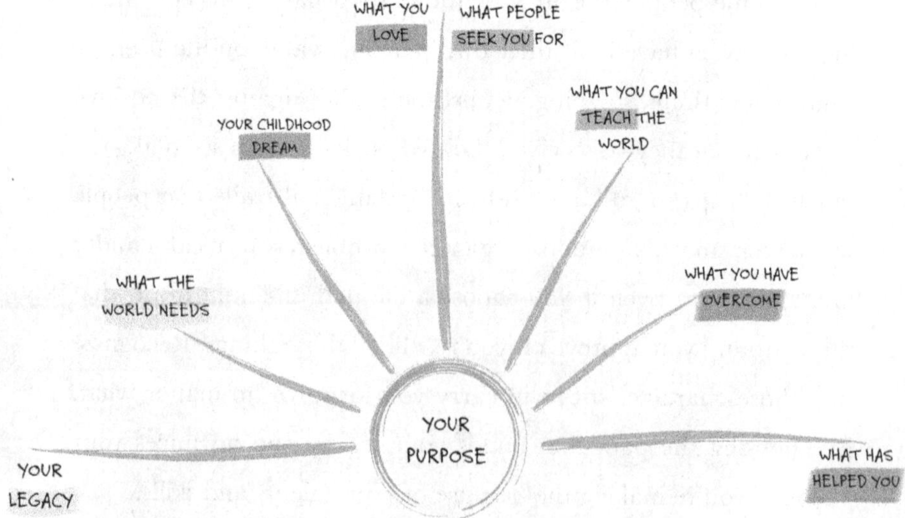

This diagram is your Purpose Sun. I love the analogy of the sun because the sun is fundamental to life. It gives warmth, light, and makes life possible. As we go through these exercises, the dawning sun reminds us of new beginnings and that change is possible. More than anything, I want you to see that you are this sun—you are light and power and warmth and an important part of this system of humanity.

I recommend that you recreate the Purpose Sun for yourself on a single horizontal sheet of paper. As you go through the following sections, transfer your notes onto your Purpose Sun. It will likely get messy and very full, but that's the idea. When completed, you'll have a meaningful and complete picture of who you are, which helps point to your purpose. No joke, some of my clients take a picture of their Purpose Sun and set it as the background on their computer so they can see it and be reminded of it every day.

YOUR LEGACY (AS PER OBITUARY EXERCISE)

Write your ultimate legacy in this section. We are going to park it here for now.

Let's move to the next section.

WHAT THE WORLD NEEDS

Through your lens, what do you believe the world needs?

Now, most of us think that people answer this question more or less the same. World peace, more money, and so on. But, actually, if they answer honestly, I have yet to meet one person who answers this question the same as anyone else. Now, I want you to get specific. If you're struggling to answer, let's take it one step further. You've been invited to the G7 summit and given endless resources (for my high achievers, you've specifically been given $2 billion and a large staff) to tackle one big issue and solve one problem. What would you pick?

Remember the exercise I did with first and fourth graders? They gave me super detailed answers. I had one kid tell me he believes the world needs clean air and he would use those funds and endless resources to purchase technology and fund engineers to remove pollution. I had another student tell me that the world needs strong negotiators to avoid wars and build joint movements. I've had answers ranging from the world needs a space for the voiceless, to the world needs storytellers and communication to bring people together, to the world needs more financial opportunities for women, to the world needs support systems. Whatever your answer is, it's unique to you. I believe the world needs the opportunity to live and build its true purpose, whether we're talking about individuals, companies, communities, or countries. Surprised?

Now, let's go back to Louis and his desire to get rid of his empathy. When we got to this question of what he thought the world needed, he answered that he believed the world needed empathy. He had been made to feel that his own great gift of empathy was the anchor holding back his progress, yet he knew inside that this was, in fact, what the world needed most. The following sessions with him were focused on building out his purpose, coming to the realization that empathy was actually his superpower and strength, and working through the limiting beliefs through an action plan, where he could be both empathetic and grow as a professional.

Now, on to your childhood dream.

CHILDHOOD DREAM

For this portion, I want you to reflect on your childhood. We all had a childhood dream, even if you forgot or blocked yours out. I recommend if you have blocked out your childhood dream, you should spend time reflecting on why you don't remember and possibly be open to therapy. This amnesia could stem from something much deeper, which a therapist or hypnotherapist can explore with you. If this is you, I have an alternate question we can explore in the meantime, which I'll get to.

For those who do remember their childhood, I want you to focus on your childhood dream or your childhood idol. Did you want to be an astronaut, policeman, fireman, doctor, teacher, superstar, or on television? This is YOUR childhood dream, and there's no wrong answer. Write it down. If your childhood dream was inspired by a particular person or event, write that down too.

Now that you've written down your childhood dream, I want you to reflect on the characteristics of that dream. What do you feel are the characteristics of the person who embodies that dream? Write down the characteristics in as much detail as possible. For example,

I had two clients whose childhood dreams were to be medical doctors. But the characteristics of the "doctor" were very different. One of them wanted to be a doctor because they wanted to help people, but another wrote about being a doctor because they were fascinated by the human body and being able to problem solve.

Believe it or not, it took my husband six months to answer this question about his childhood dream. If you're stuck, take your time and bookmark this page. It wasn't until I asked him a side question on what TV show left him amazed as a kid that a light went off in his mind and he started telling me, in great detail, how he and his family used to watch the Jacques Cousteau show every week. All of a sudden, everything made sense to him. He was like, "Oh my god, I never knew why I wanted to learn French or why I became a lifeguard and scuba diver." But he was trying to become this man whom he admired, who had this amazing calmness, independence, and adventurous life. He even wore the same beanies sometimes. Plus, he was an inventor! So, don't panic if you don't have a straight answer yet… It will come to you if you get creative and explore your childhood deeply.

Now, if you can't get into your childhood, if it's blocked, here's an alternate question:

Who do you look up to and admire now? What are the characteristics that you admire about them? For example, I admire Viola Davis. I adore her. She's kind, a bleeding heart, generous, and also very powerful.

THAT WHICH YOU LOVE: PASSIONS/INTERESTS

What do you love to do? What are you passionate about? What are your main interests? Write them in this section.

This is the standard question of "what do you love." What do you love to do in your free time? What gives you that endorphin boost? For example, maybe it's cooking, dancing, dressing up, taking pictures, or traveling. Whatever it is, list it all. It could also mean things like romance or spending time with friends, running marathons, or reading sci-fi. Whatever comes to mind, list it. Again, be as honest and detailed as you can. There are no wrong answers. One of my clients is a big guy, a broad-shouldered, martial arts expert, whose immediate response to the "what do you love question" was, "Babies!" Unexpected. But genuine.

WHAT YOU CAN TEACH THE WORLD

What topics, themes, skills, ideas can you teach the world? I want you to list them ALL. The first few will come quickly to you, based on what you do or have done for a living. In my case, I can teach the world about: environmental science, international development, teaching university… You'd be amazed by how many brilliant, accomplished, and multi-passionate people look at me straight-faced and tell me those first few things are all they could teach. I call BS on that! We just need to unpack it.

I want you to dig *way* deeper. Could you teach someone to swim? Surf? Play guitar? Speak Greek? Could you teach someone your amazing recipe for banana bread? How to dance salsa? Change a tire? If the country you live in suddenly became uninhabitable and you had to move to a new place and help create a new society from the bottom up, what could you contribute? Can you grow herbs? Build a tool shed? Do you know about first aid? Are you getting the idea? Granular. Detailed.

Great. Now, even deeper. I want you to stretch yourself to list things like soft skills. Are you a great connector of people? Negotiator? Are you a good planner? Are you really good at managing conflict? Do you have a knack for editing other people's writing? I could, for example, teach time management, how to create amazing action plans, how to facilitate meetings and workshops, how to travel, how to interview, how to write a resume, strategic communications—the list goes on.

Now, these last questions require you to dig deep—and I mean really deep. Take a deep breath because the answers to these questions will help unlock barriers that have kept you from living your purpose.

WHAT PEOPLE SEEK YOU FOR

The good and bad. What do you want to keep, add, and delete? Reflect on the past and notice what people seek you out for. When you get a phone call or a text that says, "I need your help," what are they normally looking for? When someone steps into your office and asks, "Do you have a sec?" what kind of things do they normally need?

....

....

What are the most common compliments you've heard about yourself from others? Remember, you're not bragging, but this is *not* the moment to be shy. Highlight in yellow the ones you like.

I want you to write down the things people seek you for that you're tired of people seeking you for. For example, please don't seek me for administrative logistics. Remember, it also doesn't have to be something tangible. Maybe you want people to stop seeking you for emotional support. Highlight these in red.

What do you wish people would seek you for? For what do you wish people would say, "Yeah, they're experts in that…" Highlight these in green.

I want you to save these lists. Sometimes, these things are complex. People seek us for things because we're good at them, and, at first, we agree to assist because we want to help others. But, over time, it can become an expectation. It can become a burden. My husband is someone who people turn to for safety and security, and, as much as he likes helping people feel safe, it comes at a cost to him. People come to him with their troubles, fears, and traumas, and, honestly, he wishes people would seek him a little less for this. This is the first step in identifying the boundaries you need to create (stop—red), things you need to start incorporating into your plan (add—green), and things you want to keep making time for (continue—yellow). This process will continue later in the Organization and Work-Life Integration sections of the book.

Are you starting to see some patterns? (Hint: you should start seeing some commonality between what you wish people sought you for and your legacy). Keep the list of what you want people to seek you for close. We'll use it soon.

WHAT YOU HAVE OVERCOME

What challenges and obstacles have you overcome in the past, and what did you discover about yourself?

So, for this question, I want you to also take a deep breath and be completely honest. There's no judgment. This is really just for you, so you can be imperfect, vulnerable, and list everything. This only works if you're completely honest with yourself.

I want you to list every single thing you've overcome in your life, from depression, to anxiety, to negative thoughts, to procrastination, to people-pleasing. They might range from big and systemic things, like racism or poverty, to deeply personal challenges, like introversion, fear, or addiction. Sometimes, we've had to overcome aspects of our own culture that have held us back. For some of us, we've had to overcome horrible trauma. Whatever it is, list it all.

You may wonder why I'm asking you to recall those dark places, and the answer is simple. The things you've had to overcome are likely to be the things you'll keep having to overcome. They've shaped you, and they continue to be relevant. They will be things that are likely to resurface over time and threaten to derail your progress when life gets tough. Mine are limits and boundaries—a constant repeat.

....

....

....

....

....

....

....

....

....

....

WHAT HAS HELPED YOU

Think about things that have helped you through your journey. Think back to the previous question. What are the things that helped you overcome your obstacles? If, for example, you overcame depression and anxiety, what were the tools that helped you overcome them? When you think of your darkest period, where you were struggling with X, how did you get through?

You might be asking, *Why is this important?* We each have our own tool kits—our very own. What worked for me to overcome my own depression might not work for you. So, as you look toward the future and think about the challenges you'll continue to face, these tool kits you've developed will continue to be parts of your go-to strategies. Later, when we get to the section on Resilience, we'll want to revisit this list again.

"Going against the grain—against the positive reinforcement they've received their whole lives—can seem like too much."

IDENTIFY THE OVERLAP

Now review your Purpose Sun diagram and take some time to perform some analysis. Try to identify any overlaps. For example, you may have written a similar thing in two different areas. Highlight or circle the overlaps to identify them. Use different colors and find themes and like words. If you have my VIP kit, pull out the dual highlighter, pen, and pencil, and even Post-its. You should see tons of patterns and repetition throughout the Sun. Spend some time seeing how all these elements connect. Once you find commonality, give it a phrase, a phrase that connects all the pieces together.

ESTHER'S PURPOSE DIAGRAM

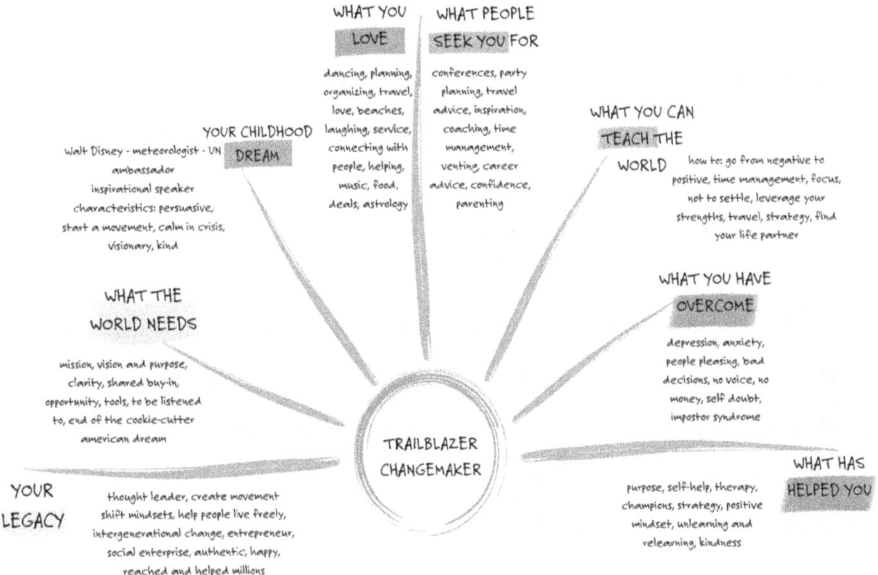

Born in Sub-Saharan Africa, Jerome came from extreme poverty. A very charismatic, bright, and kind guy, he overcame the odds to become fluent in four languages and earn a master's degree in education. He was always trying to help his family and community.

When asked, he said he believed his purpose and legacy was to leave behind financial security for his family. He was fully focused on being an NGO director and never questioned his path. His idea was that an NGO director made good money, which would secure his family's financial future.

However, once we went through this exercise, he could clearly see that his true reason for living was more than just financial. He wanted to give people hope and a voice and become a leader for his community. He wanted to be on center stage as a politician. All of his answers were around this.

Jerome struggled in technical jobs and found himself constantly procrastinating. When he procrastinated at work, he was networking and connecting with folks on political and economic issues. All the jobs he attracted and worked were desk and clipboard jobs, but he wanted to be out there connecting. He was in the wrong career—it wasn't aligned with him.

That's the thing... Our entire beings and bodies will always try to find their way to our centers in some fashion or another. From there, it became clear that Jerome needed to expand his horizons and start building on those skills and connections. Why make it hard when you can find a way to align it all?

Many people are hesitant to undertake the work of discovering their purpose, not because they don't want to know and not because they aren't longing for change in their lives but because they're afraid. Many people are afraid that by going through these exercises, they may find that they have "wasted" their lives and spent all their time on things that are completely disconnected from what they "should" be doing. They would rather continue living in ignorant bliss than risk feeling that they have failed in life. But I'm here to tell you that never once has a client felt that way after going through the purpose exercise. Much like Jerome, the truth of who you are and your deep inner purpose always find a way to leak out. It may be something that happens subconsciously or not in the way that has the impact you would like, but you're absolutely still and always YOU. The objective of the purpose exercise is not in any way to change who you are but, rather, to help you find the best possible way to live as the strongest and most authentic version of yourself. So, fear not. I encourage you to go into these exercises with honesty and optimism, knowing that you don't need "fixing" but only a pathway to greatness.

REVISING YOUR LEGACY

Now that you've completed all the parts of the Purpose Sun, I want you to revisit your legacy from the Obituary Exercise and fill in more details. Include the elements of what you want people to seek you for, what you think the world needs, the characteristics you want to grow into (hint: the person you admired as a kid or admire now), your journey and what you overcame or are overcoming (your hero's story), what you have taught the world, and what you love. This will help you be even more specific in your A to B and the powerful legacy you're leaving behind. Most of the time, we leave out these important details. However, it's time to include everything you just discovered about yourself. All of these elements have always been you and are you now. And be honest. If you want a billion dollars, put that in. Or if you want to be a nomad, write that in. There's no wrong answer. You might have figured it out by now—your legacy is you living your full purpose. It has always been there. The only difference now is that you are aware of it, so you can stop being who everyone else wants you to be, start being intentional in your everyday life, and live it to its fullest.

BONUS: For the Professionals

Carolina was a hugely talented young professional. She loved her family and going on adventures around the world. Carolina had one of those magnetic personalities that instantly makes you feel comfortable and want to engage with her. She was an expert in education and had some truly innovative ideas that could revolutionize early childhood education. She came looking for help to ramp up her career to the next level and find a job more aligned to her larger goals and a place where she felt like she could make a real impact. Although she was still relatively early in her professional career, as we spoke, it became very evident that she had brought significant transformative change to the places where she had worked. But none of this was evident in her CV or cover letter. Carolina's entire resume listed her tasks and made the entire thing sound like she was an administrative assistant. It missed mentioning how she was a strategic thinker and how she saw education as what the world needed.

These exercises are about more than your purpose. They're essential for writing your CV/resume or, if you're an entrepreneur, for making pitches or, if you're an NGO, for your case statement. I've been on hundreds of panels for jobs or grants, and I can tell you the error I constantly see is that people list "tasks" or their job responsibilities and completely fail to include their "why." They don't include what makes them unique. With the Purpose Sun and the addition of these elements, Carolina was able to secure her dream job, filtering out jobs that didn't match her and finding a position that completely aligned with who she was. Her career has absolutely taken off, and it has been amazing to see that transformation.

This same transformation happened to another client, Anna-Maria, when I worked with her to move from a managerial job to an executive position with a large international organization. The purpose exercise is such a game changer. It's the first thing I do with my clients before even editing their resume/CV. Anyone can edit (even chatGPT), but only this can reveal what makes you YOU and the value you provide to an organization, or why they should fund you and your idea. Imagine how differently the cover letter reads or how different the vibe is during an interview when you're someone who understands your purpose and legacy and speaks to the position you're applying for, not in some generic way, but knowing exactly how you'll contribute to the organization.

Maria, a recent participant in one of my programs, was able to land her dream position by understanding the connections between the Purpose Sun and her job search. This understanding led her to a role that met all her priorities: a positive culture, fulfilling work, and a good salary. Maria shared that without the knowledge about the importance of alignment and the patience to wait for the right fit, she wouldn't have even considered factors like corporate culture or negotiation. Thanks to the program, she found a job where her colleagues are engaged and she feels valued and excited to be part of the team.

OK, so now you have your purpose statement and what you want it to lead to (aka legacy). It's OK if you're feeling overwhelmed. It's a normal feeling. The next step? Assembling an action plan built just for you and your purpose.

This is where the O in POWER comes in.

ORGANIZATION

Now that you know your inner calling, your true purpose, the thing that drives you every day, what do you do now?

Now comes the time to make it happen. That's right—it's time to be intentional about making your purpose happen. You have to incorporate your purpose in your everyday life. Now that you know it, there's no turning back. As Oprah says, once you know your purpose, you have to know how every decision, big or small, helps move you closer to living that purpose.[11] You now have the filter for how you see the world in the palm of your hand. It's time to take what you know now and live intentionally. Easier said than done, right? Well, don't worry—that's why I'm here. I will walk you through it.

Let's start by first looking at your Sun, starting with your legacy. Let's take a look at your A (current state) to B (desired state).

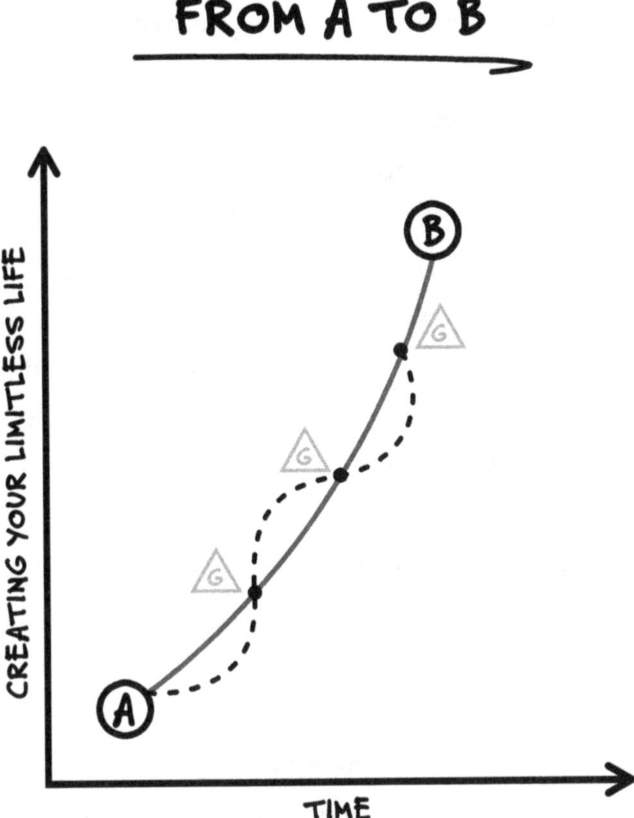

Now that we have this in front of us, let's break it down into a set of more bit-sized pieces: goals, milestones, and steps.

> **GOAL:**
>
> AN OUTCOME OR OBJECTIVE THAT SOMEONE WANTS TO ACHIEVE. IT IS BASED ON THE DESIRED RESULT THAT GUIDES ACTIONS AND DECISIONS TOWARD A SPECIFIC PURPOSE (OR LEGACY). GOALS CAN BE SHORT- OR LONG-TERM.

This is important because the majority of us *way overestimate* what we can do in one year and pile it on to the point of overload, but, at the same time, we underestimate what we can do in 5–10 years. At the moment, one year feels so LONG but if you actually stop and think, a year isn't that much time. It goes by incredibly fast. Admit it, every December, without fail, you look back at the past year and ask yourself, "Where did the time go?" Twelve months go by in a flash, and it's so easy to grossly overestimate the goals we can achieve in that time. The worst thing you can do as a high achiever is pile on too much.

Now, before you start arguing with me (I know you want to!) that the super ambitious one-year plan motivates you and that you need a high bar to reach ... remember that you're a high achiever. What happens if you don't achieve what you wrote down in that year? What happens two months from now if you hit a road bump that delays your huge goals for the year? Your brain goes into automatic fixed mindset mode, where you start filling your head with "failure." You'll want to give up, and we DON'T want that. We want to make sure the goals and steps we break down are *super* realistic and spaced out. I want to make sure you're gentle with yourself and that you also make time for rest and celebration (which we'll get to later).

So, let's use my Purpose Sun as an example. When I first fully completed it, my A to B was HUGE—*ooofff*. I went from impacting thousands to aspiring to impact millions. Also, when I did the exercise, I wasn't in the entrepreneur space. I had been applying entrepreneur skills to my government job *(do not recommend)* but hadn't fully executed building my own thing (out of fear, and so on). I was also still beating myself up for having stayed in a job that triggered my anxiety and stifled my true self. How did I not see that? But you can't undo the past, and all we can do now is take what we learned from it and move forward. That's the thing with purpose: there's no escaping it. It was creeping into all my spaces, and I was trying to make it fit everywhere other than the place it needed to be channeled.

Now, it's normal for your mind to start spinning. For example, from my legacy, it was clear I needed to build a company from the ground up and also be super active on social media. Of course, that immediately gave me heartburn. Remember, I'm a people pleaser. I was going to be frank and honest on social media. That's scary. What would my family and friends think? What would that even look like? Ugh, and I hated the way I looked on camera. Immediately, my mind was in a frenzy. So, if your mind is doing that right now, just take a deep breath. It's just the fear talking, but try with all your might to set it aside and just give the steps a chance. Baby steps.

Setting Goals

After I let my mind spin, I took a notebook and wrote down everything I could think of that needed to be done. It was a lot, but it felt good to have my brain dump on paper—something I could go back to later to expand on and categorize. So, if going from A to B meant I needed to become a global influencer, I had to break that down into goals.

Big goals were:

1. Pivot myself toward a new space (niche)

2. Create a platform to communicate my message to the world
3. Build and monetize a program that provides enormous value to the world
4. Expand my reach and credibility
5. Launch a company and system that could scale

Now, at that time, that's all I could come up with, which was OK. Remember, this exercise is not something you just do once. It's something you revisit and tweak every year. You won't have all the answers, but you can start with what you know. *Note: later, we'll add the other parts of purpose.*

"'Making time' really means making choices about your time."

At the time, I didn't know what platforms I should use. Heck, I barely knew social media. I didn't know how to create a program and didn't even know the basics of growing a business. My fancy degree in environmental science wasn't helping me much now! I knew how to showcase programs and leverage money in my career but not outside in the entrepreneur space. However, I knew from my Purpose Sun that I had a lot of the fundamental skills (from what I could teach and what people sought me for). I have them, and they're part of me. I had to pause, take a breath, and remind myself of this. I just needed to learn a new way to apply those skills.

I had to see it like college. College is four years. Remember, when I started, my college experience was on the path to failure (see how I separated the concept of failure and didn't turn it on myself?) because I didn't know the system yet. You will have that feeling of failing at some point in this process, but, remember, growth isn't a straight path. The trick is to climb back from the lows and ride the highs.

That takes us to my next point: people often make the mistake of thinking these goals follow a linear order or are self-contained modules that you work on one at a time. They aren't. You take steps for each one at the same time, little by little. Think of it as a job. If you're a development practitioner, or health specialist, or a programmer, at any moment, you're usually juggling multiple projects with different start and end dates. It's rare when we have only one responsibility at a time. If you're a manager, part of your job is about business and your technical expertise, but you also have to devote time and energy to managing people. Even at the supermarket, you could be a cashier who also closes the store (my job) or a bagger who opens the store. While you have both responsibilities, you undertake them at different times of the day and give different types of energy to each at varying moments. Same with these goals.

Your goals will happen concurrently over the next 5–10 years, so the first step is to categorize them. Which ones are short- and which are long-term? Think realistically about how long each one could take. Then I want you to intentionally add *50–100 percent more time.* I know you're a high achiever and you get your stuff done, on time, with quality. But this is your life and your purpose. I want you to take it slowly, make the journey part of the joy, and build in plenty of time for the randomness that life will surely throw your way.

Let's use my goals as an example again:

1. Pivot myself toward a new space (niche)
   Time frame: My guess (1–1.5 years). Adjusted (2–2.5 years)
2. Create a platform to communicate my message to the world
   Time frame: My guess (3–6 months). Adjusted (6 months to 1 year)
3. Build and monetize a program that provides enormous value to the world
   Time frame: My guess (1–2 years). Adjusted (2–4 years)
4. Expand my reach and credibility (at large scale)
   Time frame: My guess (2–4 years). Adjusted (4–6 years)
5. Launch a company and system that could scale.
   Time frame: My guess (1–3 years). Adjusted (2–6 years)

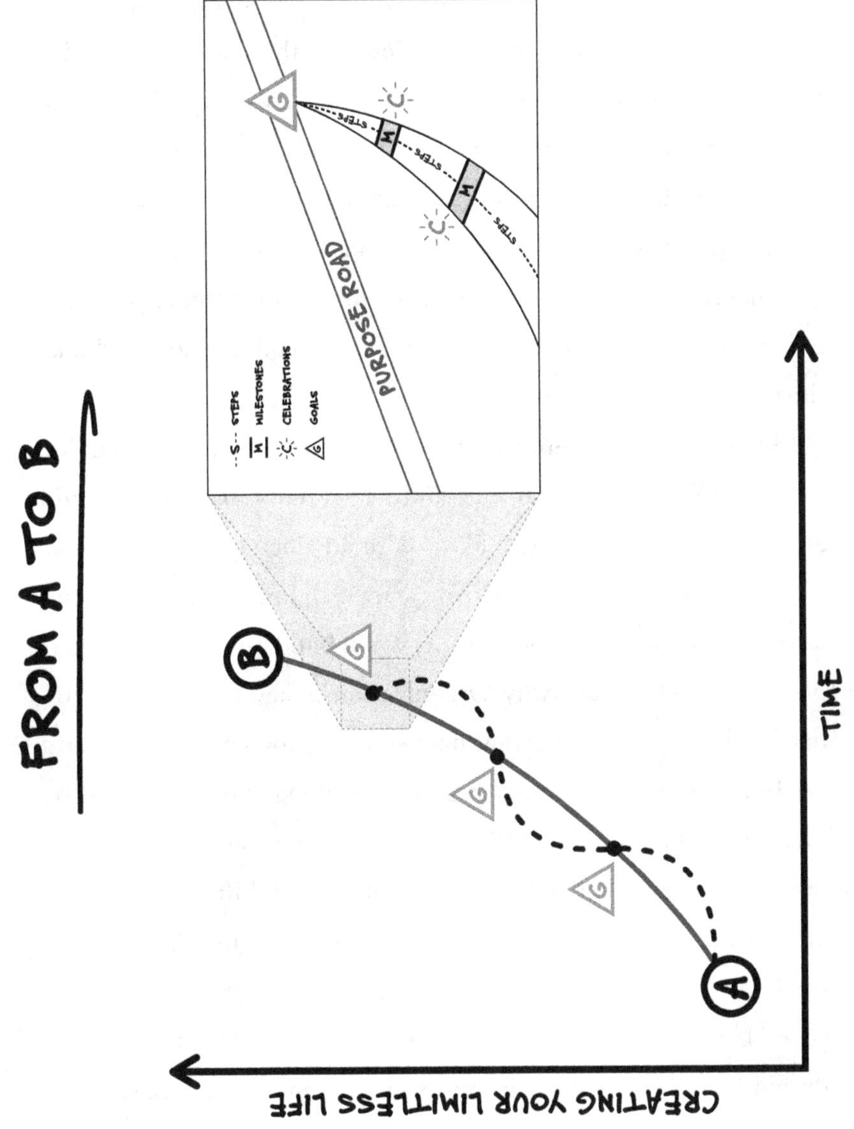
FROM A TO B
A
B
G
TIME
CREATING YOUR LIMITLESS LIFE
PURPOSE ROAD
STEPS
M
C
S -- STEPS
M MILESTONES
C CELEBRATIONS
G GOALS

Once I completed this exercise, I was able to consider how I would buffer my time, how long I would have to work as a contractor or consultant as I built my business, and how much patience the process would require. Are you seeing why the one-year intensive plan doesn't get you there? This is a plan for your life. When you consider your 5–10-year plan, do you think, *Ugh, I can't wait that long!* If you do get that feeling, remember that this is your legacy, and a legacy takes a lifetime to build and will last even longer. This is your investment, not just in yourself but in the impact you want to leave in the world. So, yes, it's a big undertaking, and it will take time.

But keep this in mind always: the point is to make your life better NOW, not just at the end. The point of purpose and alignment is to make it feel like you're advancing and living your own purpose every single day. You start with low-hanging fruit and as you move forward, little by little, you'll build momentum as your plan advances. That's why Organization is key to the plan. You need to build the systems that help you see progress every day and celebrate your wins, however small, all along the way. You'll be living it every day. Remember also that each person's A to B is different, so each person's timeline will also be different. If you've already been on the path to alignment, your A to B may be relatively small, and your goals may be achievable within the next couple of years. If your B is very different from your A (a complete change, a dramatic difference in scale, and so on), your timeline may easily look more like mine, potentially extending to well over a decade.

The best thing I can tell you is not to stress—baby steps—and to keep flexible. I also recommend that you review this book and your plan every year. I recommend purchasing the accompanying workbook. Review your goals and your progress and adjust your timelines wherever you need to.

Breaking Goals into Bite-Sized Milestones

So, what do we do with these goals? We break them down into milestones.

> **MILESTONE:**
> SIGNIFICANT EVENT OR ACHIEVEMENT THAT MARKS A SPECIFIC POINT IN THE PROGRESS TOWARD A GOAL.

Let's use my second goal as an example.

Goal two was: create a platform to communicate my message to the world, with an adjusted time frame of six months to one year.

Here are some examples of what the relevant milestones might be:

1. Identify a super specific niche that I know very well (for example, high achievers)
2. Determine which platform would be best for my niche
3. Learn the basics of how to use the platform
4. Post consistently for thirty days (repeat this milestone for every thirty days)
5. Learn a subskill of the platform (for example, video)
6. Learn another subskill of the platform (for example,

Instagram stories)

7. Learn another subskill of the platform (for example, copywriting)
8. Develop a branding strategy
9. Create a content strategy

We can keep adding to this but, for now, write as many milestones as come to mind. Fight the urge to write your milestones as tasks—these are still goals, only a little smaller. If you're describing the HOW, then you're writing about tasks. For example, if milestone three said, "Learn the basics of how to use the platform by registering for a course," you're focusing on the task of registering for the course. That comes later. Right now, I want you to think about the milestone itself and its relevance to your larger goal.

When I started adding to my list, I realized that even my adjusted time frame was probably not super realistic, so I added more time…

Time frame: My guess (3–6 months). Adjusted (6 months to 1 year). Revisited (1–2 years).

All of this was just for goal two. Repeat the process of drafting milestones for each of your big goal categories.

One Step at a Time

Next, we'll break our milestones down even further and consider the steps required for each one. This is where you start to consider the outputs and products required to reach the milestone. Let's use "branding strategy" as an example.

For branding strategy, these are the steps I foresee:

STEP:
PROGRESS COVERED UNDER A GIVEN ACTION.

1. Complete market research
2. Draft mission, vision, purpose
3. Create brand identity: logo and slogan
4. Write copy for brand messaging
5. Select brand fonts and colors

There's more, but we're not done yet, and this is plenty to get started.

Small Tasks Are the Foundation of Everything

Now that you have your steps, we can break these down into tasks. A task is a piece of work that is undertaken to achieve a step. This should feel very familiar and comforting. We spend most of our workdays and lives working on tasks, the things that fill our to-do lists. I keep this part of the process last and very defined to ensure that the intention and purpose of tasks are clear. So many of us spend our lives just "doing," with no intention, and never stop to question. An endless and unstructured list of tasks will make you feel like you're on the hamster wheel, just spinning and spinning, never getting anywhere. Instead, this progression from goal, to milestone, to step, to tasks gives a clear reason and objective for each one. You're able to see how every effort and every result contributes to the larger goal. You've turned your to-do list into a strategic implementation plan. So, let's break down one of the steps into tasks. As an example, I'll use my "brand colors" step.

Select brand colors:

1. Research the feelings of colors
2. Research the meanings and psychology of colors
3. Pick ten colors I like and see if they match the feelings and meanings I want to portray
4. Test the ten colors on Canva
5. Narrow down to five top colors
6. Test these colors on branding websites and see if I like the combo
7. Test how my pictures and shots look with my colors as background
8. Share with a test audience and make any adjustments
9. Upload branding colors into Canva
10. Change branding colors on platform or website

Now, repeat this for each step and milestone. I'm sure you can imagine that this exercise can become really long and complex if you have a big A to B like I did. At this point, you might want to think about using some sort of visual aid, like a whiteboard, a Gantt chart, calendars, or planners to help you organize and break it all down.

Then there's the other fallacy: the planner, the calendar, the app—*That's what will solve my problem.* Just because you have a hammer, it doesn't mean you know how to build a house. The same is true here. The tools work great if the plan is right, you know how to use it, and you have complete clarity. That's what all this is about: bringing clarity to the plan that builds your legacy. So, pick the tracking tool that you like and dedicate some time to it. The most important thing is that you're able to see it and revisit it.

I can tell you this: there's something about using some form of pen and paper method that's better, especially when you're just getting started. It feels good to write it down. It's somehow more real to see it in your own handwriting, and the kinesthetic motion of writing out the words imprints them more strongly in your mind and memory. An article in *Forbes*, "Neuroscience Explains Why You Need to Write Down Your Goals If You Actually Want to Achieve Them," goes further and explains how the neurological process helps with encoding the information in your brain, hence remembering it and labeling it as important long-term.[12]

There are tons of apps out there, and they're sexy, but, especially at first, learning to use the app can distract from the basic point. Experiment with a few methods and see what works best for you.

It's also important to say that this process of listing your tasks should start you thinking about efficiency and potential outsourcing. I knew that having a website would be an absolute necessity, but spending the time and energy to learn how to create my own wasn't worth it for me. I replaced "build website" with "hire a web developer/designer." You don't have to do it all by yourself.

Whatever you choose, just don't shelf it. Keep it close. Keep it visible. Look at it every day.

BONUS: Taking It One Step Further

WARNING: This will change your life.

This is for super high achievers, who want to take their organizational skills to the next level. Those impeccable beings, who love to thrive beyond the usual. Are you ready? Here we go!

Start with the "Now" Tasks

Start with the step and the set of tasks you want to work on *right now*. Take those steps and plot them out on your calendar, remembering that the related tasks are often spread over several months. If you're using a calendar app, be sure to allocate time to the tasks each week.

Note when you expect to complete each task *and* make sure you make a little time to celebrate in some small way. As you feel more comfortable, incorporate another step and its set of tasks into your calendar. Eventually, you'll map out your full set of goals, milestones, steps, and tasks.

List All the Demands

Here's what you'll quickly learn: the calendar works best when it acknowledges ALL the demands on your time—work, goals, kids, family, everything. Cue the questions (I know you've got some!).

How do I fit it all in? How do I prioritize? How do I keep all the other stuff from swallowing my goals? Are you sure I can do this?

This is where my method kicks in. It's the method I've developed and used every single day for years. It keeps me from feeling overwhelmed, keeps me focused, and keeps me moving forward. I have my "hot" and "cold" color coding strategies for aligning my time in my day, knowing when I can multitask and when I need to focus. That way, I know what tasks are essential, which can be postponed, and which can be outsourced. It's a lifesaver! It takes the overthinking out of my day and helps me stay productive in all the right places. It also stops me from multitasking when I need to devote time to focusing.

That feeling of being pulled in a thousand different directions is one that so many of us suffer from. The demands on our time are huge, and, as high achievers, we pile on even more. Creating an organizational system and a time plan based on moving you along your steps, milestones, and goals makes a tremendous difference.

WORK-LIFE INTEGRATION

A strategic time plan that brings together all the key spheres of your life is essential to achieving work-life integration. Beyond merely managing your schedule, it's about crafting a purposeful, balanced life that aligns with your personal and professional goals. By having your priorities clearly laid out and everything in your life mapped out, you create an environment where work and personal life aren't in constant battle for your time. Instead, they coexist harmoniously.

With this method, time blocks are not just meeting slots or work tasks. They also encompass personal time, family moments, relaxation, and self-care. By respecting these time blocks as you would a business appointment or work meeting, you're able to integrate your work demands with your life goals effectively. It's about giving equal importance to all facets of your life, ensuring that you're not only successful in your career but also nurturing your relationships, pursuing your passions, advancing your legacy, and maintaining your health.

When you're organized, you gain clarity and can make deliberate choices about what tasks deserve your attention and when. This helps prevent the feeling of being overwhelmed and reduces the risk of burnout. Time management, in this sense, isn't just a productivity tool. It's a strategy for living a fulfilling life in alignment with your purpose.

It wasn't until I met Erika Cramer, "The Queen of Confidence" and best-selling author of *Confidence Feels Like Sh*t*, that I shifted my language from work-life balance to integration. Erika is a mom of two, business entrepreneur, author, podcaster, among many other things. Despite running a highly successful organization, speaking on stage, and managing explosive professional growth, she never loses sight of her roots, her vision of helping women entrepreneurs, and the importance of her family.

When I interviewed her, I asked her what her secret was, and she frankly described her attitude toward work-life integration. Usually, when we hear people talk about the importance of work-life balance, that perspective assumes that work and life are two opposing forces and that it's a zero-sum game, where more of one means less of the other. Erika certainly doesn't see it like that. Instead, she sees it more like a large puzzle that all weaves together when you're congruent with who you are and you match your personality with the way you do business.

In our interview, Erika said:

"I think our world is out of balance, and we all want to have balance, but we don't have to take the all-or-nothing approach. We often think, *How can I be a great mom, the best mom in the whole world, and be a wife, and run a successful business?* We worry that if we have a great business, we'll neglect our kids. So, I like the idea of integration because I love my work and when you do the work you love, which, Esther, is what you talk about in your book, and you're doing your work on purpose, then you're on fire and on purpose at the same time.

"So, when I'm at work, it feels so strange for me to just cut off the work when I go home and step into the role of mother. I am the mother who runs my company. I'm also the wife who works with my husband. I am the businessperson who has clients, and I'm a daughter too. I am all of these parts, and they are all a part of me. And I think, as women, we're naturally multifaceted, multidimensional beings. We want to do all the things and honor all parts of our lives. I believe that we can be all the things *if* we learn to integrate them well.

"When you're in flow and you love what you do, work isn't work. With that said… it's still taking energy from you, and there's a fine line between giving and overgiving. Overgiving often ends in burnout. If I give myself to every part of my life and every person who asks for it, then I'll have nothing left. I'll become drained, exhausted. I think that's the dark side of overachieving. A lot of high achievers feel they have something to prove, and they often extend themselves beyond what's sustainable long-term."

"Truth is, you don't owe anyone any explanation, and they don't owe anything to you."

If you're going to go for the life of your dreams, achieve your legacy, live your purpose, and be on fire, you'll have to make some sacrifices. Some nights, you might get less sleep because you're up late writing your book. And you might let go of being the friend or family member who shows up to every gathering. But you also need to learn to sacrifice the opinions of others and let go of the naysayers in your life. From the outside, much of it sounds cute: follow your dreams, live your best life, and achieve your legacy. But then when you're in it, reality can feel like a slap. *Oh, like, this is hard. It's hard work.* That's why I think a lot of people don't hit their dreams—because they're not willing to prioritize and sacrifice. That's why it takes more than motivation or a day planner. You need a system and a strategy with a clear goal to keep you going when the sacrifices get tough.

Integration isn't always pretty, but it's not all sacrifice, hustle, and grind either. The ultimate way to work-life integration is to see it as a dance—awkward at first, lots of push and pull, and, eventually, a flow. I definitely don't have it all sorted either, but it's a dance that you need to practice every day. Integration is more achievable than "balance," because balance feels like we can never attain it. It's always an effort to keep life balanced and the moment you get it, something tips the scales, and life is off-balance again. The dance of work-life integration is more achievable—the push and pull is built in—and it's so much more fun!

For me, the ultimate embodiment of the work-life integration dance was shifting to remote work. This change didn't just make professional sense. It also allowed me to intertwine my personal and professional lives seamlessly. With Paul and I both working from home, our day-to-day interactions gained a new dimension. The mundane transformed into the memorable, from sharing spontaneous hugs and picking our music playlist for the day to sharing business ideas over our morning oatmeal. Before, when we worked in the same building and even on the same office floor, we barely saw each other because I never had time for lunch or a break. So, for us, this change was huge.

Our home became a playground for work and life, a place where we could participate in our kids' dance shows, take them to school, and pick them up. We weren't just parents who worked. We were working parents, who were fully present in our children's lives. In my case, the work-from-home model was ideal, allowing me to spend about 75 percent of my time at home and the remaining 25 percent traveling for work. This arrangement allowed me to be 100 percent present in whichever role I was in at any given time.

Beyond merely facilitating interaction with my family, remote work gave me the space to engage in self-care and exercise, critical for someone like me, who's prone to overwork. I realize that the perfect work-life integration formula might differ from person to person, and that's perfectly OK! The whole point of my method is that it's not a one-size-fits-all approach. Instead, it's a finely tailored strategy that aligns with you, your purpose, and what works best for *you*.

I propose that we all look at Work-Life Integration and strive to create a situation where your work aligns with your life purpose and path. Find the ways to integrate your work into the set of activities that add value and joy to your life.

Valuing Yourself and Your Time

I've never liked the phrase, "You need to make time." Some of my clients, after working with me, think I must be some kind of magician, but I'm sorry to say that I can't literally create time. Nobody can. As you start to go through your tasks and add them to your calendar, you'll soon find out that even the smallest movements mean that something has to give. "Making time" really means making choices about your time.

I like to think about it like remodeling a house. You've realized that your house's style and decor aren't what you want anymore. Do you just buy all new stuff and add it in with what you already have? Of course not. That would make the problem so much worse. You'd have no space and no style at all. You have to clear out some of the old stuff first. But do you just get rid of everything you had and start from zero? I doubt it. Some of those things, you still love.

They appeal to you. So, you figure out what's working and what's not, get rid of the things that don't match or align with the new design, and keep the things that have meaning and value. But the key lesson is this: you *must* get rid of stuff!

Working with your time is the same. I know your "time house" is already packed, and adding more "furniture" will just bring chaos. So, first you need to know what you've got to get rid of. Let's start with what you wrote under "what you want people to stop seeking you for." This is your first indication of what needs to stop happening in your life. Now, you don't have to do it overnight, but you do need to start deciding what you want to start limiting and putting boundaries on.

You may ask, "What's the difference between a limit and a boundary?" I'll try my best to explain: a limit is a rule or restriction that an individual places to manage themselves (internal), and a boundary is the emotional and physical limits they place on others to protect themselves from being overwhelmed or to make more time for themselves (external). A limit is a mental line that you commit to not crossing. A boundary is a "fence" that you put up to protect yourself and to adjust the behaviors of others. Both are essential in bringing balance to your life, helping you build the mindset that keeps you moving forward, and creating in others a set of expectations about you that differ from what they're used to.

If, for example, you decide that you're no longer going to engage in gossip, only positive conversation that uplifts people, that's your limit. It's a line that you decide for yourself that you will not cross. If you start gently turning down requests from family and friends to plan their events or organize their travel, that's your boundary. It's retraining others to have a different expectation of what you will and won't do. At first, you may get pushback and even hurt the feelings of those around you—you're acting differently from what they expect, and change is hard. But, over time, you'll see that limits and boundaries help create new and clearer expectations, and others will learn to have more respect for your time and your skills. It all boils down to expectations.

Good boundaries are really important for making progress toward your legacy and purpose. You can't be everything for everyone and do everything for everyone all at the same time. Take a moment to let that soak in. And here, you might be confused. "Wait, Esther, I thought you said, 'You can have it all.'"

Yes, you can have *it* all. But *it* is what's aligned with you and your purpose. *It* does NOT include everything that you never wanted or were only doing out of obligation.

I'm not saying that you can always eliminate 100 percent of the things you don't want to do. This part of the program is about valuing yourself and being intentional with your time. Some of your time will necessarily be devoted to the mundane, the routine, and to things that advance the objectives of another person or organization. Valuing your time means containing the time that doesn't serve you and creating systems to make sure time for other people doesn't completely swallow up that which you need for you and your goals.

I have a couple of time rules that help: the 50/50 Rule and the 10/10 Rule.

50/50 and 10/10—Two Rules That Change the Game

When I work with clients in business or large organizations, I have them incorporate the 50/50 rule at work. It means that at least half of your job should be aligned with you and your skill set (that is, it supports the skills or what you want to be sought out for in your Purpose Sun). The other half should be activities that help push and promote the group's or team's mission and purpose.

Good application of the 50/50 rule helps you enjoy and appreciate your job more, as you see how aspects of your work incorporate the skills and activities that are meaningful to you. At the same time, you'll have an awareness of where the other 50 percent of your time is going. The 50/50 rule can also apply to your homelife. You should aim to spend 50 percent of your time on things that have to get done at home (for example, cleaning, laundry, errands), but the other 50 percent should go toward building relationships, spending time with loved ones, and so on.

If we dissect this one level further, there's the 10/10 rule, which states that at least 10 percent of your personal time and 10 percent of your professional time should be about advancing your goals. This translates to about 1–2 hours per day. So, included in the four hours of your work time that's aligned to you and your skills (50/50 rule), 45 minutes to an hour needs to help you move toward your own big goals (10/10 rule). The difference between the 50/50 and 10/10 rule matters a lot.

Let's take a look at the 50/50 and 10/10 rules in action.

Bianca had a master's degree in chemistry and worked for a huge corporation. She led a team, headed up the innovation section, and traveled for work often. She was all about the science and loved her job but lately had been feeling disconnected, focusing too much on the lab and not enough on people. Bianca also had a soft spot for her artsy side. She grew up reading books by Isabel Allende that blend magic into everyday life, and becoming a published writer played a big part in Bianca's Purpose Sun and legacy.

When she crafted her 50/50, she specifically added things that she wanted to be sought out for. Bianca decided to start collaborating with the public outreach team at work, which generated articles and sponsored public events. In doing so, she was able to carve out more face time with colleagues and found fun ways to talk about new medicines as "curative spells" and compared new nanotechnology-based materials to the hardness of dragon scales. Great! That helped fill her purpose cup at work, but how did she advance her goal of becoming a writer?

Bianca enrolled in an online creative writing course. At first, it was just a two-hour commitment every week, not quite her 10/10, but it was a really important start. She knew that her improved writing would help with strategic communications, while building toward her goal of becoming a published writer. Bianca's 50/50 aligned her to her purpose every day, and her 10/10 helped make gradual progress on her legacy goals. It doesn't have to be perfect. The key is to start being intentional about how you use your time.

See table.

Figure 1: Application to Work - Bianca (Chemist in Corporation)

** Highlighted is the 10 percent that's tied to advancing professional development goals*

50% tied to what you want to be sought out for at work	Generating articles	Public events	Innovation	Strategic communications	Collaboration and networking
50% tied to job description	Management	Research	Technical writing	Quality control	Experiments

Now, you may be saying to yourself, *That's a lot of math to sort out and in so much detail.* But let's face it—if you don't budget the time and explicitly put it in there, it won't happen. We have birthday parties, homework, car repairs, sick parents, sports, and sometimes life just gets in the way. Creating balance means that we have to be intentional and prioritize our time. You have to manage your life and time with the larger goal in mind. This means you have to create boundaries. You must say no to things that don't serve you. When people nag you about the things you don't want to be sought out for, you need a system that helps you not just say "fine" and give in. I actually sometimes show people a screenshot of my time-blocked calendar. "As you can see, my time is completely programmed. Maybe I can find you a one-hour slot in a couple of weeks."

Why Limits and Boundaries Matter

Recently, I was asked if I thought that a four-day workweek would solve work-life balance and employee burnout. Overall, no! I can see how a four-day workweek would help people create a stronger division between work time and non-work time. Plus, an additional day off could help parents recharge a bit. But without prioritization, time rules, and a clear purpose to guide direction, people will continue to spin, procrastinate, and make no real changes. A darker view suggests that a four-day workweek also opens the possibility for more stress at work, as deadlines are compressed and the shorter week serves to grind employees harder from Monday to Thursday.

Rather than sticking to a rigid schedule, I champion the concept of core hours and core days. For example, expecting people to be in the office and interact with colleagues from Tuesday to Thursday allows employees to balance focused work with other obligations. At the same time, I don't buy into the idea of a one-size-fits-all approach. If one person is more productive in the early morning and another thrives in the evening, and if neither of them need to be in public-facing roles, why not tailor a schedule to suit their individual needs? We often set up these rigid boundaries but when we boil it down, it's all based on the perception that someone's not pulling their weight and the fear that expectations aren't being met. The solution? Lay out clear expectations and keep moving forward.

As I've mentioned, my approach isn't necessarily one where I'll tell you to slow down or work less. I can guarantee you that now—fulfilled, aligned, and thriving—I work harder than I ever did before. But I'm working for me, furthering my own goals, on my own terms. And that makes all the difference.

My high achieving clients don't want to slow down. They want their hustle to have meaning.

Boundaries and limits are even more important for high achievers because they provide balance and structure in their lives. They provide clarity on and expectations about what behaviors are appropriate for themselves and others. Limits and boundaries help prevent burnout, stress, overwhelm, loss of self, and promote happiness and productivity. They help high achievers prioritize time and energy, making time for themselves and their growth. They also reduce overall resentment and increase RESPECT from others, one of the major pain points for high achievers, because they show discipline, responsibility, and, above all, truth to self.

As I mentioned earlier, us high achievers tend to have this crazy FOMO (fear of missing out). We just can't bear the thought of missing out on any opportunities. We feel like every little thing, whether it's an outing, an event, or anything at all, could be a chance to make connections or achieve something great. We have this belief that if we skip out on something, we'll be kicking ourselves for missing out on a chance to grow and achieve.

That FOMO is what drives us to pack our schedules like there's no tomorrow. We don't even stop to think if the invitation or outing is really aligned with what we want or if it'll actually lead to the growth we're looking for. We just go all in and stretch ourselves thin. But you know what? That's where setting limits comes in handy.

Believe it or not, even the things we love and find exciting need to be limited. I know it sounds crazy, but focusing on just a few things is actually the fastest way to success. As I'm writing this book, for example, I had to say no to an amazing weekend getaway. But don't worry, I've got a plan to take a break once this is all done. That's why having a strategy and a long-term plan is so important. Don't be afraid to spread things out and give yourself some breathing room. It'll keep you balanced, prevent burnout, and help you make the most of each opportunity without getting overwhelmed by FOMO.

Just because you miss out on it now, it does not mean you are missing out on it forever.

Delays are not denials. You're hopefully starting to see that a big part of living a life with balance and integration comes down to regulating your thoughts and your reactions to others. This is one of the hardest things to do, and it's why we need rules like 50/50 and a clear idea of the limits and boundaries that serve us. Let me give you some examples.

I love party planning, and I'm great at it. Amazing, actually. Weddings, bachelorette parties, baby showers, birthdays, work celebrations, VIP events, huge corporate events. I go all out, and I love being the master of ceremonies. So, you can imagine how often I get pinged for that sort of thing. It got to the point where it was taking too much time away from working on me and my legacy.

I decided to put a limit on personal events. It was something internal in me and something I wanted people to stop seeking me for. But it wasn't easy. I had created an expectation, and people kept asking me to organize and host events. But I realized that these activities, as much as I love doing them, no longer served my purpose. Very often, the things you have to limit are things you like but aren't really good for you. Limits are self-regulation, and boundaries are self-defense.

Another example is limiting the amount of social media scrolling you do to avoid comparison and negative thoughts. It could also mean literally using a timer to limit the amount of time you spend overthinking in certain situations.

Boundaries, on the other hand, are restrictions you place on things you dislike or hate. In terms of boundaries, people expected me to do their administrative work. "Can you call my doctor?" "Can you schedule my oil change?" "Can you order something for me from Amazon?" "Can you find me a cheap ticket?" These tasks, I did not love at all. They weren't listed as a positive anywhere on my Purpose Sun, but there was a lot of external pressure to do them. I don't know how common it is across cultures but in my Latino, immigrant household, I handled household responsibilities from a very early age, and the expectation that I would always do those things never went away. This expectation translated to all my circles. Even though I lived in different states, different time zones, and different countries from those who wanted my help, the expectation was still there.

So, I knew I had to put a strict boundary around administrative tasks for others. I also had to decide if I would stop completely or allow it sometimes. If I decided to allow it, what would that look like? One task per week? Per month? How long would I allow? Ten minutes? One hour? While my limit on personal party planning was a strict line I wouldn't cross, my boundary on administrative tasks was more like a fence. I had to decide where to put my fence, how tall it would be, and if there would be a door to let some things in. I decided that I would limit administrative requests to one hour per week. This was outside my own responsibilities in my home. The first step is identifying your own limits and then moving to boundaries.

"Never push your purpose aside—stay resilient!"

Setting Limits, Placing Boundaries, and Dealing with Pushback

The exercise of setting limits and boundaries is going to feel uncomfortable at first. The process of moving from what people seek you for now to what people will seek you for later is going to be hard in the beginning. Humans are habit oriented. Others will want to reach out to you for what they feel comfortable with. At the same time, humans can be conditioned. So, little by little, people will learn that you don't want to do certain things anymore. What you have to remember is to use your purpose as your guide. Remember the list you made of things you want to be sought out for—the highlighted green ones? Time to bring it out and use it as your guide.

OK, so how do you express a limit and a boundary? It starts with setting clear expectations. Let's use another example: you constantly get asked to organize all the fundraisers—work, kids, school, charities, everybody.

Limit

"After this next fundraiser, I'll no longer volunteer for any fundraisers."

It sounds simple, but this will be a big change for others. How do you let them know about your limit? Your communication tools will be really important.

How to communicate and set clear expectations

You: "I just wanted to let you know I won't be able to organize any more fundraisers after this fundraiser."

Person X: "Oh no, why? You're amazing at it."

You: "I've been really reflecting on my life, and I'm starting to make more time for (fill in the blank)."

Person X: "Bummer, you really were the best at it."

You: "Yeah, but what's cool is I'm making time for some big things coming up in my life."

Remember, the "fill in the blank" has to come from your purpose!

Now, if the person starts super pressuring you, you'll need to set a boundary. So, let's continue the conversation by setting a boundary.

Person X: "Well, again, this sucks because we really need you. Can't you give up something else?"

You (putting a boundary): "It means so much that you value me in that space. Seriously, it means so much coming from you (if you

mean it). But that will be my last one. Let me know if you ever want to hear about my new initiatives (you could offer to help find a replacement if you want, but it's not required)."
Person X: "Cool, of course."

Now, let's do that again with putting a boundary and still getting pushback.

Person X: "But hey, quick question—will you at least come to all of the events?"
You (knowing you can't because they will guilt you into fundraising): "I really can't."
Person X: "But why not? Are you saying you won't even come to support us? What do you have to do that's so important?"

Let's stop here for a moment. The tendency—more evident with women—is the need and desire to explain the why. We want to explain why because we don't want to hurt the other person's feelings, and we feel guilty for letting them down. We also value the relationship with them and have this belief that if we're not there for them, we'll lose it. We attach value to our act rather than ourselves. We also feel this enormous responsibility (revisit the people-pleasing section if needed) to others and feel that if we say no, we're not "reliable." But there's more to this...

You also want the why. As high achievers, we feel that everything is our fault and our responsibility. We want to know why people cancel on us or set boundaries because we want to know it's not us. We want that external reassurance because it's how we're used to determining our worth and since we want and expect this ourselves, we also provide it to others. Truth is, you don't owe anyone any explanation, and they don't owe anything to you. They may just be tired. They may be juggling a lot of different things. They may just want to rest. There could be 1001 reasons. Also, the reason they give you if you request one may not even be honest. I say this because in addition to practicing giving no explanations, you can't expect them to either. In the end, it's not the explanation that we're really looking for or that they are looking for. It's the reassurance that they are valued and important. Let's continue with the example.

You (resisting the urge to explain the 101 reasons why and instead, more effectively, going to the root of why they want to know why): "You know that's not true. I truly value my relationship with you and the rest of the team, and I'll definitely miss you all. I can't wait to see the pictures and hear all about it. I'll be there in spirit."

Person X: "OK, we'll miss you there."

Note: never say sorry or apologize for your boundaries and limits. You've done nothing wrong.

The Truth About Saying "No"

Let's start with a game of true or false.

True or False?

Saying no is unkind.

False.

Truth:

1. Saying no is being honest.
2. There's nothing worse than doing something you don't want to do and the other person believing that you do want to do it.
3. You can say no in a kind way.

Saying "no" is often misconstrued as rudeness or indifference, when, in reality, it's an act of kindness, not only to others but to ourselves as well. It sets clear boundaries and respects our own time, energy, and capacities, preventing us from overextending ourselves, which can lead to burnout or resentment. Moreover, when we say "no" to tasks or requests that aren't aligned with our purpose or priorities, we make room to say "yes" to those that are, directing our energy to the people and activities that mean the most to us. At the same time, it gives others the opportunity to step up, learn, and grow. This may seem like a rationalization, but, as high achievers, we too often take responsibility away from others and make them dependent on us. Therefore, a well-placed "no" can serve as a catalyst for personal growth and foster better relationships based on understanding and mutual respect, the building blocks of kindness.

Let's unpack with an example of what I mean by an opportunity for others to step up:

Your partner needs an appointment today, but you only have time to deal with scheduling on Friday. You want to say no but also set the expectation of the days and times you can do these things. You want him to either step up or respect your time bounds. You're communicating via text.

Partner: Can you make an appointment today (Monday) for our car and medical?

You: Baby, (whatever form of endearment), great idea—we do need to make those medical and car repair appointments. I'm so glad you remember these things. I take care of all appointments on Fridays after 12 p.m. because you know how it is—they keep us on hold for hours, and I found these are the best times to reach people. You're much more up to speed on the urgency of these things. If you think we need it before then, do you think you can do it for us? I would really appreciate it. I'll give you access to that calendar where I put all the appointments (or things) we have to schedule. I'm also happy to put it in the Friday slot so we can manage together :) I'm so happy we're in this together.

Response: Cool, I can't wait until Friday, so I'll just go ahead and call.

As people pleasers, we think we're being nice by taking everything on and being there for everyone. The thing is, saying yes to something you don't want to do is really dishonest. Imagine you have a friend who goes with you to yoga class every Saturday. You see it as this great moment, where you both grab a coffee, chat, and exercise. You think she enjoys it too. Imagine if she never really liked it and was only doing it because she felt obligated to and couldn't say no. It taints the experience. It would be better if she said she could no longer go and you found another girlfriend who *actually* loved it as much as you do. Or maybe you could find another activity that you both love. Either way, knowing that she had hidden her true feelings all along would be hurtful.

You have to flip that switch in your brain and know that saying yes to something you don't want to do is unkind, and saying no is honest. It's more about the delivery and setting clear expectations than actually saying no.

We often feel that we can't say no because we fear the other person's reaction or fear they'll stop liking or accepting us. But reality is, it's not saying no that they're upset about. It's the delivery, the lack of transition, and the unexpectedness of the answer. For example, most people pleasers reach a moment in their lives where the people-pleasing gets to be too much, and they explode. The other person is taken aback and tends to have a forceful, negative response. The people pleaser then retreats, thinking that if they ever say no, the other person will unfriend them or explode.

Let's revisit Katia's dog sitting example we discussed earlier.

Frank: "I need you to dog sit this weekend."

Katia: "I'm not sure."

Frank: "I really need this."

Katia: "Again, I'm not sure."

Frank: "Come on, I need you to do this."

Katia *(exploding!):* "No, I can't, and, actually, I've always hated it."

Frank: "WTF, I can't believe you."

(FIGHT!)

Now… let's analyze this. Katia got pushed too far and exploded. The ugliness at the end didn't happen because she said no but, rather, because of how she communicated it. The other person was taken aback and super confused. Remember, everybody believed that Katia *loved* dog sitting. Either way, it's not because Katia said no. It's because she changed expectations without any preparation. People need time to learn that behaviors and expectations should be expressed *before* the ask.

Katia's position is tough too. Frank is someone she cares about, and she doesn't want to hurt or disappoint him. Thinking about having to say no when he asks causes her anxiety and sets her on a cycle of rumination and foreshadowing conversations and scenarios. But, if anything, this highlights the importance of setting those limits and boundaries. They help you craft tactics to preempt the situations that could cause explosions like you just saw between Katia and Frank.

Let's do this again. This time, Katia expresses the boundary *before* Frank requests the dog sitting. Katia sets the expectation up front. Note, Frank has not asked for a dog sitting yet but will soon.

Katia (over coffee): "Oh, guess what? I decided to start taking cooking classes. I wanted to let you know that I won't be able to dog sit anymore."

Frank: "Oh no, for real?"

Katia: "Yeah, with this new thing, I won't be able to do it anymore but would love to come over sometimes and visit Doggie Nico."

Frank: "Ah, man, you were the best, but thanks for letting me know. I'll have to find someone else. Are you really sure?"

Katia: "Yeah, I'm sure…"

NOTE: I highly recommend that if you struggle a lot with boundaries and limits to first seek a therapist to understand the root causes of why you're struggling with these things. HINT: most of the time, it's linked to your personal history, childhood, and story. After working with a therapist, you can bring this information to a coach like me, and we can write scripts and stick Post-its all over your wall to help you enforce your boundaries. Just like anything, with practice, you will get better.

It's YOUR Turn to Set Some Limits and Boundaries

OK, we spent a long time on boundaries and limits. But it was important to do so because to make more time for your purpose and your legacy, you'll need to create limits and boundaries, while minimizing feelings of guilt and self-doubt. Your eye has to clearly see your purpose and inner compass at all times.

Now, the examples discussed also apply to your job and relationships. You may be doing WAY too much in your job and need to examine your role there. It may mean changing positions within the same organization, finding another job, or starting to set boundaries little by little. The same goes for your personal life, with your parents, children, siblings, friends, and so on. You may need to examine your workload in your job *and* in your home. Are there adjustments you can make to reduce high-functioning anxiety or stress and make living your legacy easier? What are the other things you need to do to prioritize your purpose?

After you've cleaned your house, so to speak, I recommend that you do a complete audit on your time. You can use popular apps like Clockify, other technology tools, or even just pen and paper. What matters is that you track everything: requests you get via messages, calls, emails, what you're doing with your full day. It seems like a lot, but you and I both know you've done it with your diet. You've counted calories and meticulously inputted everything you ate and drank, maybe lying to yourself a little on portion sizes. Think of this time audit like tracking your time snacks—the things you hadn't accounted for that are still taking up time. You're tracking EVERYTHING. Once you've completed your audit, is there anything else you need to adjust? This is kind of like the final sweep in your redesigned home before you bring in your new furniture.

In my case, strangely, one thing I needed was a time zone tracker. I was wasting a lot of time figuring out time zones for meetings and finding meeting times for coworkers and clients around the world. I was seriously wasting an hour a day stressing about it. I finally created my own manual time zone calculator that I could refer to every day, especially when I traveled to Asia and Africa. I also found World Time Buddy, a website that helps me put all the times in one place. The tool helped me avoid living in constant confusion. Also, when I traveled to Europe with my kids during the summer, I decided to work the same hours as the U.S. I wanted to have time with my kids in the morning, which is something I love, and I didn't have to worry about struggling to find call times. This tweak freed up an hour of my time and also gave me more time for things I loved.

The idea is to be living your purpose and seeing the world through that lens every day, whether by working on it constantly or living it through certain elements. So, tweak what you need to tweak—you'll be surprised by what else you find.

This leads us nicely to the E in POWER.

ENJOYMENT

The last thing I want your Purpose Sun to be is one more thing to stress about or convert to a chase. You should feel energized, focused, relaxed, and at peace when you're working on your purpose. It should rejuvenate and reenergize you. It should feel amazing, and you should feel centered. Does this mean it will be easy? No, it will be tough at first. It will test you and stretch you, especially if the gap from A to B is big. Remembering and re-centering will be a daily practice. Thus, it's so important to incorporate and schedule enjoyment. I mean this beyond the things that you love!

I want you to keep a celebration calendar or chart and make sure it's always visible. On this, you'll write down and celebrate all your milestones toward making your legacy a reality and how you've lived it in your every day. You have to acknowledge progress and not let it go by. If you don't take these moments to pause, reflect, and give yourself some kudos, you'll feel like you've never stopped. You have to stop and acknowledge your milestones so you can see your progress and maintain motivation and momentum to keep going. Although we often forget to celebrate ourselves, we're quick to criticize and be harsh on ourselves. Stopping to celebrate helps balance the negative thoughts and, when self-doubt creeps in, reminds you that you've come far.

Keep to Your Intention

Further, I want you to take it to the next level and add another celebration: keeping to your intention. My favorite way to do this is to pick a word every year—and I don't mean a New Year's resolution. You may ask, "Why not a New Year's resolution?" Easy—resolutions often become just another item on our achievement checklist, potentially leading to stress and disappointment. Also, remember what I said before: we overestimate what we can achieve in one year. Instead, selecting a single word as your guide for the year allows for a more flexible, inspiring, and personal journey of growth. This word sets the intention for the year. If you go back to my purpose, for example, the year before leaving my job, I chose "courage." I tracked all the little actions that were tied to living my purpose and that led to me having that courage. The next year, I selected "freedom." I tracked how I lived my freedom every day. If you don't have a word, pick one. Pick one that sets your intention for the year and is tied to your purpose and legacy. Chart it, write it on your bathroom mirror, and celebrate it.

By charting your intention, you'll see all the progress you've made that year. You can revisit it when you have self-doubt and see how far you've come. You'll see how your small tasks led to steps, then to milestones, and then to goals. I want you to have in mind how you'll celebrate. Visualize it! Commit to it. We need these pumps to keep us going. For example, as I write this book, I'm planning to visit Japan, South Korea, Australia, and Fiji when I finish it. This book is a huge milestone for me, and I want the celebration to match the significance. It's my reward and celebration.

Celebrate Good Times!

We need those boosts of dopamine in our brains to neutralize negative thoughts. I encourage you to visit your celebration calendar or chart every day, every week, every month, every quarter, and then again at the end of the year to see how far you've come. It's worth noting that I did something similar to this with annual employee reviews when I was managing a large team. We would set their goals and identify milestones and the necessary steps to accomplish them. At our regular meetings throughout the year, we were sure to highlight and celebrate progress, and the big review at the end of the year became so much easier because we had been tracking successes all along.

It's also worth saying that your celebrations don't have to all be trips to Fiji! On the contrary, celebrate every piece of progress along the way. You learned how to make a logo on Canva? Take yourself out for coffee. You made a huge breakthrough in understanding your purpose and legacy? Take a quick trip to the beach with the kids. You get the point. Incorporate celebration and make it part of the journey every day.

This will train your brain to be positive, to reward, and to view your journey as outcomes rather than tasks.

You'll see changes in how you view yourself, your confidence, the way you interview for jobs, how you show up, and more. Let me celebrate along with you.

- Tag me **#beactchange** in your celebrations, and I will cheer you on.

"Dime con quién andas y
te digo quien eres."

Schedule Fun, Rest, and Relaxation

Lastly, schedule those vacations and find time for the things you love. Schedule them and make them your intention in your planning. As high achievers, we need rest, and we need to take breaks. And it's never too early to plan them. I actually plan my vacations for the year in January. Advance planning sets clear boundaries and limits with my employers and clients and communicates clear understanding of when I'll be out. Did you know that breaks make you more able to problem solve and be creative? Breaks actually make you more productive. Same with vacations. And if you find yourself on vacation, taking 2–3 days just to unwind before you can actually start enjoying yourself, that's a sign that something is unbalanced (revisit W). Take the break, the vacation, and celebrate. Your body and mind need it so you can create the life you desire.

Adding to that, embracing more enjoyment in your life not only elevates your personal happiness, but it also significantly influences those around you. Take, for example, the transformation in my relationship with my daughter. Following my decision to quit my job and move toward a lifestyle more aligned with my purpose, the positive impact on her was immediate and profound.

A few months later, she made an impassioned post on my Instagram, inspiring others to pursue their dreams just as I had. This was a significant shift for her. Before, she had felt like she was lacking a present and attentive mother, which left her feeling lonely and abandoned. Now, with my newfound happiness and availability, she felt loved and safe. She was so moved by this transformation that she felt compelled to share the importance of happiness and fulfillment with others.

Every day, she expresses her joy that we transitioned from our big house to our smaller apartment, purely because it resulted in me being happier. Her happiness blossomed in response to my own, affirming that there's no price tag on such profound emotional well-being. This ripple effect of positivity is one of the many priceless outcomes of aligning your life with your true purpose and passions. Paul and Maximo would agree the same happened to them…

Now onto the final letter in POWER: R.

RESILIENCE

R is what makes POWER the word it is, and it's one of the most important letters in the entire POWER sequence. The R reflects the realities of life. Life happens. Our loved ones get sick, spouses lose their jobs, kids struggle, divorce, house repairs—the list goes on.

Shit hits the fan.

This type of stress starts to cloud our brains, to the exclusion of all else. For many people, the instinctive reaction is to want to create a "safe" life, one manufactured to avoid the downturns of existence. I think this is a really difficult way to live, always worrying about what might happen and, as a consequence, missing out on so much good that the world has to offer. Plus, as the saying goes, you make plans, and the universe laughs. Reality happens. Resilience is how you react to the inevitable ups and downs that will come your way.

Stress Is the Enemy of Resilience

It reminds me of when I was giving a workshop and a participant, Mia, was so stressed that she couldn't think clearly. Mia was plagued by doubts about her career path, financial future, and personal abilities. She worried about finding the right job, and fears of being "too old" or "not prepared enough" were gnawing at her, day and night. These thoughts chipped away at Mia's resilience by leaving her more vulnerable to adversity. Any small hurdle would knock her down, and Mia's lack of resilience had become a major roadblock.

Chronic stress affects our mental processes, reinforcing the limiting beliefs that we fill our heads with and damaging our ability to bounce back and keep moving forward. This lack of resilience makes it really easy for us to lose sight of what's important and our purpose. Thus, it's so important to have systems in place to manage "life as it happens." The goal is to keep moving forward, even in times of chaos. This is how we keep ourselves in the sphere of a growth mindset and out of the fixed mindset. A limited ability to show resilience in the face of adversity is one of the key features of the fixed mindset, generally stemming from the perception that failure is inherent to you and not something over which you have control.

Have Your Tool Kit Ready

So, how do we develop resilience? For this, let's revisit your Purpose Sun. Do you see that section titled "What you have overcome"? Well, guess what? Those are things you will be constantly overcoming. The things you listed there are the things that will always hold you back and get in your way. But there's some good news: what you filled out right next to it in the "What has helped you" section is your tool kit.

Let me give you an example. Marco suffered greatly from self-doubt, and he listed it as one of the things he had overcome and had to keep overcoming. The one thing that helped him through his years was reading books, particularly about inspirational individuals. So, as part of his resilience plan, we made sure that we included reading as part of his daily routine, either when he went to bed, got up, or both. This helped keep Marco's mind from wandering into the negative and gave him that extra boost he needed every day.

We could also use one of the examples from my Purpose Sun, where I listed depression as something I'm constantly overcoming. One of the things that has always helped me is reminding myself of the impact I've had on others and how I've helped them find or live their purposes. Thus, every day when I wake up, I read my testimonials. I have them in a folder. I also have them in my Instagram highlights so they're easy to access. This sets my day on a positive note and reminds me why I'm on this planet. You've seen how my sixteen-year-old self reacted to depression and darkness, and I don't plan to ever go back to that place. My tool kit helps give me perspective and keeps me positive and focused on what matters.

That's the thing—we have our tool kits already. We have the things that have worked before. The mistake we make is believing that we only needed them once or that we only bring them out when we're already in crisis. Instead, if we incorporate elements of our tool kits into our daily routines, we can be more resilient and have the ability to bounce back and recover easily from change or adversity. Think about how you incorporate the things from your Purpose Sun in your everyday life and how, by doing that, you can avoid ever spiraling into a crisis, even when life gets chaotic.

The resilience part of the Purpose Sun is one of its most unique features and one that most other purpose methods tend to ignore or minimize. It's not just about the things you love, can get paid for, what the world needs, and what you're good at. It also goes into the deeper levels relating to how you overcome adversity and solve problems. It's what high achievers and all of us need. Let's face it—

it's part of you and your legacy. It's what you apply to your everyday life and what you need to make your goals a reality. It's also what makes you YOU.

The Complicated Relationship Between Resilience and Vulnerability

Resilience represents our ability to adapt and bounce back from adversities, to regain our balance after life has knocked us down. We should also discuss vulnerability, which Brené Brown describes as "uncertainty, risk, and emotional exposure."[13] When you're resilient, you acknowledge the hardship and then draw on your internal resources to return to your path as quickly as possible. Resilience doesn't negate vulnerability but, rather, complements it. Being resilient doesn't mean avoiding vulnerability. Instead, it means embracing it, using the lessons learned from those moments of openness to inform our growth and then finding our way back to the path we've forged for ourselves. In essence, resilience is the antidote to the destabilizing forces that vulnerability might invite, and, together, they form a crucial part of our emotional well-being.

Understanding the distinction between reducing vulnerability and strengthening resilience is crucial, and this is something Paul and I have often emphasized in the realm of international development. Reducing vulnerability, whether it pertains to climate change, education, or employment, involves creating a safe, steady trajectory that allows for continued progress and is impervious to disruptions—be they natural disasters, political changes, or otherwise. This approach is particularly necessary in regions of high turmoil or uncertainty. It not only prevents substantial losses but also ensures stability. However, this focus on stability comes at the expense of significant growth or major successes. Being invulnerable means you stick to your predefined path, nothing more, nothing less.

You've certainly come across people whose life plans are based on reducing vulnerability. They don't travel. They don't take risks. They stick to the plan, and they don't rock the boat. But guess what? Life happens to them too. Fearing the worst, they've missed out on following their purpose and living their legacy—but you can't hide forever. The resilience approach acknowledges the ups and downs and prepares you for them.

Strengthening resilience aims to boost our capacity to rebound quickly and effectively from substantial setbacks. This approach involves creating systems to reduce the time it takes to bounce back after a fall. A big part of this is setting up contingency plans for the scenarios you fear. These are a series of if-then statements: If X bad thing happens, then I will engage Y solution. If I fail to enforce one of my limits, then I will call my coach to help with new strategies. If I start losing Instagram followers, then I will conduct a performance analysis to pivot my approaches. Rather than beating yourself up, your resilience planning will put you immediately on the path back to growth when you experience adversity and, as you look forward, will help you be more inclined to take positive risks.

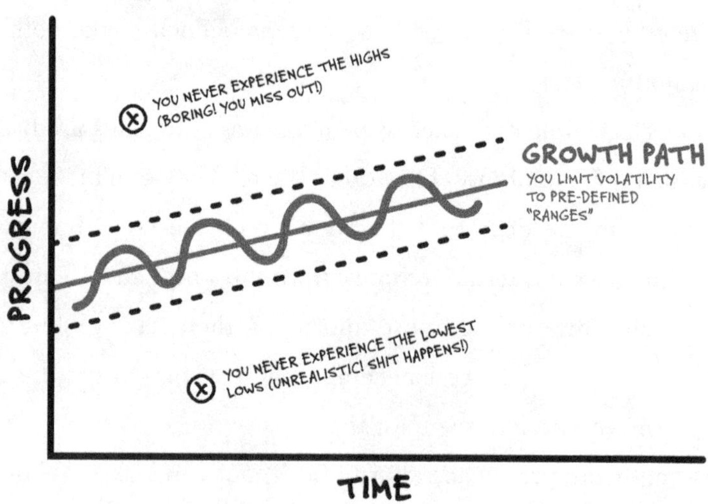

The "reducing vulnerability" approach attempts to limit volatility or risk by defining "acceptable" fluctuation and making every effort to stay within those predefined limits. This approach stems fundamentally from a desire to avoid the lows but has the side effect of also preventing episodes of high growth. A focus on reducing vulnerability also rather unrealistically assumes that the predefined limits are completely enforceable, but, in reality, unexpected and unanticipated shocks occur. You can never completely eliminate the likelihood of adverse shocks.

STRENGTHENING RESILIENCE

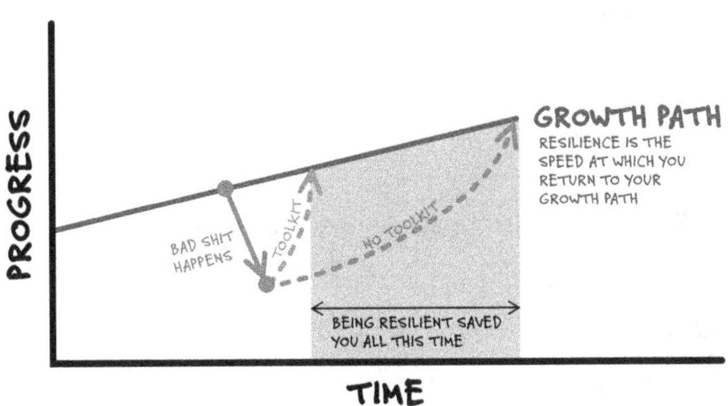

The "strengthening resilience" approach instead assumes that adverse shocks will occur and focuses instead on crafting a tool kit that returns you to a positive growth path as quickly as possible. In the absence of the resilience tool kit, it takes much longer to return to the growth path.

FLEXIBLE RESILIENCE

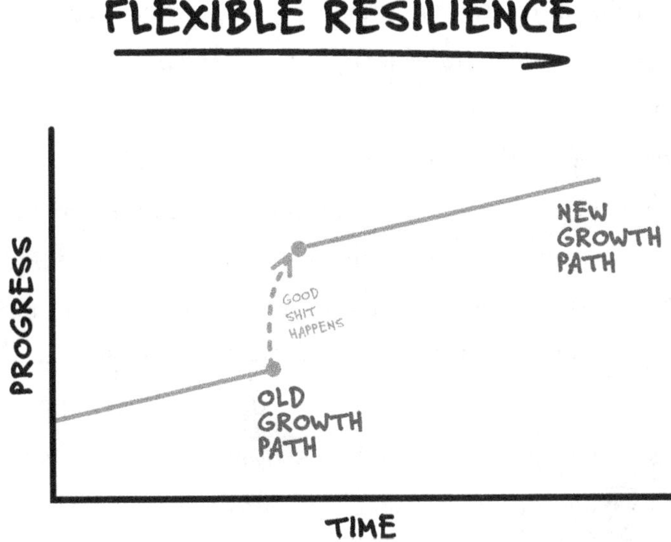

The resilience approach also grants the flexibility to take advantage of positive shocks by shifting to a new and higher growth path, something explicitly not allowed in the "reducing vulnerability" approach.

Never Push Your Purpose Aside—Stay Resilient!

I can tell you how resilience, focus, and purpose helped me during a crisis. During the summer of 2022, I took my entire family, including my parents, on a trip to Europe. Seeing my parents getting older, I felt a deep desire to take them on a trip, to really soak up some quality time together. It was one of the best things about being a remote contractor and entrepreneur. I had flexibility in my schedule, could travel with my family, and was able to work at night after touring different cities. It was amazing. My parents were going to return back to the U.S. sooner than us, while we were going to continue traveling with the kids. A week before my parents were scheduled to travel back, my dad started to feel sluggish and not himself. We thought he was just tired, so we didn't think too much about it.

Suddenly, Dad got really ill on a flight to Lisbon. He almost died on us, going full-on septic. We had to rush him to the emergency room and because of the episode, his memory was affected. It was very scary and super stressful, and I was really worried for him. We had to figure out how to help him, while also dealing with my stressed-out mom, bored kids, travel insurance, doctors, and hospitals, all in a foreign language. Luckily, Paul is fluent in Portuguese. On top of all that, we had to keep my extended family informed. Oh, and I still needed to get the work done that I was hired to do. We were all tired and worried, and I had to dig deep to not let it drag me down. I had to rely on my resilience.

It would have been super easy to get caught up in this chaos and the added stress. It would have been easy to put my purpose on the back burner through this whole thing. For me, I knew two things: one, working on my purpose brings me calm and focus, and two, sticking to my calendar is one of the strongest tools in my resilience tool kit. No matter how bad the situation was getting, sitting and drowning in it would have been the worst thing to do. Instead, I pulled out my calendar, scheduled and blocked my time, and worked on my purpose and my projects one hour a day before bed, even in days of crisis—even at the airport. And it was a good thing I did, because he didn't end up having surgery until March 2023 (don't even get me started again on the medical system in the U.S.). Imagine if I had neglected my calendar and put my purpose aside—I would have lost almost a year of progress. And I was running out of time. With Dad's memory fading more each day, I knew I had to get this book finished. Because I employed my resilience tools, working on my purpose kept me positive for both of my parents and allowed me to be more helpful than ever. I was able to spend time with him while his memories were still clear, be there for my mom, and keep the kids' spirits high with joy. Focusing on my resilience tools helped me reenergize and keep my own inner light in heavy times, which translated to less stress and anxiety and reduced the toll on my physical and mental well-being.

Lastly, for your birthday this year, I further challenge you to request testimonials from your friends to create a legacy video. On October 24, 2022, my amazing husband reached out to all of our closest friends and requested videos. He asked them to answer how I impacted their lives. In the end, I had over fifty videos and 1.5 hours of content from friends from all my walks of life. It was amazing and so beautiful. I cried tears of joy and gratitude. It was amazing how many people came through for me.

All birthdays should be celebrated like this—like funerals. To me, a legacy video serves as a reminder to keep enjoying my life and of the impact I've made in the world. It reminds me why I'm here and gives me the resilience to move forward.

- Do this on your birthday or do it for someone else—and hashtag #beactchange in your video!

BUILDING YOUR COMMUNITY OF CHAMPIONS

We have a saying in Spanish that translates to, "Tell me who you're with, and I'll tell you who you are." "Dime con quién andas y te digo quien eres." The closest English equivalent I've seen is: "You're the average of the five people you spend the most time with." That might be a bit of an oversimplification, but it certainly speaks to the importance of community and the circle of people we surround ourselves with. Before anything else, I want you to analyze your own community and circle that's around you. Those around you will influence your thoughts, your actions, and ultimately, your success. Are you around people who just vent and complain about their lives, work, spouses? People who drink all the time and just talk about the past? Are you around people who put you down or mock your projects? Or are you around people who are positive, idea oriented, and who cheer you on? Do you surround yourself with your champions?

Remember that self-doubt and insecurity are already common traits for high achievers. How do you think that a negative circle of people affects your willingness and ability to pursue your purpose and legacy? You guessed it: it's hugely detrimental. Our minds already swing toward the negative, and you don't need the voices of those around you adding to it. Sadly, most people don't have enough positive voices around them and are surrounded by naysayers who, honestly, just crap on ideas due to their own fears. You need a space where your ideas won't be shut down, a place where you can get out of your own head and not have to be "perfect."

Through my story, you've seen that I had to make an effort throughout my entire life to find new circles. Middle school, high school, graduate school, the workforce, and even now. The workforce was the hardest. Because aside from a few notable exceptions, the majority of folks were in that first, negative category. Every weekend was about drinking, and all people did was talk about work and complain about colleagues. Not about their purpose, not about ideas, just about people and situations at work. And I get it: they were exhausted and burned out from trying to survive in the same toxic system. We commiserated but I also knew that whenever I wasn't there, it was certain that they were talking about me too. There was no balance or space to even consider our purpose. Complaining and being negative was how others knew they belonged. It was the way they bonded.

I knew right then that if I ever wanted to live my purpose, I needed out of that cult and stifling atmosphere, so I found new communities. It was either with local staff from that country, my champions within the organization, or connecting with other groups. I would volunteer in communities, reading books on weekends, and make an effort to reach beyond my circles. When I finally left the diplomatic service, as mentioned earlier, I found a new community of entrepreneurial women and coaches. I met women online, largely from Australia, who had ideas and positivity. This community helped and encouraged me to keep moving forward, and all were aligned with my values and outlook. From there, I found other communities and, eventually, a community near where I lived. It's definitely possible to improve your situation, but it takes clarity of purpose and intentional action.

It's not so hard to understand, right? The people around us influence our thoughts, our feelings, our actions, our "vibe." What's harder to see is that these circles, whether positive or negative, always spiral. The negative voices, the gossip, the complaining all accumulate and drag you down—if you let them. Our minds already tend toward the negative, so why push our thoughts further in that direction?

It's important to know that positive circles also spiral up. When you have a community of champions, you'll find that you uplift yourself by uplifting others and that the positivity and light you shine on them is reflected back on you tenfold.

So, don't give up on looking for your community. It's out there, but it may not exist in your neighborhood yet. That's the beauty of our global world. You can find a community for just about anything that's aligned to your purpose. Community is also a space for your brain to register that people are people. We all have struggles. We all share these challenges, and you're not alone. You don't have to be perfect for everyone, and there are spaces where you can feel heard and seen.

A positive community also helps you see that you're not alone in your struggles. If you haven't watched the documentaries by Jennifer Lopez or Selena Gomez, two of the highest of high achieving women in the entertainment space, I recommend that you check them out. Not as a fan or a groupie, but because they speak honestly and openly about how they suffer in silence through depression, insecurity, stress, and perfectionism. These traits are super common in many high achievers, but superstars have to live it out under the public eye, which I can only imagine amplifies everything. But if you look closely, you see how they get through it all: they have an amazing community of champions—people they trust, who uplift them and help pull them out of the darkness.

So, what about you? Who are your people? Pull out a pen and paper and make a list of the people who have championed you, cheered you on, and inspired you, even if only in some seemingly small way. Start there, and don't be afraid to be the person who brings people together and creates the community of champions.

"IF WHAT YOU WANT DOESN'T EXIST, CREATE IT YOURSELF."

Dr. EZ

PART THREE:

THINKING BIGGER

SCALING UP

How Purpose and Intention Relate to Business, International Development, and More!

This has been one amazing ride that we've taken together to find your purpose and intentionally live it. I've hinted at this all along, but one of the coolest things is that it doesn't just apply to individuals. Finding your purpose, aligning your actions, and living it every day apply to businesses, nonprofits, communities, countries, and more. It's something that teams, offices, and entire organizations struggle with, and it can impede their scale and growth completely. Having a clear mission, purpose, and vision not only allows the organization to be extremely clear when communicating a business pitch, submitting a funding application, or jockeying for a seat at the table, but it also attracts talent and employees that are aligned.

For example, the biggest struggle I saw in over a decade of working in international development was that NGOs and local organizations had a difficult time identifying their mission and purpose or forgot it along the way. Similar to individuals, they were clouded with international (external) priorities, pushed into chasing typical funding opportunities for security, becoming organizations that fit in rather than being who they wanted to be. This leads to frustration from employees who want to do impactful work, lack of long-term sustainability in projects and initiatives, and overall stagnation. From what I saw too often, "growth" was really just the proliferation of bureaucratic processes. Thus, the exercise of untangling why they started the organization to begin with, from both the individual and team points of view, is essential to the long-term sustainability of the group. It also attracts the employee who wants to be there and can see their purpose aligned with the group's, which leads to increased productivity and loyalty.

This entire purpose exercise can be performed with an organization or team in pretty much any industry. It's not just another retreat or planning session. Instead, each participant has the opportunity to understand their own strengths, their optimal role within the organization, and how their own values and purpose align to the mission, vision, and purpose of the organization. The more you can bring everyone into this process of shared visioning, the more buy-in you'll have long-term.

SCALE BEYOND BELIEF

If you successfully build a community, team, or organization with shared visioning, you can scale beyond belief. You'll have team members who are there because they believe in the higher purpose and outcome and see the linkage to themselves. You'll be clear on what you need to filter out and say no to and what opportunities to seek. Also, you'll be clear on your messaging.

Think about an organization that has a clear vision and purpose and the employees they attract. For example, Apple. They're very clear on their mission and purpose and the type of impact they want to create in the world. They select employees who share this. Their decisions are grounded in their objectives, and their messaging is consistent. At the same time, we've all worked for organizations that are unclear, disorganized, and, as a result, struggling. Those have been my worst jobs, where I often thought, *I don't belong here*, and I knew I wasn't being valued or appreciated for what I brought to the table. Morale was low, and they were a hard places to work.

So, this purpose method is also a great filter for when you're looking to work with a business or organization. Read their published statements. Do they match with your purpose and what you think the world needs (your values)? Or are they completely unaligned? Also, don't take what's written as the ultimate truth. It's easy to craft beautiful statements that don't really get implemented. Ask questions and dig deep to make sure. When I look back now on the mission and purpose statements of the jobs or teams I've not been aligned with, I see now how I misread them.

I could also write a whole book on the topic of shared visioning and purpose in communities and organizations. It's one of my specialties, and, in many ways, this book is based on much of the work I've done with organizations and groups around the world. It has been tremendously effective and transformative. Feel free to contact us if you want to explore this more.

FROM SMALL SEEDS, BIG THINGS GROW

For now, I just want to plant the seed in your mind that purpose is so much bigger than you might have imagined. With purpose, international development and humanitarian efforts would be more sustainable. With purpose, people would be happier in their corporate jobs. Communities would be able to come together to lobby for what they needed, and developing countries would be able to have a seat at the table and leverage their comparative advantage effectively.

But don't stop there—you can take this so much further. You

can use this tool to get to know your kids or make better choices about your next partner. With this tool, you can understand what's important to your kids and what they're naturally drawn to. You can support them from a very early age in their journey to live out their purpose. It also keeps you from continuing the intergenerational pull to keep pushing the status quo onto future generations. On the partner front, you can use it for dates and getting to know your partner. If you're serious about finding not just a spouse but a true partner, the questions you've asked yourself throughout this process are the same questions you should ask of any potential partner. If your partner's vision of their legacy focuses on family and the local community, while yours involves impacting millions, it's worth discussing to see how you can support each other. I know now that had I done this exercise with my past partners, we would have realized right away, just with the section on what the world needs, that we weren't compatible. I could have saved a lot of heartache and wasted time.

But guess what? You don't have to repeat my mistakes. You have this tool now, so use these questions to get to know the people around you. You'll be surprised by what you learn about them, and you'll begin to understand how they process things.

So, what now?

My program can be used in every context. How do I know this? Because I've applied it to everything, from relationships, to companies, to communities, to countries. My cutting-edge approach, combined with my extensive experience in working in diverse settings, has been used all over the world. My dedicated team and I will help you identify your unique purpose, create intentionality in your life, achieve all of your professional and personal goals, and develop resilience, with the right skills and habits. Unlike other programs that just leave you with the general information, my team and I personalize the experience to you, using tools that are built for you. We work with you and your team one-to-one to help you overcome obstacles and create a road map that's tailored to your needs and aspirations, taking into account the tools you need for resilience.

So, whether you're looking to change your personal life, start a business, or make a difference in the world and your community, we're here to make those dreams a reality so you can go from living to thriving. What are you waiting for?

And if that's not enough, continue reading to see how my program applies to couples, companies, communities, and countries!

THE 4CS—COUPLE, COMPANY, COMMUNITY & COUNTRY

Couple

I was sitting with my client, Andre, talking about his purpose. He came to me because he felt lost and guilty for wanting more. He had tried to express to his parents that he felt like what he had wasn't enough, and they dismissed him. He was also struggling to find a partner, and he realized that he needed to work on himself first. His friend referred him to me.

Andre's family and friends misunderstood him because he was in his early thirties and worked in an NGO field that allowed him to give back to the world. Whenever he expressed his dissatisfaction, they were like, "Dude, you're giving back to the world."

"Then why do I feel this emptiness inside?"

As we proceeded through the sessions, he became aware that he wanted to have a large impact in the world. His legacy was huge, but he felt a void because he wanted to live his legacy with a partner, yet he had struggled through relationships. As we progressed, he quickly realized that a lot of the struggle he was having with relationships was due to him missing a fundamental question when going on dates. He was missing the question of scale of impact. He would go on dates and center questions around values and hobbies, but those questions were leading him on a wild goose chase.

"Oh my," he said in one of our sessions. "I realize what's happening. I value family, empathy, and work ethic, and I met so many women with the same values, yet I'm constantly turned off by them." He felt that he was being picky and complicated, but he was not aligning his purpose with theirs. He realized that was the big issue. He never asked them what impact they wanted in the world and the legacy they wanted to leave behind. Duh!

He was searching for a woman with his values but with a purpose and legacy compatible with his, which was why he was constantly turned off when they would later express wanting to live always in the same city and be in one place. He realized that he was dating in the wrong places and using the wrong filter. So, he took this information and started using it with his potential partners, and it helped remove the layers of guilt he constantly felt when ending relationships that didn't fit—because now he understood why.

I have also used this approach with couples that are in a crisis moment. One person wants to keep scaling and reaching new heights, while the other wants to slow down. In this case, the process helps each partner learn about the other and gain appreciation for each other's legacies. Sometimes, simply understanding the importance of someone's legacy, how it's part of their why and not just pursuit for the sake of ambition, helps the other person understand where it's coming from. Having that clarity is important, as is what you do with it. Essentially, it's up to you.

I learned all of this the hard way. I was so obsessed with love and being married that I didn't use this filter. I dated men who fit other check marks but not the ones who matched my legacy. That's why I spent so many years living with regret and anger at myself for wasting so much time and letting that one man go. He was the closest match for my legacy until I met Paul. When I met Paul, we spoke of our legacies, and we spoke about the impact we wanted to create in the world. We asked ourselves those hard questions, which allowed us to grow together.

You may ask why that's so important. Well, the thing is, if your legacies don't match, then how will your future? If Paul wasn't on the same page as me about building this empire and me helping people live out their purpose, this wouldn't work. If he only wanted me to stay home and focus on him and the children, I would eventually feel trapped and want to escape. Same with him. Part of his legacy is to leave a large, relatable imprint on the world. If I didn't like to travel and wasn't open to different cultures, I would be limiting him. Eventually, we would have come to a crossroad of me wanting to build a business and him wanting to live overseas, which would have either led to resentment in one party, one person sacrificing, or one of us escaping. When we both analyze our pasts now, we realize how much could have been avoided had we asked this fundamental question around legacy. We can go back in time to the exact moment when we realized how much that answer would have changed things. Fortunately for you, I'm giving you this insight now. Ask those questions. Probe while dating. Share your purpose with your partner.

Bonus: if you have kids, it will help you get on the same page and understand your offspring better.

Need help, I'm here. I regularly work with couples.

Company and Organization

I've worked with hundreds of companies and organizations. Whether it has been to help them with their corporate social responsibility arm, help an NGO build a solid case for funding, submit a grant application, serve as president and grow funding, help bring their board together, or manage my own teams on a shared mission, vision, and purpose (MVP), I've seen the power of purpose in teams, companies, and organizations.

An article published by Gartner delves into how the pandemic has reshaped individuals' feelings about work, with a particular focus on the importance of purpose, underscoring that this emotional shift is likely to persist.[1] Workers want to know how they fit in an organization and ensure that their purpose aligns with the organization's or team's MVP. For so many, the pandemic was a wake-up call and a time to reflect on what matters most. With so many deaths and day-to-day fear, it was the closest the world came to the Obituary Exercise on a large scale. That experience has created a worldwide demand for companies and organizations to be clear on what their purpose is and to appreciate that employees want to live with purpose and balance.

The good news for you is that if you're running a team, office, business, or large corporation or company, you can take this exercise and apply it to your team. As a certified purpose facilitator, I've facilitated these discussions in the forms of workshops and retreats, helping teams come together to codevelop their mission, vision, and purpose. Codevelopment is essential because employees feel connected to the shared MVP when they create it, rather than just having it pushed on them by management. Being a part of the statement's creation or being a part of "revisiting" helps bring commitment and understanding of how and why it was developed. Employees get a voice, and they can visualize how they contribute to the MVP. For the most effective buy-in, the process should begin by first understanding the purpose of the individual and then, together, working on the MVP for the team and organization. By understanding themselves and the process, it's easier for each person to engage in the conversation about the team, organization, or unit.

With this completed, the organization, team, or unit is clear in their messaging. They can then use this messaging to apply for funding, showcase their results to upper management, collaborate with others with a similar agenda, and, most importantly, attract and retain people aligned with the MVP.

Using this approach, I've helped NGOs fundraise millions of dollars, helped small businesses immensely grow their social media platforms, and created teams that work better together. This process is also key to productivity, strategy, and general contentment at work. Everyone is clear how they fit, what their work contributes to, and the long-term vision. It also helps individuals with their own CVs and resumes, along with the company's communication and outreach products. If you're struggling with this or want it for your team, reach out, because it will transform everything. It's a game changer.

Community (Town, Municipality)

"Listen more, guide less. Help others unlock their own change."

When I first visited the northern border between the Dominican Republic and Haiti, I wasn't sure what to expect. There were so many narratives about this region based on politics, news sensationalism, historical tensions, and word of mouth. What I did know was that there was a development need and that it was time to give them a voice—and for us to listen.

As we approached the city of Montecristi, I was in awe of its spectacular beauty. This region is home to hundreds of shipwrecks, coral reefs that are claimed to be 300–400 years old, and one of the largest coral reef barriers in the Caribbean. With huge mountains and crystal clear waters, you get the feeling you're in coastal California and Tahiti at the same time.

But the most beautiful thing I encountered there was the community. At that time, I worked as the director of a large office with multiple units, and I was testing a different way of helping people. I had been exposed to the world of international and humanitarian aid since I was a child, and I remember, even then, wondering if the goods and things we were giving people were actually the things they wanted and needed.

When I finally got to a position of power, I decided it was time to shake things up and move away from the traditional model of "helping" and delivering aid. Instead of going with our own ideas about what people needed, we would visit the communities and just listen. And when I say "listen," I mean really, really listen to what they want and need and then fund it. So, I had the opportunity to grow my team and unit based on my new approach (if you're ever curious to know what I did and how I grew that office to approximately $100 million, check out my LinkedIn).

We had already sat down with other community members and groups, but this conversation was different. This leader was passionate and filled with purpose. Roberto was a fisherman, who had a dream of owning a diving shop. It was something he had wanted to do since he was a child, and he built it little by little. He started off with having one set of gear to multiple and then one boat to several, slowly building his dive shop. Roberto still fished, was part of the cooperative, and was someone who *never* wanted to leave his community—even with hundreds of offers—because he was committed to developing the community.

"It's important to know that positive circles also spiral up."

When I sat down with him and his group, he had a standard presentation ready. You know, the presentation and pitch he thought we wanted to hear because he had given it dozens of times to people in similar positions. When he finished, I said, "Thank you so much for this presentation. This was lovely. However, I want to hear what *you* really want and need. We're actually just here to listen. There's no agenda, no preconceived ideas, and we are open." His face completely changed. I saw the people in the group look at each other, and then they all got really excited. They went on to tell us all about the ongoing challenges and the frustrations with previous aid projects. The energy and passion were all-consuming. But at the same time, they felt confused. Confused because no one had ever asked them that question. They never had the space to articulate their mission, vision, or purpose, mainly because no one had ever wanted to listen. Just like many other communities and countries I had visited, they were feeling the weight of donor fatigue and growing tired of feeling dragged down. Everyone wanted to fund their own ideas, so, like so many communities around the world, they just gave everyone proposals based on what they wanted to hear. It's not surprising. Donors often expect these local organizations and communities to provide in-kind contributions—essentially, a condition that donors require these small organizations to show some "skin in the game" and gratitude. These passion-fueled and resource-starved organizations that are dedicated to helping some of the most underserved populations now have to volunteer their time and resources. This leads to a scenario where volunteers and communities are worked to the point of exhaustion, barely treading water, and compromising the quality of their primary objective. They needed the money, and they wanted better for their community, so they did what they thought they had to do.

But the "skin in the game" approach is flawed. The true demonstration of commitment is not in grinding people down to the point of burnout, but rather in shared vision and buy-in. There's nothing more irritating than when I hear those fallacies and see donors and individuals do this to people who are barely treading water. The fear of judgment, the fear of burdening others, and the fear of appearing weak or ungrateful can create a silence around this issue. That's the thing: the world of international development is marked by passion, purpose, and a common desire to make a significant difference. Countless individuals, myself included, enter this realm with hearts ablaze, eager to effect positive change. But beneath this earnest dedication, a toxic undercurrent erodes the vigor and spirit of those in the sector. From high-profile NGOs to donor organizations, there exists a chronic syndrome of overwork and undercompensation. People's time, energy, and talents are frequently undervalued. The expectation of unpaid volunteer work, combined with a stark lack of adequate compensation and overtime pay, paves a relentless path toward burnout. So, they silence themselves and just tell donors what they want to hear. But I was there to listen. I was there to spark change.

Thus, over the years, I partnered with the community and the organization Roberto worked with. The organization's leader was equally committed to this approach, and I had the honor of joining them in developing their own mission, vision, and purpose journey, using the same methodology. Together, we tested different mediums and learned from each other the different ways to develop shared buy-in and visioning. Through their vision and networks, they made a huge impact, and I was able to repeat this in different locations. Over several years, we proved that listening and funding the shared mission, purpose, and vision of communities leads to sustainability and long-term success of the programs and interventions. I grew so close to this community. My family and I would celebrate our birthdays there, and I learned to scuba just to be able to see the ocean through Roberto's eyes.

Further, I was able to show the connection between their purpose and larger international priorities and initiatives, as well as the importance of local communities and organizations communicating their purpose to donors and funders. While I'm very vocal about the need for international development institutions to consciously shift toward a more localized model (I have many podcast interviews and talks on this), there's also an opportunity for local organizations to better communicate their own vision, mission, and purpose and align it with their funding proposals. Further, when given the opportunity for capacity building, they can express their needs to make their vision a reality.

I was able to expand this work beyond. Being on the board of several NGOs, serving as a coach and mentor, and working with communities across the world has taught me that this struggle is worldwide. With that in mind, I know that this work is key and is applicable to international development professionals who want to help communities untangle their mission, vision, and purpose after they followed the cookie-cutter model, and it failed. Sound familiar to the individual plight? It's also applicable to community members who have never been asked what they actually want and don't know where to start.

In the international development context, I used a different visual model from the Purpose Sun because I had to keep my own views and interests separate. I represented an organization, not myself. With that said, I strongly believe the Purpose Sun is the place to start if you want to make that change in the world. It's a tool that holds all these concepts together. Your legacy is your impact. The things you want to be sought out for are the services you want to provide. What you can teach the world is your comparative advantage, and your childhood dream is your aspiration. It's all the same.

Country

Let's go back to when Paul and I met. Remember that vision we had that we turned into a project together? Our project was to help a development agency create five-year strategies in countries all around the world. It was an extremely fulfilling time, where we traveled the world, met with stakeholders and staff working abroad, and had the opportunity to meet government officials in all levels and ranks of government, as well as community members and leaders. Paul continued working on these types of projects for years to come. In our observations, we found that the most challenging aspect was getting everyone to have a shared mission, vision, and purpose. With so many pushes and pulls from international donors, political motivations, constituents, citizens, private sector, and other local and international actors, it was difficult to come together on what to prioritize. Again, does this sound familiar to our lives? It's all related.

For example, I remember one country, which we'll call Pluto. For Pluto, developing tourism was the highest priority. They saw that as their comparative advantage (aka what they wanted to be sought out for). It was something they believed they could do in five years. However, at the same time, studies and analysis showed that water and sanitation were needed. The Plutonian diaspora abroad pushed the country to focus on education so people could invest in companies within the country. These interests that felt so distant from each other had many overlaps, but they couldn't see it.

In this case, it wasn't that outsiders were going to dictate priorities. Instead, there was a need to agree internally on what the short- and long-term visions for the country would be. Given all the competing priorities, interests, money, and pressure, Pluto had a hard time deciding what to focus on first.

The model discussed in this book helped guide those discussions. It can bring people together for a shared mission, vision, and purpose, which could then be translated into a prioritization and alignment exercise. Further, it can assist countries in petitioning for funds from different donors, helping to clarify and understand priorities. Focusing on shared mission, vision, and purpose has the potential to be truly transformative in the arena of international affairs.

CONCLUSION:

LOOK HOW FAR WE'VE COME ...

As we close this transformative journey through the pages of *Creating Your Limitless Life*, I hope the candid accounts of my experiences, as well as the stories of others, have resonated with you and have filled you with the fervor and courage to conquer the world that lies before you. By utilizing the three key steps—discovering your purpose, laying out your road map, and arming yourself with the right tool kit—you hold the power to manifest any dreams your heart harbors.

Remember, the only limitations that exist are the ones we place upon ourselves. We all possess the capacity to lead a limitless life, to reach uncharted territories of personal and professional fulfillment. This is the essence of our shared human experience, and it is this boundless potential that I've aimed to encapsulate in this book.

Thank you for embarking on this journey with me and allowing me to share my story with you. It is my heartfelt hope that it will guide and inspire you to craft the life you truly desire. Hasta la próxima—until we meet again in the limitless expanse of possibility.

"The time to upgrade your legacy is now."

ABOUT THE AUTHOR

Dr. Esther Zeledón is more than just a senior development advisor, a localization expert, and a transformational coach—she is a catalyst for change. Her deep well of expertise has empowered a diverse range of entities, from governments and donors to NGOs, communities, businesses, and individuals, helping them articulate their purpose and elevate their impact. She is a transformative force that guides others toward lasting, impactful change that inspires them to live limitlessly.

With a PhD and MS from UC Berkeley and a BA from Swarthmore College, Dr. Zeledón's worldview and depth of knowledge is further augmented by her extensive travels and deep connections to people and communities around the globe.

Born in Nicaragua and raised in the U.S., Dr. Zeledón is a proud Latina and mom to Xilónem and Máximo. She readily admits her addiction to chocolate, and when not changing lives, you can find her traveling the world, dancing, and living her limitless life together with her soulmate.

beactchange.com

ACKNOWLEDGMENTS

To my parents, Sonia and Sergio, the ones who started it all, I thank you from the bottom of my heart. You've given so much. You've loved so much. You've sacrificed so much. And all for me and my siblings. I'm on a mission to give you back everything you've given us. And even then, it wouldn't be enough.

In memory of Dr. Benjamín Zeledón, who fought bravely for his convictions. I want you to know that your sacrifice will never be forgotten. It has kindled a fire in me to continue the fight. To my ancestors, thank you for being my guiding stars. Your courage and strength flow in my veins, emboldening me to take a stand and raise my voice. I am here because of you.

Paul, my love, you're not just my husband and partner, but the silent coauthor of this journey. Although my name might be on the book, this story is just as much yours. You are my rock, my champion, my love. Together, we've dreamed this, built this, lived this. Here's to us.

To Xilonem and Maximo, my children, my cheerleaders, thank you for believing in me, for celebrating my victories, and for being a constant source of joy. I'm crafting this legacy for you and because of you.

To Sonia, my sister, my closest confidant, thank you. I'm at a loss for words to fully express my gratitude. From your encouragement and guidance to your constant belief in me, you've made a world of difference. As my mentor, you showed me how to turn opportunities into successes. Your steadfast support and love have been invaluable. Thank you for being not just a sister, but a driving force in my life.

To my brothers, Maximo and Benjamin, I'm deeply grateful for our shared history and intertwined lives. You've enriched my story in ways you may never fully realize. To Maximo, your big heart taught me invaluable lessons in empathy and generosity. To Benjamin, as my youngest sibling, caring for you deepened my understanding of life, and our shared summers enriched our bond.

To my lifelines—Rita (RIP), Alexis, Elizabeth, Mauricio, Pauline, Lilyvania, Jason, Helena, Yoselin, Sari, Keno, and so many more (you know who you are), this wouldn't have been possible without your unwavering support. You've stood by me, cheered me on, and loved me every step of the way. I love you to the moon and back!

A heartfelt shoutout to Dean Publishing. Your dedication transformed my dreams into reality, giving life to this book in ways beyond my imagination. You're more than a publishing company. You're visionaries, illuminating every author's best work. To Nat, a brilliant beacon in this universe—your guidance helped me unravel, articulate, and shape my vision. Our synchronous journey and friendship are treasures I will always cherish.

To Erika, my business coach, your narrative ignited a spark

within me, propelling this journey. You're a living testament to your legacy, and I'm eternally grateful to have your guiding influence. Your generosity and unyielding passion for empowering women is truly remarkable.

To all my followers at @beactchange, thank you for your support and companionship on this journey. Your encouragement, your engagement, your stories—you've become a vibrant community that I'm so proud to be a part of.

And finally, a heartfelt thank you to my clients, mentees, extended family and friends, and to all the people who have opened their worlds to me, letting me be a part of their journeys. It is through your trust and your stories that I have found my purpose and am able to live it daily. I am humbled and forever grateful for each of you. You've reminded me that we all can be limitless!

In conclusion, thank you, everyone, for being a part of my journey, for helping me create something beautiful. We did it!

Introduction

1 Hughes, Langston. n.d. "Harlem." Poetry Foundation. Accessed April 25, 2023. https://www.poetryfoundation.org/poems/46548/harlem.

2 Coehlo, Paulo. 2006. *The Witch of Portobello*. New York: Harper Collins, 73; Coehlo, Paulo. 1993. *The Alchemist.* New York: Harper Collins, 126.

Part One

1 Guido, Clemente et al. 2014. *El General Benjamín Zeledón y sus Valientes*, 65. Alcaldía de Managua. https://www.managua.gob.ni/wp-content/uploads/2016/06/ZELEDON.pdf.

2 Redfield, James. 1993. *The Celestine Prophecy: An Adventure*. Hoover, Alabama: Satori Publishing, 64, 206, 207.

3 Gene Keys. n.d. "Gene Keys." Accessed June 27, 2023. Website. https://genekeys.com/.

4 Smith, Samantha. 2017. "Most Think the 'American Dream' Is within Reach for Them." Pew Research Center. Published October 31, 2017. https://www.pewresearch.org/short-reads/2017/10/31/most-think-the-american-dream-is-within-reach-for-them/.

5 Kochhar, Rakesh, and Stella Sechopoulos. 2022. "Black and Hispanic Americans, Those with Less Education Are More Likely to Fall Out of the Middle Class Each Year." Pew Research Center. Published May 10, 2022. https://www.pewresearch.org/short-reads/2022/05/10/black-and-hispanic-americans-those-with-less-education-are-more-likely-to-fall-out-of-the-middle-class-each-year/.; Hill, Latoya, Nambi Ndugga, and Samantha Artiga. 2023. "Key Data on Health and Health Care by Race and Ethnicity." KFF. Published March 15, 2023. https://www.kff.org/racial-equity-and-health-policy/report/key-data-on-health-and-health-care-by-race-and-ethnicity/.

6 World Population Review. 2023. "Standard of Living by Country | Quality of Life by Country 2023." Accessed July 12, 2023. https://worldpopulationreview.com/country-rankings/standard-of-living-by-country.

Part Two

1 Seo, Hannah. 2023. "How to Stop Ruminating." *The New York Times*. Online article. Published February 1, 2023. https://www.nytimes.com/2023/02/01/well/mind/stop-rumination-worry.html.

2 Jones, Allie. 2023. "Katherine Schwarzenegger Pratt's Picture-

Perfect Life." *The New York Times*. Published February 06, 2023. https://www.nytimes.com/2023/02/06/style/katherine-schwarzenegger-pratt.html.

3 Bethune, Sophie. 2022. "More than a Quarter of U.S. Adults Say They're So Stressed They Can't Function." American Psychology Association. Published October 19, 2022. https://www.apa.org/news/press/releases/2022/10/multiple-stressors-no-function.

4 Baken, Sezen. 2023. "Australia's 'Laid-Back' Workers Rank Among the World's Most Stressed." The New Daily. Published June 15, 2023. https://thenewdaily.com.au/life/2023/06/15/workers-stressed-australia-work/.

5 Gawande, Atul. 2017. "Want to Get Great at Something? Get a Coach." TED. Video, 16:37. Accessed July 17, 2023. https://www.ted.com/talks/atul_gawande_want_to_get_great_at_something_get_a_coach/.

6 Gawande, Atul. 2017. "Want to Get Great at Something? Get a Coach."

7 Kobau, Rosemarie. 2010. "Well-Being Assessment: An Evaluation of Well-Being Scales for Public Health and Population Estimates of Well-Being among U.S. Adults." *Applied Psychology: Health and Well-Being*, vol. 2, no. 3: 272-297. https://doi.org/10.1111/j.1758-0854.2010.01035.x.

8 Leading Effectively Staff. 2023. "Create (Better) Culture: The Keys to Wellbeing and Leadership." Center for Creative Leadership. Published February 17, 2023. https://www.ccl.org/articles/leading-effectively-articles/create-better-culture-the-keys-to-wellbeing-and-leadership/.

9 Jung, Carl. 1973. *Synchronicity: An Acausal Connecting Principle.*

Princeton, New Jersey: Princeton University Press.

10 Roxburgh, Elizabeth C., Sophie Ridgway, and Chris A. Roe. 2016. "Synchronicity in the Therapeutic Setting: A Survey of Practitioners." *Counselling and Psychotherapy Research*, vol. 16, no. 1: 44-53. https://doi.org/10.1002/capr.12057.

11 Schwartz, Brie. 2019. "In Oprah's New Book, *The Path Made Clear*, She Shares Her Greatest Life Lesson Yet." Oprah Daily. Published March 26, 2019. https://www.oprahdaily.com/life/a26930708/oprah-path-made-clear/.

12 Murphy, Mark. 2018. "Neuroscience Explains Why You Need to Write Down Your Goals If You Actually Want to Achieve Them." Forbes. Published April 15, 2023. https://www.forbes.com/sites/markmurphy/2018/04/15/neuroscience-explains-why-you-need-to-write-down-your-goals-if-you-actually-want-to-achieve-them.

13 Brown, Brené. 2013. *Daring Greatly: How the Courage to Be Vulnerable Transforms the Way We Live, Love, Parent, and Lead*. London: Penguin.

Part Three

1 Turner, Jordan. 2023. "Employees Seek Personal Value and Purpose at Work. Be Prepared to Deliver." Gartner. Published March 29, 2023. https://www.gartner.com/en/articles/employees-seek-personal-value-and-purpose-at-work-be-prepared-to-deliver.

Printed in the USA
CPSIA information can be obtained
at www.ICGtesting.com
LVHW091440131024
793698LV00042B/488